BECOMING
LESS SEPARATE?

SCHOOL DESEGREGATION,
JUSTICE DEPARTMENT ENFORCEMENT,
AND THE PURSUIT OF UNITARY STATUS

UNITED STATES COMMISSION ON CIVIL RIGHTS

SEPTEMBER 2007

UNITED STATES COMMISSION ON CIVIL RIGHTS

The U.S. Commission on Civil Rights is an independent, bipartisan agency established by Congress in 1957. It is directed to:

- Investigate complaints alleging that citizens are being deprived of their right to vote by reason of their race, color, religion, sex, age, disability, or national origin, or by reason of fraudulent practices.
- Study and collect information relating to discrimination or a denial of equal protection of the laws under the Constitution because of race, color, religion, sex, age, disability, or national origin, or in the administration of justice.
- Appraise federal laws and policies with respect to discrimination or denial of equal protection of the laws because of race, color, religion, sex, age, disability, or national origin, or in the administration of justice.
- Serve as a national clearinghouse for information in respect to discrimination or denial of equal protection of the laws because of race, color, religion, sex, age, disability, or national origin.
- Submit reports, findings, and recommendations to the President and Congress.
- Issue public service announcements to discourage discrimination or denial of equal protection of the laws.

MEMBERS OF THE COMMISSION

U.S. Commission on Civil Rights
624 Ninth Street, NW
Washington, DC 20425

(202) 376-8128 voice
(202) 376-8116 TTY

www.usccr.gov

This report is available on disk in ASCII Text and Microsoft Word 2003 for persons with visual impairments. Please call (202) 376-8110.

Cover Photos:

Little Rock, Arkansas, September 1958. African American students arriving without incident at Van Buren High School, Little Rock, Arkansas. *Photo courtesy of Library of Congress: U.S. News & World Report Magazine Photograph Collection.*

Washington, DC, September 1954. H.B. Sanders, right, gives instructions to members of a 10th grade class at McKinley Technical High School as the new District of Columbia public school term opens Sept. 13. *Photo courtesy of Library of Congress: New York World-Telegram and the Sun Newspaper Photograph Collection.*

Kids in a classroom responding to the teacher's question. Nancy Louie, 2004. *Photo: istockphoto.*

BECOMING
LESS SEPARATE?

School Desegregation,
Justice Department Enforcement,
and the Pursuit of Unitary Status

Letter of Transmittal

The President
The President of the Senate
The Speaker of the House

Sirs and Madam:

The United States Commission on Civil Rights transmits this report, *Becoming Less Separate? School Desegregation, Justice Department Enforcement, and the Pursuit of Unitary Status,* pursuant to Public Law 103-419. The purpose of the report is to examine what effect the increase in the number of schools obtaining unitary status has had on the racial balance of schools that were previously under court order. Specifically, the report examines whether levels of integration tend to erode as consent decrees are lifted.

To that end, the Commission collected data as to the legal status of school districts in seven states: Alabama, Georgia, Florida, Louisiana, Mississippi, North Carolina, and South Carolina. The Commission then analyzed this data to determine if obtaining unitary status was associated with greater levels of racial clustering or reduced integration within districts. In addition, the Commission examined the Educational Opportunities Section (EOS) of the Department of Justice, which is charged with the primary enforcement role in this area to determine what effect its policies and actions have had on the racial balance of school districts.

The findings indicate that the increase in the number of jurisdictions obtaining unitary status has not had a negative effect on levels of integration. Moreover, the evidence indicates that the substantial number of districts that have obtained unitary status since 2000, at least partly through the actions of EOS, exhibit higher levels of integration than those districts that obtained such status in prior decades.

The report also indicates that certain factors, unrelated to the legal status of a school district, have a more significant effect on levels of racial balance. Among these are the size of a district's student population, the percentage of white student enrollment, and the state in which the district is located. The Commission urges that these factors be further examined and that school districts and the communities of which they are a part take the steps necessary to address the vestiges of state based discrimination.

On August 2, 2007, the Commission approved this report. The vote was as follows: Chapters 1–5 and the appendices were approved by Commissioners Braceras, Heriot, Kirsanow, Reynolds, Taylor, Thernstrom, and Yaki, with Commissioner Melendez not present. Chapter 6 was approved by Commissioners Braceras, Heriot, Kirsanow, Reynolds, Taylor, and Thernstrom; and objected to by Commissioners Melendez and Yaki. The report includes a separate statement submitted by Commissioners Melendez and Yaki.

For the Commissioners,

Gerald A. Reynolds
Chairman

TABLE OF CONTENTS

FIGURES

TABLES

EXECUTIVE SUMMARY

For almost a century following the end of the Civil War, many state and local governments, particularly in the South but not exclusively so, operated a crippling system of state-sponsored segregation. The nation's elementary and secondary school students were most affected by these policies.

It was not until 1954, in the decision of *Brown v. Board of Education of Topeka*, 347 U.S. 483 (1954), that the Supreme Court finally ruled that *de jure* racial discrimination in education was unconstitutional. To address the damage caused by the intentional segregation of schools, the Court sanctioned an extraordinary level of federal intervention. Many of those in the affected areas reacted to the process of integration with massive resistance, which sometimes included outright violence.

In response to continued resistance, Congress enacted the Civil Rights Act of 1964, which authorized the Department of Justice to take an active role in enforcing anti-discrimination laws. The Act allowed the Department of Justice to initiate or intervene in lawsuits to desegregate schools.

In addition, Title VI of the Act made school districts that engage in racial discrimination ineligible for federal funding. This provision, when combined with the Elementary and Secondary Education Act of 1965, (which provides financial assistance to schools serving areas with concentrations of children from low income families), exerted a substantial influence on school districts as federal funding for education increased.

In recognition of the continued resistance to desegregation, the Supreme Court in the decision of *Green v. County School Board of New Kent County*, 391 U.S. 430 (1968), established specific standards by which desegregation efforts should be judged. The Court established that a school system that successfully transitioned from a segregated, racially dual system to an integrated one would be classified as "unitary."

Throughout the 1960s and 1970s, judicial oversight continued to grow. Given the extent of resistance, this extraordinary federal intervention was both necessary and unavoidable. But it was not without costs. By its nature, judicial supervision supplanted the decisions of locally elected officials and professional educators with those of an unelected judge without special training or expertise in education policy.

By the 1990s, many court orders had been in place for decades, and the state-sponsored schemes of segregation had been addressed. It was at this point in time that the Supreme Court acknowledged the historical importance of local elected control over elementary and secondary schools and held that federal judicial supervision should end when the effects of past intentional discrimination are remedied. To that end, the Court clarified the means by which school districts might obtain unitary status and receive relief from judicial oversight. These cases were *Board of Education of Oklahoma City Public Schools v. Dowell*, 498 U.S. 237 (1991), and *Freeman v. Pitts*, 503 U.S. 467 (1992). In these decisions, the Court held that the award of unitary status is appropriate when a school district demonstrates that it has complied with the court's desegregation order for a reasonable period of time and has exhibited a good faith commitment to the constitutional principles *Brown* established.

The Department of Justice (DOJ) has the primary enforcement role in addressing cases of school desegregation. Through its participation in the judicial process, it can help or hinder those school districts that seek unitary status. Until recent years, few districts were released from judicial supervision. Since fiscal year 2000, the number of districts obtaining unitary status has increased dramatically, with DOJ's docket of elementary and secondary school desegregation cases declining from approximately 430 cases to 266 cases. Indeed, almost 56 percent of the districts that have obtained unitary status over the last several decades have done so since 2000.

The purpose of this report is to examine the effect that this increase in the number of school districts obtaining unitary status has had on the racial balance of schools that were previously under court order. In other words, do school districts tend to revert to racial clustering—as some would say, do they "resegregate"—after they are released from judicial supervision? Justice Stephen Breyer recently raised this very issue, when he claimed that many school districts are maintaining or extending their integration efforts because they fear what Justice Breyer calls "the evident risk of a return to school systems that are in fact (though not in law) resegregated . . . ."[1] Justice Breyer's argument implicitly raises an important question, which this report attempts to answer: Does judicial supervision appear, in the aggregate, to maintain racial integration and does that integration tend to erode as court orders are lifted?

To that end, the Commission collected data as to the legal status of school districts from seven states which historically have had a substantial number of school districts under judicial supervision: Alabama, Florida, Georgia, Louisiana, Mississippi, North Carolina, and South Carolina. Since surprisingly little data on this issue was available, the Commission reviewed each district within these states to determine if the school system was currently under a court order, had never been under a court order, or had obtained unitary status. The Commission believes that this constitutes the most comprehensive and current record of the legal status of school districts ever undertaken. The Commission then analyzed the district data to determine if obtaining unitary status was associated with greater levels of racial clustering or reduced integration within districts.

A cursory view of the data, comparing only African American and white student enrollment, suggests that unitary districts have greater levels of racial concentration than districts that remain under court order and that the latter have higher levels of racial concentration than districts never under judicial supervision. However, when one adjusts for other factors, such as the size of a district's student

---

[1] *Parents Involved in Cmty. Sch. v. Seattle Sch. Dist. No. 1*, 127 S. Ct. 2738, 2802 (2007) (Breyer, J., dissenting). Although terms like "segregation" and "integration" are often used loosely to describe patterns of racial concentration, some commentators have been careful to distinguish between *de jure* segregation and voluntary residential clustering. Justice Thomas, in his concurring opinion in *Parents Involved*, made the following distinction:

> In the context of public schooling, segregation is the deliberate operation of a school system to "carry out a governmental policy to separate pupils in schools solely on the basis of race."

> ...

> Racial imbalance is not segregation. Although presently observed racial imbalance might result from past *de jure* segregation, racial imbalance can also result from any number of innocent private decisions, including voluntary housing choices.

Id. at 2769 (Thomas, J., concurring) (citation omitted); *see also Parents Involved in Cmty. Sch. v. Seattle Sch. Dist.*, 426 F.3d 1162, 1197, 1220 (9th Cir. 2005) (Bea, J., dissenting) ("As an introductory note, I call attention to the majority's frequent misuse of the terms 'segregation,' 'segregated schools,' and 'segregated housing patterns.' ... The racial imbalance in Seattle's schools results not from *de jure* segregation nor from any invidious exclusion of nonwhite minorities from the schools. Instead, it results from racially imbalanced residential housing patterns, an issue which the District does not contend it can alter.").

population, the percentage of white student enrollment and the state in which the district is located, the legal status differences are not statistically significant, even when only these two racial groups are considered.

Similarly, when unitary districts are compared with court supervised districts over time, there is no statistically significant difference in the levels of racial balance between the two categories. If districts experienced greater racial imbalances after obtaining unitary status, one could expect that the levels of racial balance between the categories would differ substantially, especially over time, with the unitary districts becoming less integrated than those supervised by the courts. Within the parameters of this study, however, this did not occur.

Moreover, when the analysis includes other racial and ethnic groups, such as Hispanics, Asian Americans and Native Americans, the results indicate that school districts, on average, are substantially more integrated than would appear from a comparison of just the black-white balance alone. This is especially relevant given that districts are facing drastic demographic changes in school-age population, with white enrollment decreasing and Hispanic, Asian, and other minority student populations expanding substantially. When the analyses include these other groups, and show changes in schools' racial/ethnic composition over time, no substantial overall increases or decreases in the racial balance occur in the decade this study examined.

These findings indicate that the increase in jurisdictions obtaining unitary status has not had a negative effect on the levels of integration. Moreover, the evidence further indicates that districts that have obtained unitary status since 2000 exhibit higher levels of integration than those districts that obtained such status in prior decades.

Ironically, while large districts have been released from judicial supervision more frequently than small districts, it is the smaller districts which show significantly less racial clustering. On average, administrators in districts with enrollments of 1,000 to 9,999 students need to shift less than 37 percent of their pupils to achieve perfect racial balance. Officials in larger court-supervised districts would need to reassign, on average, 43 percent or more.

Given these results, the increase in the number of districts obtaining unitary status is not surprising and does not suggest any significant subsequent increase in racial isolation among students in the affected schools.

Many of the original desegregation orders have been in place for decades. In the Commission's study, 98 percent of the districts ever under court order were placed under supervision in the 1970s or earlier. A majority of them remain under court order today. The purpose of these orders was to address state sponsored schemes of segregation and to remedy the effects of intentional discrimination. While each case must be examined on its own merits, there is little doubt that the process of review should continue.

The Commission urges the Department of Justice to examine those districts that have been under court order the longest and increase its efforts to ensure that such districts address the lingering effects of state sponsored discrimination. In addition, the Commission asks social scientists, academicians, and relevant government agencies to determine why many small school districts are not seeking unitary status when they evidence higher levels of integration than many large districts that were released from judicial supervision. Finally, the Commission recommends that state boards of education determine what, if any, non-legal reasons might affect the decisions of school districts within their jurisdiction not to seek unitary status.

CHAPTER 1: INTRODUCTION

Over fifty years have passed since the decision of *Brown v. Board of Education of Topeka* in which the Supreme Court held that state-sponsored racial segregation of schools is unconstitutional.[1] Initially, desegregation was either ignored or actively resisted. Even a decade after the *Brown* decision most school districts had taken few or no steps to implement a program of racial desegregation. This resistance resulted in litigants seeking and obtaining the federal judiciary's extraordinary intervention in the area of public education.

In an effort to craft effective remedies that would compel school districts to operate integrated schools, the Court revisited school desegregation several times after *Brown*. Most significantly, the Court's decision in *Green v. County School Board of New Kent County*,[2] spurred widespread federal court supervision of school districts that were operating racially dual systems. In *Green*, the Court held that federal courts should monitor school districts until the vestiges of *de jure* segregation were eliminated. In making this assessment, a federal court must, to the extent practicable, look at every facet of school operations. Not until a school district successfully transitioned from a segregated, racially dual system to a unitary one would it be released from court supervision.

The *Green* standard, however, did not provide clear guidelines as to when such court supervision of public schools should end. Accordingly, in the early 1990s, the Supreme Court revisited the general standards for unitary status in two cases: *Board of Education of Oklahoma City Public Schools v. Dowell*[3] and *Freeman v. Pitts*.[4] In *Dowell*, the Court ruled that a declaration of unitary status is appropriate if a school district demonstrates that it has complied with a judicial desegregation order since it was entered and the vestiges of past discrimination are eliminated.[5] In *Freeman*, the Court extended *Dowell* and held that a school district need not achieve unitary status as to all aspects of school administration to obtain partial relief in those areas in which success has been achieved.[6]

By outlining the process by which local control of school districts could be reestablished, *Dowell* and *Freeman* provide a roadmap for school districts to seek unitary status. As time has passed, more and more school districts have sought and obtained release from court supervision. For example, although as recently as 2000, the number of school desegregation cases on the Department of Justice's open case list was approximately 430,[7] as of May 2007, this number had decreased to 266.[8]

---

[1] *Brown v. Bd. of Ed. of Topeka, Shawnee County, Kan.*, 347 U.S. 483 (1954).

[2] *Green v. County Sch. Bd. of New Kent County, Va.*, 391 U.S. 430 (1968).

[3] *Board of Ed. of Oklahoma City Public Schools, Independent Sch. Dist. No. 98, Oklahoma County, Okla. v. Dowell*, 498 U.S. 237 (1991).

[4] *Freeman v. Pitts*, 503 U.S. 467 (1992).

[5] *See Dowell*, 498 U.S. at 249–50.

[6] *See Freeman*, 503 U.S. at 497–99.

[7] U.S. Department of Justice, Civil Rights Division, Response to U.S. Commission on Civil Rights' Interrogatories and Document Requests, Response to Interrogatory Requests 2 and 26, May 17, 2007.

[8] *Id.*

This report seeks to examine the effect of these changes by analyzing the current extent of judicial oversight, the impact that obtaining unitary status has on racial balance within school districts, and the role the Department of Justice plays in the process.[9] The following topics are addressed:

The continuation of federal supervision raises concerns related to federalism, interference with the traditional prerogative of state and local control of schools, and the scope and propriety of judicial remedies such as busing. To understand why this level of federal intervention continues, despite these concerns, it is necessary to consider the evolving role of the courts in unitary status cases following the decisions in *Green* and later in *Dowell* and *Freeman*. Such an analysis is presented in chapter 2 of this report.

The Department of Justice (DOJ) has played an active role in this area and has intervened in many federal desegregation cases. The DOJ's elementary and secondary school desegregation docket, which currently includes approximately 266 cases, is handled by the Civil Rights Division's Educational Opportunities Section (EOS). EOS is charged with enforcing federal statutes that prohibit discrimination in public education and is authorized to initiate or intervene in such suits pursuant to Titles IV, VI, and IX of the Civil Rights Act of 1964.[10] EOS is thus responsible for overseeing these cases on behalf of DOJ. Little commentary exists on the role of EOS in such litigation and the overall structure of this important section of DOJ. Chapter 3 of this report describes the functions of this section.

Chapter 4 sets forth the Commission's research cataloging the legal status of school districts in seven states. The Commission shows when the districts came under court order and the timing and frequency with which they gained judicial recognition of unitary status. The chapter further examines whether the frequency with which districts obtain unitary status is related to district size. Finally, for districts remaining under court order, this chapter provides information as to the intent of such districts with regard to gaining unitary status.

Chapter 5 examines whether school districts' legal status (i.e., as unitary, court-supervised, or nonlitigated entities) is related to student racial concentrations. First, the Commission analyzes whether districts that obtained unitary status show more or less racial and ethnic integration than those remaining under court order. Second, the statistical analyses examine whether different types of districts are more or less integrated now than in 1992 when the criteria for attaining unitary status were established. Finally, for districts with unitary status, the Commission analyzes whether schools become more racially concentrated after they are released from judicial oversight.

Finally, chapter 6 details the Commission's findings and recommendations arising out of the research and analysis.

---

[9] Pursuant to the Commission's statute: "The Commission shall submit to the President and Congress at least one report annually that monitors federal civil rights enforcement efforts in the United States." Civil Rights Commission Amendments Act of 1994, 42 U.S.C § 1975a (c)(1) (2007).

[10] Civil Rights Act of 1964, Pub. L. No. 88-352, 78 Stat. 252 (1964) (codified in sections of 42 U.S.C.).

CHAPTER 2: HISTORICAL AND LEGAL BACKGROUND

Race Relations in the United States

Almost a century after the Civil War, parts of the United States continued to operate legally-sanctioned systems of racial segregation. Although the passage of the 13th, 14th, and 15th Amendments to the Constitution ended slavery, granted equal rights to all citizens and extended the right to vote, most African Americans continued to face opposition to the exercise of these rights.[1]

The legal system of racial segregation had the explicit approval of the Courts and extended to the issue of education. In the 1896 decision of *Plessy v. Ferguson*, for example, the Court discussed the parameters of legal separation of the races and used the following example of allowable segregation:

> The most common instance of this is connected with the establishment of separate schools for white and colored children, which has been held to be a valid exercise of the legislative power even by courts of States where the political rights of the colored race have been longest and most earnestly enforced.[2]

For decades, state sponsored segregation of schools was a matter of settled law. Indeed, as late as 1927, Chief Justice Taft was able to cite numerous authorities to support his statement that segregated school systems were "within the constitutional power of the state legislature to settle without intervention of the federal courts under the Federal Constitution."[3]

Brown and *Brown II*

In the 1954 decision of *Brown v. Board of Education of Topeka*, the United States Supreme Court reversed *Plessy v. Ferguson* and held that the doctrine of "separate but equal" has no place in public education.[4] The Court found that separate educational facilities are inherently unequal,[5] and that the *de*

---

[1] *See* U.S. Commission on Civil Rights (USCCR), *Twenty Years After Brown: A Report of the United States Commission on Civil Rights,* 1974; U.S. Commission on Civil Rights, *Desegregation of the Nation's Public Schools: A Status Report,* February 1979; U.S. Commission on Civil Rights, *With All Deliberate Speed*, Clearinghouse Publication No. 69, November 1981.

[2] *Plessy v. Ferguson*, 163 U.S. 537, 544 (1896).

[3] *Gong Lum v. Rice*, 275 U.S. 78, 86 (1927) (these authorities were: "Roberts v. City of Boston, 5 Cush. (Mass.) 198, 206, 208, 209; State ex rel. Garnes v. McCann, 21 Oh. St. 198, 210; People ex rel. King v. Gallagher, 93 N. Y. 438; People ex rel. Cisco v. School Board, 161 N. Y. 598; Ward v. Flood, 48 Cal. 36; Wysinger v. Crookshank, 82 Cal. 588, 590; Reynolds v. Board of Education, 66 Kans. 672; McMillan v. School Committee, 107 N. C. 609; Cory v. Carter, 48 Ind. 327; Lehew v. Brummell, 103 Mo. 546; Dameron v. Bayless, 14 Ariz. 180; State ex rel. Stoutmeyer v. Duffy, 7 Nev. 342, 348, 355; Bertonneau v. Board, 3 Woods 177, s. c. 3 Fed. Cases, 294, Case No. 1,361; United States v. Buntin, 10 Fed. 730, 735; Wong Him v. Callahan, 119 Fed. 381.").

[4] *Brown v. Bd. of Ed. of Topeka, Shawnee County, Kan.*, 347 U.S. 483 (1954).

[5] *Id.* at 495.

jure[6] segregation of students in public schools on the basis of race, even when physical facilities and other tangible factors are equal, is unconstitutional.[7]

The Court, however, did not initially address how quickly local school systems must desegregate. This was addressed a year later when the Court held that schools must initiate the process of desegregation with "all deliberate speed."[8]

Opposition to Desegregation

Brown helped to usher in a period of civil rights activism, as well as a backlash by those seeking to preserve the system of state-sponsored segregation. In many cases, many whites met the assertion of equal rights by African Americans with hostility, opposition, and sometimes even violence.[9]

- The court-ordered admission of nine black students to Central High in Little Rock, Arkansas, created such a fierce and violent opposition by some whites that it required the federalization of the Arkansas National Guard.[10]

- In Virginia, the decision in *Brown* produced a state-sponsored program of "Massive Resistance." In some instances, local public school systems were closed for years rather than integrate.[11]

- Rosa Parks' refusal to give up her seat on a bus sparked the 382-day Montgomery, Alabama Bus Boycott. Some whites responded to this boycott with violent opposition and bombed churches and the home of Dr. Martin Luther King, Jr.[12]

- In 1962, federal troops were called in to enforce the implementation of a court order requiring the admission of the first African-American student to the University of Mississippi.[13]

- In New Orleans, when the courts ordered that public schools be integrated in 1960, many white families boycotted the schools and the legislature attempted to cut off funding for teachers. Those who continued to attend classes were harassed at home and at school.[14]

- In 1963, the 16th Street Baptist Church, a church where Dr. Martin Luther King, Jr. frequently preached, was the target of a bomb that killed four young black girls and injured approximately 20 others.[15]

---

[6] In *Parents Involved in Cmty. Sch. v. Seattle Sch. Dist. No. 1*, 127 S. Ct. 2738, S. Ct. 2758–59, 2761 (2007) (Roberts, J., plurality), a majority of the Court reconfirmed the legal significance of the distinction between *de jure* discrimination, in which the power of the state is used to compel segregation, and *de facto* discrimination, arising out of private choices. *Id.* at 2794–96 (Kennedy, J., concurring).

[7] *Brown*, 347 U.S. at 493.

[8] *Brown II*, 349 U.S. 294, 301 (1955).

[9] *See, e.g.,* USCCR, *Twenty Years After Brown*, pp. 16–25.

[10] Ibid. pp. 17–18.

[11] *See* Jennifer E. Spreng, *Scenes From The Southside: A Desegregation Drama In Five Acts,* 19 U. Ark. Little Rock L.J. 327 (1997) (discussing Prince Edward County, Virginia's resistance to desegregation).

[12] *See* USCCR, *Twenty Years After Brown*, pp. 16–17.

[13] *See Meredith v. Fair*, 83 S. Ct. 10 (1962); *see also* Jack Greenberg, *Brown v. Board of Education: Witness to a Landmark Decision* (NY: Twelve Table Press, 2004), pp. 204–22; USCCR, *Twenty Years After Brown*, pp. 19–20.

[14] Greenberg, *Brown v. Board of Education*, pp. 183–89.

It was during this tumultuous time that President Eisenhower signed the Civil Rights Act of 1957, which created the U.S. Commission on Civil Rights.[16] The Act provided that the Commission would:

> (1) investigate allegations in writing under oath or affirmation that certain citizens of the United States are being deprived of their right to vote and have that vote counted by reason of their color, race, religion, or national origin; which writing, under oath or affirmation, shall set forth the facts upon which such belief or beliefs are based;
>
> (2) study and collect information concerning legal developments constituting a denial of equal protection of the laws under the Constitution; and
>
> (3) appraise the laws and policies of the Federal Government with respect to equal protection of the laws under the Constitution.[17]

From its inception, the Commission undertook these duties as it related to the segregation of schools through the issuance of statutory and staff reports[18] and the holding of conferences and hearings.[19]

The Civil Rights Act of 1964 and the Elementary and Secondary Education Act of 1965

A decade after *Brown*, little had changed. The extraordinary and sometimes violent opposition to desegregation had left the status quo in place. As described by one authority: "[I]n the eleven ex-Confederate states 'deliberate' amounted to glacial. There, a full decade after *Brown*, a mere 1.2 percent of black public school students attended schools that had *any* white pupils at all."[20] By making "only the

---

[15] USCCR, *Twenty Years After Brown*, p. 25.

[16] Civil Rights Act of 1957, Pub. L. No. 85-315, 71 Stat. 634 (1957).

[17] *Id.* § 104(a).

[18] *See, e.g.*, U.S. Commission on Civil Rights, *Report of the U.S. Commission on Civil Rights*, 1959; U.S. Commission on Civil Rights, *Equal Protection of the Laws in Public Higher Education*, 1960; U.S. Commission on Civil Rights, *Statutory Report for 1961, Vol. 2 Education*, 1961; U.S. Commission on Civil Rights, *Civil Rights '63*, 1963; U.S. Commission on Civil Rights, *Civil Rights Under Federal Programs*, 1965; U.S. Commission on Civil Rights (USCCR), *Federal Rights Under School Desegregation Law*, Clearinghouse Publication No. 6, 1966; U.S. Commission on Civil Rights, *Racial Isolation in the Public Schools*, 1967; U.S. Commission on Civil Rights, *Schools Can be Desegregated*, 1967; U.S. Commission on Civil Rights, *Education Parks*, 1967; U.S. Commission on Civil Rights, *Process of Change: The Story of School Desegregation in Syracuse, N.Y.*, 1968; U.S. Commission on Civil Rights, *Problems of Segregation and Desegregation of Public Schools: Synopsis of Conference Before the U.S. Commission on Civil Rights*, Staff Report, 1962; U.S. Commission on Civil Rights, *Civil Rights, U.S.A./Public Schools North and West, Camden and Environs*, Staff Report, 1963; U.S. Commission on Civil Rights, *Public Education 1963*, Staff Report, 1963; U.S. Commission on Civil Rights, *Public Education 1964 (Southern and Border States)*, Staff Report, 1964.

[19] *See, e.g.*, U.S. Commission on Civil Rights, *First Annual Conference on Education, Nashville, Tenn.*, 1959; U.S. Commission on Civil Rights, *Second Annual Conference on Education, Gatlinburg, Tenn.*, 1960; U.S. Commission on Civil Rights, *Third Annual Conference on Education, Williamsburg, Va.*, 1961; U.S. Commission on Civil Rights, *Conference Before the U.S. Commission on Civil Rights, Washington, D.C.*, 1962; U.S. Commission on Civil Rights, *Hearing Before the U.S. Commission on Civil Rights, Los Angeles, Calif. and San Francisco, Calif. Report*, 1960; U.S. Commission on Civil Rights, *Hearing Before the U.S. Commission on Civil Rights, Memphis, Tenn. Report*, 1962; U.S. Commission on Civil Rights, *Hearing Before the U.S. Commission on Civil Rights, Boston, Mass.*, 1966; U.S. Commission on Civil Rights, *Hearing Before the U.S. Commission on Civil Rights, San Antonio, Tex. Report*, 1968.

[20] Stephan Thernstrom and Abigail Thernstrom, *America in Black and White* (New York: Simon & Schuster, 1997), p. 105. Moreover, a decade after *Brown* only 2.3% of African-American students in the South attended majority white schools. *See* Erwin Chemerinsky, *Essay: Separate and Unequal: American Public Education Today*, 52 Am. U. L. Rev. 1461, 1463 (2003) (citing Gary Orfield, *Schools More Separate: Consequences of a Decade of Resegregation*, The Civil Rights Project Harvard University, July 2001, p. 29).

most minimal and grudging gestures toward desegregation," those jurisdictions invited "much more aggressive judicial intervention than otherwise would have been the case."[21]

Due in part to this opposition, and the fact that it was often undertaken under color of state law, Congress enacted the Civil Rights Act of 1964.[22] The Act was created in recognition of the fact that federal intervention and enforcement were necessary to ensure the equal rights of African Americans. The Civil Rights Act of 1964 accomplishes this by a variety of methods.

First, Title IV of the Act authorizes the Attorney General to sue a school district when a parent or parents submit a meritorious written complaint alleging that a school board is depriving a child or children of the equal protection of the laws and the complainant is unable to proceed against the school board on his or her own.[23]

Second, Title VI of the Act makes school districts that engage in racial discrimination ineligible for federal funding.[24] As federal funding of education increased, this exerted a substantial influence on school districts' decisions to undertake desegregation.[25]

Finally, Title IX of the Act authorizes the Attorney General to intervene in existing lawsuits that private parties bring "seeking relief from the denial of equal protection of the laws under the fourteenth amendment to the Constitution on account of race, color, religion, sex or national origin"—if the Attorney General certifies that the case is of general public importance.[26]

The next year, Congress enacted the Elementary and Secondary Education Act of 1965, which provides financial assistance "to local educational agencies serving areas with concentrations of children from low-income families to expand and improve their educational programs by various means (including preschool programs) which contribute particularly to meeting the special education needs of educationally deprived children."[27] With the passage of these two acts, the "federal bureaucrats combined the stick provided by Title VI of the Civil Rights Act with the carrot of significant new funding in the 1965 legislation to motivate many Southern school districts to comply rapidly with desegregation orders."[28]

---

[21] Thernstrom and Thernstrom, *America in Black and White*, p. 317.

[22] Civil Rights Act of 1964, Pub. L. No. 88-352, 78 Stat. 252 (1964) (codified in sections of 42 U.S.C.).

[23] *See id.* § 2000c-6 (2007). Appropriate reasons why the complainant cannot proceed directly on his or her own accord are inability "to bear the expense of the litigation or to obtain effective legal representation; or whenever ... [the Attorney General] is satisfied that the institution of such litigation would jeopardize the personal safety, employment, or economic standing of such person or persons, their families, or their property." *Id.* § 2000c-6(b).

[24] *See* 42 U.S.C. §§ 2000d – 2000d-7 (2007).

[25] Charles Clotfelter, *After Brown: The Rise and Retreat of School Desegregation* (Princeton: Princeton University Press, 2004), p. 26 (citing U.S. Commission on Civil Rights, *School Desegregation in Wichita, Kansas* (1977), p. 16, table 21.1).

[26] 42 U.S.C. § 2000h-2 (2007).

[27] Elementary and Secondary Education Act of 1965, Pub. L. 89-10, 79 Stat. 27, § 201 (1965) (codified as amended at 20 U.S.C. § 6301 (2002)).

[28] Clotfelter, *After Brown*, p. 26 (citing Gary Orfield, *The Reconstruction of Southern Education: The Schools and the 1964 Civil Rights Act* (New York: Wiley-Interscience, 1969), pp. 46, 77).

Green and its Progeny

By the late 1960s, the Supreme Court's patience at the slow pace of desegregation came to an end. Only a month after the assassination of Dr. Martin Luther King, Jr., the Court issued its decision in *Green v. County School Board of New Kent County*, which established specific standards by which desegregation efforts should be judged and "signaled the true beginning of federal court supervision of the desegregation of local schools."[29] It held that in assessing whether a school district had eliminated the vestiges of *de jure* segregation, federal courts must, to the extent practicable, look at every facet of school operations.[30] The Court then identified six factors that should be examined: (1) student assignment, (2) faculty assignment, (3) staff assignment, (4) transportation, (5) extracurricular activities, and (6) facilities.[31]

In addition, the Supreme Court for the first time used the term "unitary" to describe a school system that had transitioned from a segregated, racially dual system, to a unitary, desegregated system.[32]

Shortly thereafter, in 1969, the Court indicated that no further delays would be tolerated. In *Alexander v. Holmes County [Mississippi] Board of Education*,[33] the Court held that desegregation was to be achieved "at once" and that the school district in question was to "operate now and hereafter only unitary schools."[34]

In later reviewing these times, Justice Clarence Thomas noted that:

> [R]esistance to *Brown I* produced little desegregation by the time we decided *Green* ... Our impatience with the pace of desegregation and with the lack of a good-faith effort on the part of school boards led us to approve such extraordinary remedial measures.[35]

Having ordered that desegregation should proceed without further delay, the next decade of the Court's jurisprudence focused on issues of implementation. *See, e.g., Swann v. Charlotte-Mecklenberg Board of Education*, 402 U.S. 1 (1971) (authorizing the use of busing as a remedy); *Keyes v. School District No. 1, Denver, Co.*, 413 U.S. 189 (1973) (finding that if intentional segregation is found in part of school district, it is presumed to occur in all of the district); *San Antonio Independent School District v.*

---

[29] Danielle R. Holley, *Is* Brown *Dying? Exploring the Resegregation Trend in Our Public Schools*, 49 N.Y.L. Sch. L. Rev. 1085, 1089 (2004). For an account of this historic case by one of the petitioners' attorneys, *see* Greenberg, *Brown v. Board of Education*, pp. 230–32.

[30] *Green v. County Sch. Bd. of New Kent County, Va.*, 391 U.S. 430, 435 (1968). It is worth noting that the U.S. Commission on Civil Rights' report on *Southern School Desegregation, 1966–'67*, was cited in this historic decision. *Id.* at 441, n.5 (citing U.S. Commission on Civil Rights, *Southern School Desegregation, 1966–'67*, July 1967, p. 88).

[31] *Green*, 391 U.S. at 435 ("Racial identification of the system's schools was complete, extending not just to the composition of student bodies at the two schools but to every facet of school operations – faculty, staff, transportation, extracurricular activities and facilities. In short, the State, acting through the local school board and school officials, organized and operated a dual system, part 'white' and part 'Negro.'").

[32] *Id.* at 435–36.

[33] *Alexander v. Holmes County [Mississippi] Board of Education*, 396 U.S. 19 (1969).

[34] *Id.* at 20.

[35] *Missouri v. Jenkins*, 515 U.S. 70, 125 (1995) (Thomas, J., concurring). *See also, Parents Involved*, 127 S. Ct. at 2795 ("To remedy the wrong, school districts that had been segregated by law had no choice, whether under court supervision or pursuant to voluntary desegregation efforts, but to resort to extraordinary measures including individual student and teacher assignment to schools based on race.") (Kennedy, J., concurring in part and concurring in judgment).

Rodriguez, 411 U.S. 1 (1973) (holding that inequalities in school funding did not deny equal protection); *Milliken v. Bradley*, 418 U.S. 717 (1974) (holding that inter-district remedies are not permissible, unless a constitutional violation within one district produces a significant segregation effect in another); *Milliken v. Bradley II*, 433 U.S. 267 (1977) (holding that courts may order states to pay for compensatory and remedial programs for schoolchildren who have been subjected to segregation).

The strong intervention by the federal courts, as well as the effects of the Civil Rights Act of 1964 and the incentive of increased federal funding, caused previously recalcitrant jurisdictions to change their policies. The process has been described as follows:

> The Civil Rights Act of 1964, the HEW [Department of Health, Education, and Welfare] school desegregation guidelines, and a series of federal court decisions made it unmistakably plain to southerners that further delay of school desegregation would not be tolerated. As a result, the walls of the Jim Crow school system suddenly came tumbling down. In the 1963–1964 school year, barely 1 percent of southern black children attended a school that had any whites enrolled in it. By the time of the *Green* decision, in 1968, the figure was up to 32 percent. That was an impressive jump, obviously, but it still meant that two out of three black pupils in the South had no white classmates at all. *Green* and *Swann* turned up the heat so that by the 1972–1973 school year no fewer than 91 percent of southern black students were attending school with whites. By this minimal measure, at least, integration was nearly complete.[36]

But substantial federal intervention also came at a price. During this time, courts placed numerous metropolitan areas under court-ordered desegregation plans requiring them to restructure their educational systems.[37] This often removed children from their local schools and made the decisions of elected school boards subservient to those of unelected judges without expertise in the area of education.[38]

In particular, the imposition of busing caused many to question the extent of federal intervention in matters that have historically been under local control. The appropriateness of ongoing, decades-long federal court control in an area of society previously served by elected, local school boards has been questioned by recent Supreme Court jurisprudence, discussed in more detail in the next section of this chapter.[39] Justice Breyer noted in his dissent to the recent *Parents Involved* decision, "[T] his Court has repeatedly stressed the importance of acknowledging that local school boards better understand their

---

[36] Thernstrom and Thernstrom, *America in Black and White*, p. 324 (citation omitted); *see also* Clotfelter, *After Brown*, p. 26 ("The result of these developments was a breathtaking transformation of public education in many communities in the South. In the space of just a few years—principally, 1969 to 1972—levels of interracial contact in school shot up all over the South. Whereas 78 percent of black students attended schools that were 90 percent or more minority in 1968, by 1972 the share had fallen to 25 percent. These dramatic increases in interracial contact were accomplished by means of desegregation plans that reassigned thousands of students to different schools.") (citation omitted).

[37] Thernstrom and Thernstrom, *America in Black and White*, p. 330. Jurisdictions brought under court order included Boston, San Diego, San Francisco, Omaha, Minneapolis, Cleveland, Columbus, and Dayton, as well as dozens of other urban centers. Ibid. *See also* Clotfelter, *After Brown*, pp. 28–29.

[38] Thernstrom and Thernstrom, *America in Black and White*, p. 331.

[39] *Board of Ed. of Oklahoma City Public Schools, Independent Sch. Dist. No. 98, Oklahoma County, Okla. v. Dowell*, 498 U.S. 237 (1991); *Freeman v. Pitts*, 503 U.S. 467 (1992); *Missouri v. Jenkins*, 515 U.S. 70 (1995); *see also* The Hon. David S. Tatel, *Madison Lecture: Judicial Methodology, Southern School Desegregation, and the Rule of Law*, 79 N.Y.U. L. Rev. 1071, 1126–28 (Oct. 2004) (commenting, in part, on the shift in the Supreme Court's emphasis from constitutional violations and the harms of segregation to the virtues of local control).

own communities and have a better knowledge of what in practice will best meet the educational needs of their pupils."[40]

Busing was hotly contested since before it was first authorized by the Court in *Swann v. Charlotte-Mecklenberg Board of Education*.[41] Opponents of busing argue that, in addition to imposing a hardship on children, busing stifles parental involvement in school activities when their children's schools are not located in their neighborhoods and that busing children out of neighborhoods destroys communities.[42] It has been consistently unpopular with a clear majority of the general public.[43]

Court-ordered desegregation creates costs to the state and local communities.[44] The cost in maintaining desegregation plans, is at times, an adverse incentive for school districts to seek unitary status, even when they are not necessarily fully unitary.[45]

Finally, the decades-long supervision of school districts by courts may not have kept pace with the demographic changes in student population over time, mainly as a consequence of immigration and white flight. While court supervision was meant to address *de jure* discrimination between whites and blacks, there has been a steep decline in the white student population since many of these orders were put in place. In addition, growing levels of immigration have increased the number of Hispanic and Asian students, groups that were not present in large numbers when court intervention began.[46]

The situation has been described as follows: "At the time of *Brown*, the United States had two major racial groups. Non-Hispanic European Americans, or whites, were numerically dominant, representing some 88 percent of the total population. African Americans, or blacks, made up about 10 percent."[47]

That situation has changed and in its 2007 annual report on *The Condition of Education*, the Department of Education's National Center for Education Statistics reported that:

> Forty-two percent of public school students were considered to be part of a racial or ethnic minority group in 2005, an increase from 22 percent of students in 1972.... In comparison, the percentage of public school students who were White decreased from 78 to 58 percent. The minority increase largely reflected the growth in the proportion of students who were Hispanic. In 2005, Hispanic students represented 20 percent of public school enrollment, up from 6 percent in 1972. The proportion of public school students who were

---

[40] *Parents Involved*, 127 S. Ct. at 2826 (Breyer, J., dissenting) (citation omitted).

[41] 402 U.S. 1 (1971); *see also* Kenneth O'Neil Salyer, *Chalk Talk: Beyond Zelman: Reinventing Neighborhood Schools*, 33 J.L. & Educ. 283, 283 (Apr. 2004) ("Students of all ages are still failing, even those inner-city students who have to ride a bus three hours daily to the so-called 'white schools.'"); Thernstrom and Thernstrom, *America in Black and White*, pp. 330–36; *compare* U.S. Commission on Civil Rights, *Your Child and Busing*, Clearinghouse Publication No. 36, 1972.

[42] Salyer, 33 J.L. & Educ. at 287–88.

[43] Thernstrom and Thernstrom, *America in Black and White*, pp. 330–31.

[44] *See, e.g.*, Monika L. Moore, *Note: Unclear Standards Create an Unclear Future: Developing a Better Definition of Unitary Status*, 112 Yale L. J. 311, 322 (Nov. 2002) (citing James Ryan, *Schools, Race, and Money*, 109 Yale L. J. 249, 262, n. 41 (Nov. 1999)).

[45] *See, e.g.*, Cynthia Howell, "Keep monitoring LR [Little Rock, AR] schools, court is urged; Attorney for black students: 2 more years needed to gauge desegregation compliance," *Arkansas Democrat–Gazette*, Apr. 16, 2004.

[46] In its recent decision in *Parents Involved*, the Supreme Court noted the changes in the nation's racial and ethnic mix, and suggested that viewing race exclusively in strictly black-white terms was inappropriate. *Parents Involved*, 127 S. Ct. at 2754, 2760.

[47] Clotfelter, *After Brown*, pp. 33–35; *see also* Jessica E. Watson, *Note: Quest for Unitary Status: The East Baton Rouge Parish School Desegregation Case*, 62 La. L. Rev. 953, 982 (2002).

Hispanic increased more than the proportion of students who were Black or who were members of other minority groups. For example, in 2005, Black students made up 16 percent of public school enrollment compared with 15 percent in 1972. Hispanic enrollment measurably surpassed Black enrollment for the first time in 2002. Together Asian (4 percent), Pacific Islander (0.2 percent), and American Indian/Alaska Native (0.7 percent) students and students of more than one race (3 percent) made up 7 percent of public school enrollment in 2005, compared with 1 percent combined in 1972.[48]

The Supreme Court Desegregation Cases of the 1990s – *Dowell, Freeman,* and *Jenkins*

By the early 1990s, the Supreme Court revisited the general standards for "unitary status" in two cases: *Board of Education of Oklahoma City Public Schools v. Dowell*[49] and *Freeman v. Pitts*.[50]

In *Dowell*, the Court ruled that a declaration of unitary status is appropriate after a school district demonstrates, by way of the *Green* factors, that "[1] the [School] Board had complied in good faith with the desegregation decree since it was entered, and [2] … the vestiges of past discrimination had been eliminated to the extent practicable."[51] The Court further noted the importance of returning school districts to local control:

> Local control over the education of children allows citizens to participate in decisionmaking, and allows innovation so that school programs can fit local needs. *Milliken v. Bradley*, 418 U.S. 717, 742 (1974) (*Milliken I*); *San Antonio Independent School District v. Rodriguez*, 411 U.S. 1, 50 (1973). The legal justification for displacement of local authority by an injunctive decree in a school desegregation case is a violation of the Constitution by the local authorities. Dissolving a desegregation decree after the local authorities have operated in compliance with it for a reasonable period of time properly recognizes that "necessary concern for the important values of local control of public school systems dictates that a federal court's regulatory control of such systems not extend beyond the time required to remedy the effects of past intentional discrimination. *See* [*Milliken II*], 433 U.S. at 280–82." *Spangler v. Pasadena City Bd. of Education*, 611 F.2d at 1245, n.5 (Kennedy, J., concurring).[52]

The next year, in *Freeman v. Pitts*, the Supreme Court held that courts may remove judicial supervision incrementally in favor of local control. The Court stated, "As we have long observed, 'local autonomy of school districts is a vital national tradition.' *Dayton Bd. of Education v. Brinkman*, 433 U.S. 406, 410 (1977) (*Dayton I*). Returning schools to the control of local authorities at the earliest practicable date is essential to restore their true accountability in our governmental system."[53] Thus, if a school district was found to be in full compliance with one or more of the *Green* factors (student assignment, faculty assignment, staff assignment, transportation, extracurricular activities, and facilities), but not in

---

[48] National Center for Education Statistics, *The Condition of Education 2007*, "Section 1: Participation in Education," June 2007, p. 26; *see also* Gary Orfield and Chungmei Lee, *Racial Transformation and the Changing Nature of Segregation*, The Civil Rights Project Harvard University, January 2006, p. 8 (indicating that in the 2003/04 academic year, regular public school enrollment consisted of the following percentage of students: 58 % White students, 19% Latino students, 17% Black students, 4% Asian students, and 1% Native American students); Clotfelter, *After Brown*, pp. 33–35.

[49] *Board of Ed. of Oklahoma City Public Schools, Independent Sch. Dist. No. 98, Oklahoma County, Okla., v. Dowell*, 498 U.S. 237 (1991).

[50] *Freeman v. Pitts*, 503 U.S. 467 (1992).

[51] *Dowell*, 498 U.S. at 249–50.

[52] *Id.* at 248.

[53] *Freeman*, 503 U.S. at 490.

compliance with other *Green* factors, the court could elect to remove judicial supervision for the factor in which compliance had been achieved.[54]

The Court further held that "the *Green* factors need not be a rigid framework" and noted that courts may conduct an inquiry into the quality of education to determine whether other elements of the school system are in need of judicial supervision to ensure full compliance with the consent decree.[55] In other words, the Court held that the *Green* factors, while still highly relevant, were not necessarily the only measures of desegregation. The Court stated,

> The District Court's approach illustrates ... the uses of equitable discretion. By withdrawing control over areas where judicial supervision is no longer needed, a district court can concentrate both its own resources and those of the school district on the areas where the effects of *de jure* discrimination have not been eliminated and further action is necessary in order to provide real and tangible relief to minority students.[56]

Compliance is met once the vestiges of *de jure* discrimination have been eliminated to the maximum extent practicable.[57]

Under *Freeman*, courts must consider three primary factors for terminating judicial supervision:

> [1] whether there has been full and satisfactory compliance with the decree in those aspects of the system where supervision is to be withdrawn; [2] whether retention of judicial control is necessary or practicable to achieve compliance with the decree in other facets of the school system; and [3] whether the school district has demonstrated, to the public and to the parents and students of the once disfavored race, its good-faith commitment to the whole of the court's decree and to those provisions of the law and the Constitution that were the predicate for judicial intervention in the first instance.[58]

Just a few years after *Freeman*, the Court again emphasized the need to bring finality to judicial oversight in the case of *Missouri v. Jenkins*.[59] While not directly addressing the concept of unitary status, the Court reiterated the obligation of courts to "strive to restore state and local authorities to the control of a school system operating in compliance with the Constitution."[60] Thus, as noted by one authority, "the value of local control can easily become the deciding factor when courts consider motions to terminate."[61]

---

[54] *Id.* at 491.

[55] *Id.* at 492–93.

[56] *Id.*

[57] *See id.* at 493–94.

[58] *Id.* at 491.

[59] *Missouri v. Jenkins*, 515 U.S. 70 (1995) (holding that *Milliken v. Bradley II* remedies should be limited in time).

[60] *Id.* at 99 (citations omitted).

[61] Wendy Parker, *The Future of School Desegregation*, 94 Nw. U. L. Rev. 1157, 1165 (2000).

Current Practice

Active Court Orders

Although over fifty years have passed since *Brown*, many school districts are still subject to school desegregation court orders. As of May 2007, the United States remains a party to 266 suits in which school desegregation court orders are in effect.[62] There are, of course, many more such cases to which the United States is not a party, but no comprehensive list of these cases currently exists.[63] Moreover, many cases were initiated in the late 1960s and early 1970s and the original players have either moved on or in some cases passed away. In such instances, not even the school districts understand the scope of the court orders that bind them and little reliable information exists that can provide a complete picture as to the nature of ongoing court-ordered desegregation. In addition to school districts that are parties to litigation concerning desegregation, many school districts have entered into agreements with the Department of Education's Office for Civil Rights to implement desegregation plans, also known as Form 441-B plans.[64]

The extent of continued judicial oversight is particularly notable given that "the nation's schools are going through an astonishing transformation since the 1960s, changing from a country where more than four of every five students were white, to one with just 58 percent white enrollment nationwide and changing slightly every year."[65] As summarized by one report,

> High birth rates, low levels of private school enrollment and increased immigration of Latinos have resulted in a rise of Latino public school enrollment, which is now more than 7 million. Nationwide, the Latino share of public school enrollment has almost tripled since 1968, compared to an increase of just 30% in black enrollment and a decrease of 17% in white enrollment during the same time period.[66]

Given the demographic changes in the composition of student bodies across the nation, it is useful to inquire into the utility of court orders originally entered to address state-sponsored schemes of racial segregation that only considered black and white pupils.

---

[62] *See* U.S. Department of Justice, Civil Rights Division, Response to U.S. Commission on Civil Rights' Interrogatories and Document Requests, Response to Interrogatory Requests 2 and 26, May 17, 2007.

[63] *See, e.g.,* Moore, 112 Yale L. J. at 311.

[64] Title VI of the Civil Rights Act of 1964, required school districts to submit documentation indicating their desegregation status to remain eligible for federal funding to the U.S. Department of Health, Education, and Welfare's Office of Education. Those school districts that did not operate segregated schools or which eliminated segregation from its schools were required to complete and submit Form 441. Those school districts that entered into voluntary desegregation plans were required to complete and submit Form 441-B. And those school districts that were operating under a desegregation court order had to provide evidence to that effect. *See* U.S. Department of Health, Education, and Welfare (HEW), Office of Education, Revised Statement of Policies for School Desegregation Plans Under Title VI of the Civil Rights Act of 1964, 45 C.F.R. §§ 181.5–181.7 (1966) *reprinted in* USCCR, *Federal Rights Under School Desegregation Law*, "Appendix," pp. 11–21. *See also* James R. Dunn, *Title VI, The Guidelines and School Desegregation in the South*, 53 Va. L. Rev. 42, 59 (Jan. 1967) (discussing the requirement for school districts to submit Form 441-B).

Although HEW no longer exists, the requirement remains in effect. Thus, school districts must continue to provide such information to HEW's successor, the U.S. Department of Education, to remain eligible for federal funding. It should be noted that the current iteration of these regulations does not reference "Form 441-B." *See* 34 C.F.R. § 100.4(c) (2007).

[65] *See* Orfield and Lee, *Racial Transformation*, p. 8; *see also* Thernstrom and Thernstrom, *America in Black and White*, pp. 336–40.

[66] Erica Frankenberg and Chungmei Lee, *Race in American Public Schools: Rapidly Resegregating School Districts*, The Civil Rights Project, Harvard University, August 2002, p. 2.

Extrajudicial Reasons

Perhaps not surprisingly, extrajudicial considerations have affected school districts' decisions whether to seek unitary status. Anecdotal evidence suggests that reasons not to seek unitary status include: the potential loss of state or federal funds if the school district is declared unitary,[67] the desire to preserve the court mandated racial balance of staff,[68] the desire to preserve the continued use of race-conscious approaches to determine eligibility in certain programs, such as magnet schools, which might otherwise be constitutionally challenged,[69] the desire to maintain funding available to magnet schools established under school desegregation plans,[70] the financial and administrative cost of seeking unitary status,[71] the fear of changing the culture and identity of schools,[72] the belief that court orders must remain in place to protect the interests of the students,[73] the fear that unitary status will lead to the dissolution of particular school district,[74] the fear of alienating African American members of the community,[75] and simple inertia.[76]

Similar evidence suggests that extrajudicial reasons to seek unitary status also exist and include: the forgiveness of school district debts by the state,[77] the promise of increased funding to the school district by the state,[78] the pressures placed on school districts by states to dismantle desegregation plans because they are costly,[79] the pressures from white and black middle class flight,[80] an increased ability to operate

---

[67] *See* Moore, 112 Yale L. J. at 322 (citing Ryan, 109 Yale L. J. at 262, n. 41).

[68] *See* Moore, 112 Yale L. J. at 323.

[69] Some settlement agreements dismissing such suits have included clauses to preserve such programs. *See* "School Board OKs desegregation pact: Memorandum of Understanding," *Advocate*, Baton Rouge, LA, June 26, 2003.

[70] *See* Magnet Schools Assistance Program, 34 C.F.R. §§ 280.1–280.41(2006).

[71] "Not seeking termination imposes only known costs, while dismissal proceedings would require additional resources and, more importantly, an examination of how the district treats minority school children." Parker, 94 Nw. U. L. Rev. at 1160. *See also* Phillip L. Hartley, Esq., written statement to the U.S. Commission on Civil Rights, Dec. 11, 2006, p. 5; Superintendent Joseph Pye, written statement to the U.S. Commission on Civil Rights, Dec. 14, 2006, p. 2.

[72] Kids in the Wire, "The Color of Teaching: In a Small Black School, Students Tackle a Conundrum of Equity," <www.whatkidscando.org> (last accessed Jan. 31, 2007).

[73] *See* Hartley, written statement, p. 6; *see also* Charles J. Boykin, Esq., written statement to the U.S. Commission on Civil Rights, Dec. 14, 2006, p. 4.

[74] *See* Rick Kron, "Split Up County District," *Arkansas Leader*, July 3, 2006.

[75] *See* Dr. Phil Burchfield, written statement to the U.S. Commission on Civil Rights, Dec. 14, 2006, p. 3.

[76] Parker, 94 Nw. U. L. Rev. at 1160 ("[M]ost cases suffer from extreme neglect—little activity will occur for years, if not decades, but the court-ordered remedies remain in place. The clear majority of school districts appear content with their outstanding court orders."); *see also* Hartley, written statement, p. 6.

[77] *See, e.g.*, Howell, "Keep monitoring LR schools, court is urged."

[78] Ryan, 109 Yale L. J. at 265:

> District courts have responded [to recent Supreme Court desegregation cases] by approving termination agreements reached by school districts, the state, and civil rights plaintiffs. These agreements typically call for the dismantling of desegregation plans and thus a potential return to de facto segregated neighborhood schools, in exchange for a large, one-time payment from the state to the relevant school districts. For example, school districts in Prince George's County, Cleveland, Kansas City, Nashville, Dayton, and Memphis have all agreed to terminate mandatory desegregation plans in exchange for large payments from the state.

[79] *See* "Sutherland Asbill & Brennan Litigators Win Major School Funding/Desegregation Case for State of Michigan," *Business Wire, Inc.*, Apr. 17, 2002; *see also* Watson, 62 La. L. Rev. at 982.

[80] *See* Watson, 62 La. L. Rev. at 982.

the school system more freely,[81] and the desire on the part of both black and white parents to end ineffective desegregation remedies and the use of race-conscious student assignment plans.[82]

Recent Developments

A majority of the Supreme Court recently confirmed that judicial remedies must be tailored to *de jure* segregation, not racial imbalance per se.[83] Chief Justice Roberts noted that, "We have emphasized that the harm being remedied by mandatory desegregation plans is the harm that is traceable to segregation, and that 'the Constitution is not violated by racial imbalance in the schools, without more.'"[84]

Similarly, Justice Kennedy explained:

> Where there has been *de jure* segregation, there is a cognizable legal wrong, and the courts and legislatures have broad power to remedy it. The remedy, though, was limited in time and limited to the wrong. The Court has allowed school districts to remedy their prior *de jure* segregation by classifying individual students based on their race. ... The limitation of this power to instances where there has been *de jure* segregation serves to confine the nature, extent, and duration of governmental reliance on individual racial classifications.[85]

---

[81] *See* Marion County Public Schools, "Judge Grants Unitary Status to District," News Release, Jan. 16, 2007, <www.marion.k12.fl.us/dept/crs/newsdetails2.cfm?recordID=250> (last accessed Aug.29, 2007).

[82] Parker, 94 Nw. U.L. Rev. at 1159; *see also* Dennis D. Parker, *Are Reports of Brown's Demise Exaggerated? Perspectives of a School Desegregation Litigator* 49 N.Y.L. Sch. L. Rev. 1069, 1079–80 (2004).

[83] *See Parents Involved in Cmty. Sch. v. Seattle Sch. Dist. No. 1*, 127 S. Ct. 2738 (2007).

[84] *Id.* at 2752 (citation omitted).

[85] *Id.* at 2796 (Kennedy, J., concurring in part and concurring in judgment) (citation omitted).

CHAPTER 3: THE DEPARTMENT OF JUSTICE'S ENFORCEMENT EFFORTS

The Department of Justice's (DOJ) involvement in desegregation cases derives from Titles IV, VI, and IX of the Civil Rights Act of 1964.[1] Title IV of the Act authorizes the Attorney General to sue a school district when a parent or group of parents submits a meritorious written complaint alleging that a school board is depriving a child or children of the equal protection of the laws and that the complainant is unable to proceed against the school board on his or her own.[2] Similarly, upon a referral from the Department of Education, the Attorney General may bring suit against a school district which discriminates "on the ground of race, color, or national origin" pursuant to Title VI of the Act.[3] Title IX of the Act authorizes the Attorney General to intervene in existing lawsuits that private parties bring "seeking relief from the denial of equal protection of the laws under the fourteenth amendment to the Constitution on account of race, color, religion, sex or national origin" – if the Attorney General certifies that the case is of general public importance.[4] The component within DOJ that is charged with carrying out these duties is the Educational Opportunities Section (EOS) of the Civil Rights Division (CRD), which is the subject of this chapter.[5]

While the Act provides DOJ with the authority to bring suit against segregated school districts directly or to intervene in such cases, the agency has a far wider range of options to achieve its ends. For example, it may file amicus briefs in support of plaintiffs or serve as an advisor to schools or courts on designing desegregation plans and the effectiveness of alternative strategies.[6] Furthermore, as many of the school desegregation lawsuits have been placed on the courts' inactive docket (due primarily to the age of the cases), DOJ officials can allocate additional resources and staff to these cases, enabling greater activity in these stagnant cases that can result in further relief for plaintiffs or an eventual finding of unitary status.[7]

---

[1] Civil Rights Act of 1964, Pub. L. No. 88-352, 78 Stat. 252 (1964) (codified in sections of 42 U.S.C.).

[2] *See* 42 U.S.C. § 2000c-6 (2007).

[3] Under Title VI of the Civil Rights Act, federal funding may be withheld from school districts that discriminate "on the ground of race, color, or national origin." 42 U.S.C. § 2000d (2007). In such instances, the Department of Education may refer the case to DOJ for legal action. *See* 34 C.F.R. § 100.8 (2007).

[4] 42 U.S.C. § 2000h-2 (2007).

[5] U.S. Department of Justice, Civil Rights Division, Educational Opportunities Section, "Overview," <http://www.usdoj.gov/crt/edo/overview.htm> (last accessed July 22, 2007) (hereafter cited as "EOS Overview").

[6] The Educational Opportunities Section's fiscal year 2002 performance measures track, for example, "Motions, Pleadings and Proposed Orders Filed," "Settlement Negotiations Conducted," and "Modification Proposals/Petitions Approved." U.S. Department of Justice, Civil Rights Division, Financial Operations Staff, *FY 2002 Congressional Budget Submission*, p. G-52 (hereafter cited as "FY 2002 CRD Cong. Budget Submission" and similarly for other years). Today, the section's overview describes the unit's efforts to achieve consent decrees and favorable decisions that enhance districts' desegregation. For example, these efforts led to a settlement agreement that dismissed a case but retained federal court jurisdiction to enforce the agreement. EOS Overview, p. 1.

[7] For example, in fiscal year 1979 the DOJ planned to devote increased resources to student desegregation cases in large metropolitan areas and anticipated many more student assignment cases for court action as a result. Executive Office of the President, Office of Management and Budget, *Special Analyses, Budget of the United States Government, Fiscal Year 1979*, "Special Analysis N, Civil Rights Activities," p. 282 (hereafter cited as "FY 1979 OMB Special Analyses"). Also, in fiscal year 1991, a unit within the Educational Opportunities Section (EOS) gave increased emphases to monitoring districts' compliance with the court orders under which they were operating and initiated enforcement action against a number of districts that were in noncompliance. FY 1993 CRD Cong. Budget Submission, p. G-35. In fiscal year 1981, DOJ announced its new policy to pursue litigation and remedies not only to assure equal access to education, but against discrimination in the *quality* of elementary and secondary educational opportunities based on race or national origin. Executive Office of the President, Office of Management and Budget, *The Budget of the United States Government, 1983,* "Special Analysis J, Civil Rights

This chapter examines the organizational strengths as well as the resources DOJ brings to bear on desegregation issues; shifts in policy or emphases that extend, expand, or contract the number or length of time school districts are under DOJ or court supervision; and, finally, DOJ workload and accomplishments. The presentation analyzes information from the early 1990s through May 2007.

Organizational Strengths, Weaknesses, and Resources

Structural Placement of the Educational Opportunities Section

The Department of Justice's Civil Rights Division (CRD), established in 1957,[8] is responsible for the enforcement of federal statutes prohibiting discrimination on the basis of race, sex, disability, religion, and national origin. CRD's responsibilities include discrimination in housing, employment, education, voting, lending, public accommodations, access to services and facilities, activities that receive federal financial assistance, and the treatment of juvenile and adult detainees and residents of private institutions.[9]

In 1969, the Educational Section of the CRD was formed. The Education Section "was charged with enforcing federal statutes prohibiting discrimination on the basis of race, sex, disability, religion, and national origin in public schools."[10] In 1979, the Education Section was joined with the Housing Section and merged into the General Litigation Section "in an effort to jointly combat segregation in those areas."[11] This merger only lasted until 1984, when the General Litigation Section was re-divided into the current Educational Opportunities Section (the focus of this chapter) and the Housing and Civil

---

Activities," p. 14 (hereafter cited as "FY 1983 OMB Special Analyses"). *See also,* Executive Office of the President, Office of Management and Budget, *Special Analyses, Budget of the United States Government, Fiscal Year 1985,* "Special Analysis J, Civil Rights Activities," p. J-9 (hereafter cited as "FY 1985 OMB Special Analyses"). Finally, in 2002, EOS emphasized timely reviews of unitary status that resulted in obtaining full unitary status and dismissal, or partial unitary status. FY 2002 CRD Cong. Budget Submission, p. G-43.

[8] *See, e.g.,* Department of Commerce, Justice, and State, the Judiciary, and Related Agencies, *Appropriations for 2005: Hearings before a Subcommittee of the Committee on Appropriations, House of Representatives, 108th Cong.,* p. 528 (2004) (hereafter cited as "FY 2005 Cong. Appropriations Hearings").

[9] *See* ibid., p. 528.

The Commission on Civil Rights has reviewed enforcement efforts of several sections of the Department of Justice's Civil Rights Division in past reports. *See, e.g.,* U.S. Commission on Civil Rights, *Voting Rights Enforcement & Reauthorization: The Department of Justice's Record of Enforcing the Temporary Voting Rights Act Provision,* May 2006; U.S. Commission on Civil Rights, *Federal Efforts to Eradicate Employment Discrimination in State and Local Governments,* September 2001; U.S. Commission on Civil Rights, *Helping State and Local Governments Comply with the ADA: An Assessment of How the United States Department of Justice Is Enforcing Title II, Subpart A, of the Americans with Disabilities Act,* September 1998; U.S. Commission on Civil Rights, *Federal Title VI Enforcement to Ensure Nondiscrimination in Federally Assisted Programs,* "Chapter 3: The Coordination and Enforcement Role of the Department of Justice," June 1996, pp. 55–158; U.S. Commission on Civil Rights, *Ten-Year Check-Up: Have Federal Agencies Responded to Civil Rights Recommendations? Volume II: An Evaluation of the Departments of Justice, Labor, and Transportation,* September 2002. The *Ten-Year Check-Up* is a sequel to the reports on the American with Disabilities Act and Title VI.

[10] Asheesh Agarwal, Deputy Assistant Attorney General, U.S. Department of Justice, letter to David Blackwood, General Counsel, U.S. Commission on Civil Rights, July 19, 2007, p. 1 (hereafter cited as "DOJ correspondence, July 19, 2007").

[11] Ibid., p. 1; *see also* Executive Office of the President, Office of Management and Budget, *Special Analyses, Budget of the United States Government, Fiscal Year 1981,* "Special Analysis J, Civil Rights Activities," p. 298 (hereafter cited as "FY 1981 OMB Special Analyses").

Enforcement Section.[12] Currently, the Educational Opportunities Section (EOS) is one of approximately 10 components within CRD.[13]

EOS's section chief reports to one of three deputy assistant attorney generals, who reports to the Assistant Attorney General for CRD.[14] Currently, each deputy assistant attorney general manages three or more sections. In recent years, the deputy overseeing EOS has been responsible for other sections, such as the Voting Section and the Coordination and Review Section.[15]

Although there is evidence that suggests that EOS was at one time structured into components such as a Compliance Monitoring Unit and a Litigation Support Unit,[16] EOS is currently not divided into units.[17]

Budget and Staffing of the Educational Opportunities Section

EOS's ability to accomplish its mission and function is related in part to its budget and staffing and the scope of its responsibilities. Since at least 1969, CRD has had responsibility for school desegregation issues on behalf of DOJ and frequently reported planned budget amounts for its equal educational opportunities activities.[18] Not until CRD established EOS in FY 1984, did budget submissions contain enacted amounts strictly designated for such functions.[19]

---

[12] *See* DOJ correspondence, July 19, 2007, p. 1.

[13] *See* U.S. Department of Justice, Civil Rights Division (CRD) organizational charts in Fiscal Year (FY) 1993 to FY 2004 CRD Cong. Budget Submissions.

[14] *See* ibid.

[15] *See* CRD organizational charts in FY 2002 to FY 2004 CRD Cong. Budget Submissions; CRD organizational charts in FY 2005 Cong. Appropriations Hearings, p. 533, and Science, The Departments of State, Justice, and Commerce, and Related Agencies, *Appropriations for 2006: Hearings before a Subcommittee of the Committee on Appropriations, House of Representatives, 109th Cong.*, p. 604 (2005); U.S. Department of Justice, "Organization, Mission and Functions Manual, February 2006," [Civil Rights Division's Organizational chart and mission and functions statement], <http://www.usdoj.gov/jmd/mps/mission.htm>, last updated Feb. 29, 2000, (last accessed July 3, 2007).

The Coordination and Review Section works with other federal agencies under authority of Title VI of the Civil Rights Act of 1964 and other statutes to ensure that the government's programs and funding recipients do not discriminate in the provision of services and benefits. *See, e.g.,* FY 2005 Cong. Appropriations Hearings, p. 541.

[16] *See* FY 1993 CRD Cong. Budget Submission, p. G-34.

[17] *See* U.S. Department of Justice, Civil Rights Division (DOJ/CRD), Response to U.S. Commission on Civil Rights' (USCCR) Interrogatories and Document Requests, Response to Interrogatory Request 12, May 17, 2007.

[18] For example, the planned budget for the Department of Justice's equal educational opportunities program in FY 1975 was $2.8 million. *See* Executive Office of the President, Office of Management and Budget, *Special Analyses, Budget of the United States Government, Fiscal Year 1975*, "Special Analysis L, Federal Civil Rights Activities," p. 179 (hereafter cited as "FY 1975 OMB Special Analyses").

[19] *See* Executive Office of the President, Office of Management and Budget, *Special Analyses, Budget of the United States Government, Fiscal Year 1986*, "Special Analysis J, Civil Rights Activities," p. J-21 (hereafter cited as "FY 1986 OMB Special Analyses"). Also see the Civil Rights Division's organizational chart showing the Educational Opportunities Section, dated Oct. 30, 1983, and budget information in *Department of Commerce, Justice, and State, the Judiciary, and Related Agencies Appropriations for 1986: Hearings before a Subcommittee of the Committee on Appropriations, House of Representatives*, 99th Cong., pp. 1401–1405 (1985).

Note that the lack of a budget line item for the equal educational opportunities function, while not protecting against reallocations of its funding and staffing to other missions, at times can provide flexibility for augmenting its resources from the Division's coffers. For example, in April 1979, the Civil Rights Division consolidated its equal education opportunities and housing functions to address the interrelated problems of residential segregation and segregation of public schools. *See* FY 1981 OMB Special Analyses, "Special Analysis J, Civil Rights Activities," p. 298. In fiscal year 1980, the Department of Justice increased the planned budget approximately 43 percent for the combined education/housing function over the FY 1979 amount for equal educational opportunities. *See* Executive Office of the

While CRD's budget grew during the 1990s, seemingly to accommodate the legislated expansion in mission and functions, EOS's enacted funding remained relatively level. Figure 3.1 shows EOS's enacted budget and inflation adjusted trends. When established in FY 1984, EOS's enacted budget was $1.5 million. By FY 1991, the amount increased to $2.3 million, but even with steady annual growth, it remained at or below $3.0 million in FY 1999. However, EOS's allocation increased to $5.6 million by FY 2006, with a small reduction in FY 2005 having little effect overall. Adjusting amounts to year 2000 dollars flattens, but does not erase these evident trends. In constant 2000 dollars, EOS's budget was $2.3 million in FY 1984, approximately $2.8 to $3.0 million (relatively constant) between FY 1991 and FY 1999, $3.6 million in FY 2000, and rose to $4.8 million in FY 2006.

Figure 3.1
The Department of Justice's Budget for the Civil Rights Division's Educational Opportunities Section, 1984 and 1991 to 2006

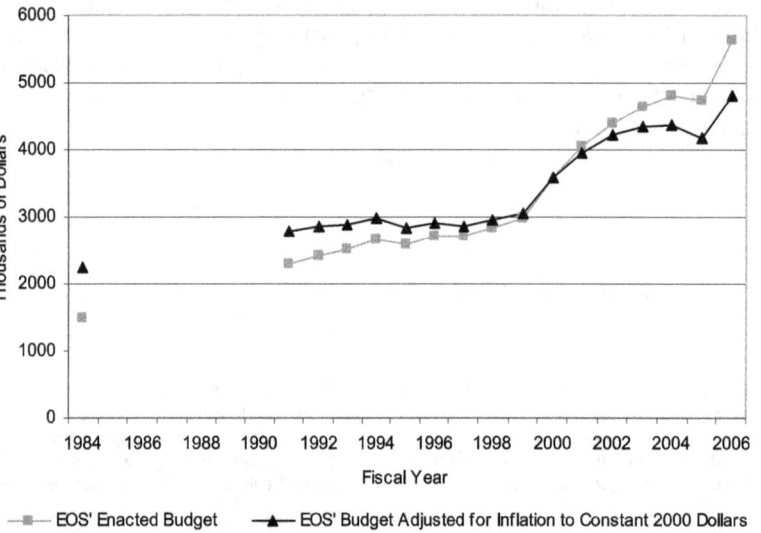

Caption: Adjusted for inflation to constant 2000 dollars, EOS's budget remained relatively level, between 2.8 and 3.0 million dollars, through the 1990s. In FY 2000, the section's budget began to climb. Adjusted for inflation, this climb resulted in an overall increase of approximately 1.8 million dollars between FY 1999 and FY 2006.

Sources: U.S. Department of Justice, Civil Rights Division, Financial Operations Staff, *FY[s] [1993 to 2004] Congressional Budget Submission*; Departments of Commerce, Justice, and State, the Judiciary, and Related Agencies, *Appropriations for 1986: Hearings before a Subcommittee of the Committee on Appropriations, House of Representatives, 99th Cong.*, 1401–1433 (1985); Departments of Commerce, Justice, and State, the Judiciary, and Related Agencies, *Appropriations for 2005: Hearings before a Subcommittee of the Committee on Appropriations, House of Representatives, 108th Cong.*, 526–571 (2004); Departments of Commerce, Justice, and State, the Judiciary, and Related Agencies, Appropriations for 2006: Hearings before a Subcommittee of the Committee on Appropriations, House of Representatives, 109th Cong., 568–615 (2005); and U.S. Department of Justice, FY[s] [2003 to 2007] Budget [and Performance] Summary, <http://www.usdoj.gov/05publications/05_3.html> (last accessed Oct. 17, 2006).

President, Office of Management and Budget, *Special Analyses, Budget of the United States Government, Fiscal Year 1980*, "Special Analysis J, Civil Rights Activities," p. 268; and FY 1979 OMB Special Analyses, "Special Analysis N, Civil Rights Activities," p. 282.

EOS's budget is partly tied to the section's staffing level. DOJ reports that the number of on-board, full-time permanent employees assigned to EOS for each of the following years are 30 in FY 1991, 30 in FY 1992, 30 in FY 1993, 32 in FY 1994, 33 in FY 1995, 32 in FY 1996, 29 in FY 1997, 30 in FY 1998, 28 in FY 1999, 33 in FY 2000, 33 in FY 2001, 34 in FY 2002, 33 in FY 2003, 33 in FY 2004, 26 in FY 2005, and 31 in FY 2006.[20] This information is found in Figure 3.2.

Figure 3.2
The Department of Justice's Staffing in the Civil Rights Division's Educational Opportunities Section, 1991 to 2006

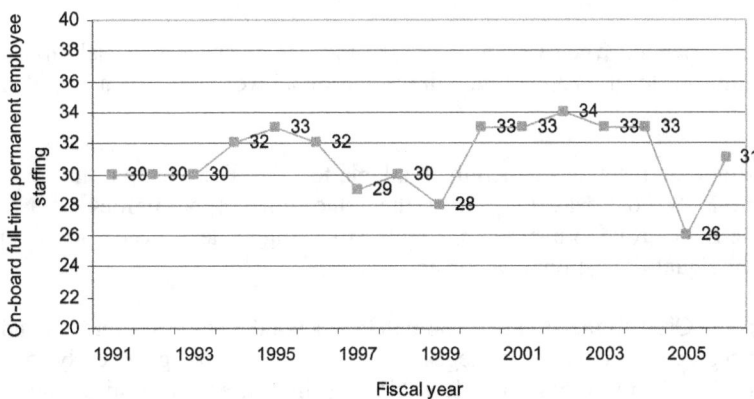

Caption: Since 1991 EOS's on-board full-time permanent staffing has ranged between 26 and 34 employees. EOS had 30 staff in the early 1990s; the number rose to 33 in 1995, then dropped to 28 by 1999. In fiscal years 2000 and 2001, the full-time staffing increased to 33, then to 34 in 2002. It returned to 33 in fiscal years 2003 and 2004, then dropped to 26 in fiscal year 2005. In 2006, EOS had 31 permanent full-time staff on board.

Source: U.S. Department of Justice, Civil Rights Division, Response to U.S. Commission on Civil Rights' Interrogatories and Document Requests, Responses to Interrogatory Request 23, May 17, 2007.

It appears that between FY 1990 and FY 2000 nearly two-thirds of EOS's staff members provided support, while approximately one-third were attorneys. In FY 1996 to FY 1999, the permanent positions included 19 support staff and 11 attorneys. The increase in FY 2000 provided for four additional attorneys, but only two additional full-time equivalents. The FY 2000 appropriation augmented low-level support staff by two to 21 positions. The FY 2001 increases raised full-time equivalents for attorneys to 14 and for support staff to 23.[21] After FY 2001, it is unclear how many of EOS's employees are attorneys and support staff.[22]

---

[20] DOJ/CRD, Response to USCCR Interrogatories, Response to Interrogatory Request 23.

[21] FY 1998 to FY 2004 CRD Cong. Budget Submissions.

[22] *See* DOJ/CRD, Response to USCCR Interrogatories, Response to Interrogatory Request 23.

Broad Educational Opportunity Missions and Functions

In addition to enforcing desegregation of elementary and secondary schools under Titles IV, VI, and IX of the Civil Rights Act of 1964,[23] EOS also enforces:

> [T]he Equal Educational Opportunities Act of 1974 (EEOA), and Title III of the Americans with Disabilities Act, as well as other statutes such as … Section 504 of the Rehabilitation Act, the Individuals with Disabilities Education Act, and Title II of the Americans with Disabilities Act upon referral from other governmental agencies. The Section may intervene in private suits alleging violations of education-related anti-discrimination statutes and the Fourteenth Amendment to the Constitution. The Section also represents the Department of Education in lawsuits.[24]

Notably, EOS's responsibilities expanded when Congress passed the Americans with Disabilities Act and the Individuals with Disabilities Education Act, although the additional workload was not evident in the ensuing years.[25]

Special emphases further constrain the resources generally available to EOS. For example, in the early 1990s, one explicit long-term EOS goal was to protect the educational opportunities of Native Americans,[26] and in this decade EOS strove to insure non-English speaking students access to effective educational experience under the Equal Educational Opportunities Act.[27]

Finally, EOS's authority under the Civil Rights Act of 1964 extends beyond elementary and secondary school desegregation to cover segregation issues in colleges and universities. During the early to mid-1990s, DOJ devoted many of EOS's resources to a few high profile cases concerning same-sex colleges[28] and since 2000, EOS "worked with the states to complete the desegregation process in its four statewide higher education desegregation cases (Alabama, Louisiana, Mississippi, and Tennessee)."[29]

DOJ indicates that it does not categorize the percentage of resources it devotes to elementary and secondary school desegregation efforts.[30]

---

[23] 42 U.S.C. §§ 2000c-6, 2000d, 2000h-2 (2007).

[24] EOS Overview. *See* Equal Educational Opportunities Act of 1974, Pub. L. No. 93-380, 88 Stat. 515 (codified at 20 U.S.C. §§ 1701–1758 (2007)); Americans with Disabilities Act, Pub. L. No. 101-336, 104 Stat. 327 (codified at 42 U.S.C. §§ 12101–12213 (2007)); Rehabilitation Act of 1973, Pub. L. No. 93-112, 87 Stat. 355 (codified in sections of 29 U.S.C.); Individuals with Disabilities Education Act, Pub. L. No. 102-119, 105 Stat. 587 (codified as amended at 20 U.S.C. §§ 1400–1482 (2007)).

[25] Budget submissions first articulate the EOS's responsibilities under Section 504 of the Rehabilitation Act of 1973 and the Americans with Disabilities Act (ADA) in the fiscal year 1997 request. *See* FY 1997 CRD Cong. Budget Submission, pp. G-27–G-28. The Section's statutory authority for the Individuals with Disabilities Education Act appears first in the fiscal year 2000 request. *See* FY 2000 CRD Cong. Budget Submission, p. G-52. Although the Section anticipated receiving one or two Department of Education referrals per year under Section 504 and ADA, such cases failed to materialize in fiscal years 1996 and 1997, the only periods for which EOS reported details of statutory authority. *See* FY 1997 CRD Cong. Budget Submission, p. G-59; FY 1998 CRD Cong. Budget Submission, (Workload/activity performance indicator 5); FY 1999 CRD Cong. Budget Submission, p. G-89.

[26] *See* FY 1993 CRD Cong. Budget Submission, p. G-33; FY 1994 CRD Cong. Budget Submission, p. G-23.

[27] *See* FY 2000 CRD Cong. Budget Submission, p. G-51; FY 2001 CRD Cong. Budget Submission, p. G-49.

[28] *See United States v. Virgina*, 518 U.S. 515 (1996) (concerning the Virginia Military Institute); *United States v. Jones*, 136 F.3d 342 (4th Cir. 1998) (concerning the Citadel).

[29] *See* DOJ/CRD, Response to USCCR Interrogatories, Introductory Text.

[30] *See* ibid., Response to Interrogatory Request 24.

Department of Justice Policy Directions

DOJ's approach to ensuring equal educational opportunities has evolved over time. Changes are evident in (1) the strategies or approaches DOJ has promoted for combating segregation (e.g., busing and magnet schools), (2) the emphasis on quality of education, extending the analysis beyond an examination of the equality of educational inputs to their outcomes, and (3) increased or decreased activities in school desegregation cases.

Strategies for Desegregating

An evolving agenda of proposed strategies has accompanied the more than five decades of school desegregation efforts in the United States. In 1982, DOJ shifted from pursuing mandatory busing to promoting magnet schools with superior course offerings that would attract a voluntarily integrated enrollment.[31] The new DOJ policy recognized that court-ordered, race-conscious pupil assignment plans that rely upon forced busing typically resulted in the undesired effect of huge decreases in student populations, particularly white pupils.[32]

In support of this change, DOJ intervened in support of local school boards' efforts to modify such orders.[33] In so doing, DOJ was "acting to defend the abiding interests of black and white students and parents against those who would (in the name of desegregation) resegregate school systems and denude local citizens and their school boards of the capacity to engage in a critical set of good-faith educational policy decisions."[34]

DOJ also obtained consent decrees requiring school districts to implement desegregation plans that relied primarily on the use of magnet schools to encourage voluntary student desegregation.[35]

Broadening Analysis to Apply to Quality of Education

In 1982, DOJ articulated a new policy of pursuing school districts that discriminated on the basis of race or national origin in the quality of education they provided.[36]

---

[31] *See, e.g.,* FY 1983 OMB Special Analyses, "Special Analysis J, Civil Rights Activities," p. 14; FY 1985 OMB Special Analyses, "Special Analysis J, Civil Rights Activities," p. J-9; FY 1986 OMB Special Analyses, "Special Analysis J, Civil Rights Activities," p. J-22.

[32] *See* FY 1986 OMB Special Analyses, "Special Analysis J, Civil Rights Activities," p. J-22.

[33] *See* ibid.

[34] Ibid.

[35] *See* ibid.

[36] *See* FY 1983 OMB Special Analyses, "Special Analysis J, Civil Rights Activities," p. 14.

> In fashioning remedies for alleged *de jure* segregation, the Civil Rights Division has continued to reject the proposition that future discrimination in pupil assignment is an appropriate remedy for past discrimination in pupil assignment. Such mandates, which frequently include forced busing, not only exclude students … from educational programs based solely on their race or national origin; but frequently simply reassign students from one poor school to another, and typically result in significant enrollment losses—followed by racial isolation more severe than existed before.[37]

Thus, in 1983, DOJ began securing remedies that would not only assure equal access to education, regardless of race or national origin, but would also assure equal access to quality education.[38]

The Educational Opportunities Section's Desegregation Enforcement Activities

Detailed information exists for EOS enforcement efforts during the FY 1994 through FY 2002 period through DOJ budget documents, and the Commission obtained information through May 2007 regarding certain aspects of these efforts.[39] This section endeavors to provide an analysis of this information.

There has never been a clear and consistently maintained record of the number of schools under court order to desegregate or of the school system's progress in achieving compliance such that the legal system need no longer intervene. In the early 1970s, DOJ reported that it was supervising 235 education cases representing 540 school districts.[40] In the late 1970s, the agency reported the figures less definitively—more than 200 cases, representing some 500 school districts.[41] In 1984, DOJ documents indicated that the United States was a party to "approximately 525" suits involving mostly Southern elementary and secondary school districts and that since 1964 courts had declared approximately 150 districts unitary.[42]

After the Supreme Court's *Dowell* and *Freeman* decisions,[43] the number of school districts that obtained unitary status in cases in which the United States was a party substantially increased. From FY 1991 to May 2007, 178 school districts received unitary status, decreasing the total number of suits with DOJ involvement from approximately 444 to 266.[44] This decrease has been pronounced since 2000, at which time approximately 430 suits were active.[45]

---

[37] FY 1985 OMB Special Analyses, "Special Analysis J, Civil Rights Activities," p. J-9; *see also* FY 1986 OMB Special Analyses, "Special Analysis J, Civil Rights Activities," p. J-22.

[38] *See* ibid.

[39] *See* DOJ/CRD, Response to USCCR Interrogatories.

[40] FY 1975 OMB Special Analyses, "Special Analysis L, Federal Civil Rights Activities," p. 179; Executive Office of the President, Office of Management and Budget, *Special Analyses, Budget of the United States Government, Fiscal Year 1976*, "Special Analysis M, Federal Civil Rights Activities," pp. 215–16.

[41] Executive Office of the President, Office of Management and Budget, *Special Analyses, Budget of the United States Government, Fiscal Year 1977*, "Special Analysis M, Federal Civil Rights Activities," p. 236; Executive Office of the President, Office of Management and Budget, *Special Analyses, Budget of the United States Government, Fiscal Year 1978*, "Special Analysis M, Federal Civil Rights Activities," p. 247.

[42] FY 1986 CRD Cong. Budget Submission, p. J-21.

[43] *Board of Ed. of Oklahoma City Public Schools, Independent Sch. Dist. No. 98, Oklahoma County, Okla. v. Dowell*, 498 U.S. 237 (1991); *Freeman v. Pitts*, 503 U.S. 467 (1992).

[44] DOJ/CRD, Response to USCCR Interrogatories, Response to Interrogatory Requests 2 and 26.

[45] Ibid.

The Department of Justice's List of Schools Under Court Order Today

As of May 17, 2007, the United States remains a party to 266 school desegregation lawsuits. These cases are primarily, although not exclusively, concentrated in the southeastern United States.

Table 3.1
The Department of Justice's Tally of School Desegregation Lawsuits in mid-2007 by State

State	Number of Cases	State	Number of Cases	State	Number of Cases
Alabama	53	Georgia	67	South Carolina	7
Arizona	1	Illinois	2	Tennessee	12
Arkansas	3	Indiana	2	Texas	14
California	1	Louisiana	30	Utah	1
Connecticut	1	Mississippi	53	Virginia	3
Florida	12	North Carolina	4		

Caption: The United States remains a party to 266 school desegregation lawsuits. The majority of these lawsuits, approximately 90 percent, are concentrated in the southeastern United States.

Source: Compiled by the U.S. Commission on Civil Rights from U.S. Department of Justice, Civil Rights Division, Response to U.S. Commission on Civil Rights' Interrogatories and Document Requests, Response to Interrogatory Request 2, May 17, 2007.

Workload and Accomplishments

The detailed workload and performance measures tracked during the management era of the Government Performance and Results Act[46] provide the most comprehensive perspective on the everyday tasks of EOS. These measures in large part ceased to be reported after FY 2001.

As mentioned above, the workload and performance measures represent all of the missions and functions assigned to EOS, not just those relating to elementary and secondary school desegregation. The documents emphasize activities with respect to colleges and universities, students with disabilities, and language issues, leaving unclear how much of EOS's efforts are devoted to elementary and secondary education.[47]

Complaint Receipts and Processing

Between FY 1991 and FY 2001, EOS reported that it received between 200 and 500 desegregation-related complaints a year.[48] Approximately 75 percent of these complaints came from citizens or community groups; the other roughly 25 percent from Congressional referrals or other controlled correspondence.[49] In nearly every year, CRD reports indicate that EOS has responded to all complaints

---

[46] Government Performance and Results Act of 1993, Pub. L. No. 103-62, 107 Stat. 285 (1993) (codified at 31 U.S.C. § 1101 (2007)).

[47] *See* EOS Overview.

[48] *See* FY 1993 to FY 2003 CRD Cong. Budget Submissions.

[49] *See* ibid.

within one year of receipt.[50] EOS refers approximately 20 percent of these complaints to other DOJ sections and other federal agencies, such as the Department of Education.[51]

EOS classifies any correspondence concerning school districts that are not operating under a desegregation order to which the United States is a party as "matters."[52] Matters may concern issues with the potential of generating a new case.[53] EOS receives 0 to 20 matters in any year, but maintains a workload of 20 to 55 pending matters from year to year.[54] The Section closes between 0 to 17 matters each year.[55]

EOS received a dozen or fewer referrals and letters about noncompliant schools from the Office for Civil Rights of the Department of Education (OCR) each year from FY 1991 to FY 1999 and 20 a year thereafter.[56] These do not appear to concern desegregation.[57]

Case Initiation and Case Intervention

In its examination of the DOJ's litigation during the era when most of these cases were brought, the Commission found that whether the agency commenced a suit depended on several factors in addition to the prerequisites found in the Act.[58] First, DOJ had to receive a written meritorious complaint of discrimination from a parent unable to bring his or her own suit.[59] In addition, DOJ weighed whether or not the litigation was a key case which would set important precedent, whether it raised difficult problems of proof, whether it was representative of key issues such as desegregation involving rural or urban areas, and whether the case would be the first before a particular judge. DOJ also gave special attention to districts whose federal funds were terminated for failure to comply with Title VI of the Civil Rights Act of 1964 and the statute's accompanying regulations.[60] It is unclear which, if any, of these factors DOJ uses today in evaluating whether to bring suit.

---

[50] *See* ibid.

[51] *See* ibid.

[52] *See* ibid.

[53] *See, e.g.,* FY 1997, CRD Cong. Budget Submission, p. G-60.

[54] *See* FY 1993 to FY 2003 CRD Cong. Budget Submissions.

[55] *See* ibid.

[56] Pursuant to Title VI of the Civil Rights Act, federal funding may be withheld from school districts that discriminate "on the ground of race, color, or national origin." 42 U.S.C. § 2000d (2007). In such instances, the Department of Education may refer a case to DOJ for action. *See* 34 C.F.R. § 100.8(a) (2007) ("If there appears to be a failure or threatened failure to comply with this regulation, ... compliance with this part may be effected by ... a reference to the Department of Justice with a recommendation that appropriate proceedings be brought to enforce any rights of the United States under any law of the United States (including other titles of the [Civil Rights] Act [of 1964]), or any assurance or other contractual undertaking... .").

[57] *See* FY 1993 to FY 2003 CRD Cong. Budget Submissions.

[58] U.S. Commission on Civil Rights (USCCR), *Southern School Desegregation, 1966–'67,* July 1967, pp. 42–43.

[59] *See* 42 U.S.C. § 2000c-6(b) (2007) (Appropriate reasons why the complainant cannot proceed directly on his or her own accord are inability "to bear the expense of the litigation or to obtain effective legal representation; or whenever ... [the Attorney General] is satisfied that the institution of such litigation would jeopardize the personal safety, employment, or economic standing of such person or persons, their families, or their property.").

[60] *See* USCCR, *Southern School Desegregation*, pp. 42–43.

Since FY 1991, EOS has not initiated any new traditional desegregation lawsuits and has indicated that they are not aware of any such federal suits being instituted by other parties.[61] Moreover, EOS has not intervened in any ongoing desegregation lawsuits during this time period.[62]

Investigations and Compliance Reports

Between FY 1991 and FY 2001, EOS reported that it initiated between 5 and 16 investigations of school districts each year. The number completed is reported as 2 in FY 1995 and 10 in FY 1996. EOS's use of the number of investigations completed as a performance measure ceased before information on actual numbers completed were reported for FY 1997 and thereafter. Despite the low number of investigations initiated and completed each year, EOS maintains a large number of on-going investigations of school districts under court order, which ranged from 265 to 450 for FY 1990 to FY 2007.

Between FY 1991 and FY 2001, DOJ reported that it received and reviewed between 145 and 200 compliance reports each year.[63]

In FY 2000, EOS reported sending 94 information request letters to school districts and made plans to send such correspondence to 97 school districts in FY 2001 and FY 2002.[64] It is unclear what triggered these letters.

Case Reviews

In FY 1999, EOS began to extensively review desegregation cases to which the United States is a party.[65] Between FY 1999 to July 2007, EOS initiated more than 265 such reviews. These reviews may include one or more activities, such as: (1) desk audits; (2) site visits; (3) interviews with school officials, students, and community groups; (4) analysis of school data on student assignment and race/ethnicity; (5) evaluations of school policies; (6) reviews of civil rights complaints filed with the

---

[61] *See* DOJ/CRD, Response to USCCR Interrogatories, Response to Interrogatory Request 6.

[62] *See* ibid., Response to Interrogatory Request 10. (DOJ indicates that, "[t]he determination to intervene in an ongoing elementary/secondary school desegregation case is subject to a review of the facts, consideration of the statutes under which the case was brought, and the requirements of Federal Rule of Civil Procedure 24.")

[63] *See* FY 1993 to FY 2003 CRD Cong. Budget Submissions.

[64] FY 2002 CRD Cong. Budget Submissions, p. G-52.

[65] *See* DOJ correspondence, July 19, 2007, p. 1.

Department of Education; (7) requests and review of other related information directly from school districts; (8) review of publicly available data, such as census, historical, state department of education, and U.S. Department of Education data; and (9) the evaluation of information from national civil rights groups.[66] EOS states that "[t]he monitoring is case specific" and does not track the types of monitoring for each case.[67]

Based on such reviews, when EOS determines that the school district has achieved unitary status, it joins with the school district in a consent motion to dismiss the case.[68] If EOS determines the school district has not met its obligations, staff works with the district to achieve unitary status.[69]

Modifications to Desegregation Plans

Many schools under court order must submit modifications to their desegregation plans to DOJ for review and comment. In FY 1995, EOS received 17 proposals for modifications to desegregation plans.[70] The section classified 11 of them as major changes and 6 as minor changes. Between FY 1996 and FY 1999, EOS received 22, 25, 30, and 17 modification proposals respectively.[71] Of these requests, EOS "approved" 14, 20, 25, and 20 each year, respectively.[72] In FY 2000 and FY 2001, 17 and 15 modifications were approved respectively.[73] This data appears in Figure 3.3.

---

[66] *See* DOJ/CRD, Response to USCCR Interrogatories, Response to Interrogatory Request 4.

[67] Ibid.

[68] *See* ibid.

[69] *See* ibid.

[70] FY 1997 CRD Cong. Budget Submission, G-59.

[71] FY 1998 CRD Cong. Budget Submission; FY 1999 CRD Cong. Budget Submission, p. G-89; FY 2000 CRD Cong. Budget Submission, p. G-97; FY 2001 CRD Cong. Budget Submission , p. G-91.

[72] EOS indicates that it "does not approve modifications to desegregation orders because only the court can approve such a change." DOJ correspondence, July 19, 2007, p. 2. But DOJ budget documents use the term "approve" seemingly to indicate plans which DOJ reviewed and consented. FY 1998 CRD Cong. Budget Submission; FY 1999 CRD Cong. Budget Submission, p. G-90; FY 2000 CRD Cong. Budget Submission, G-98; FY 2001 CRD Cong. Budget Submission, G-92.

[73] FY 2002 CRD Cong. Budget Submission, p. G-52; FY 2003 CRD Cong. Budget Submission, p. G-45.

Figure 3.3
Modification Proposals: The Number EOS Received and the Number Approved by the Courts, 1995 to 2001

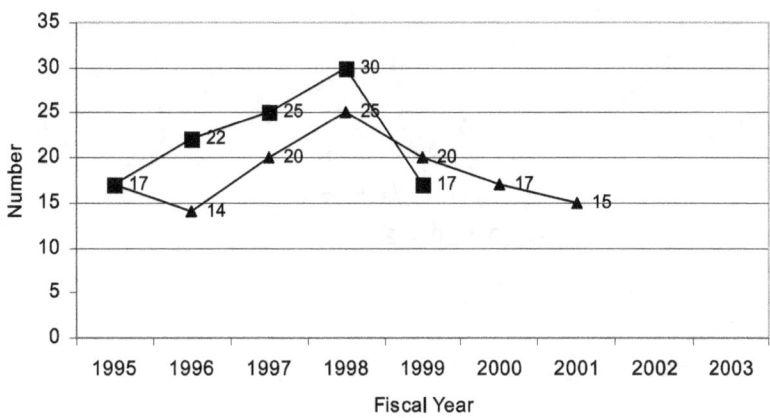

—■— Modification Proposals Received

—▲— Responses to Proposals/Petititons to Modify Desegregation Plan (Approvals)

Caption: In FY 1995, the Department of Justice received 17 modification proposals. The number of received proposals and approved proposals rose overall until 1998, with 30 received proposals and 25 approvals, and then began a decline until 2001. DOJ ceased maintaining this data after 2001.

Source: Department of Justice, Civil Rights Division, Congressional Budget Submissions, FY 1997 to FY 2004.

Reviews of the Unitary Status of School Districts

DOJ reported that between from FY 1991 through May 2007, 178 school desegregation cases were dismissed.[74] Moreover, all such cases were dismissed after a finding of unitary status was made by the court.[75] Figure 3.4 provides the number of closed cases for each of these years.

---

[74] DOJ/CRD, Response to USCCR Interrogatories, Response to Interrogatory Request 2.

[75] Ibid.

Figure 3.4
Department of Justice Reports the Number of School Desegregation Cases Closed, 1991 through mid-2007

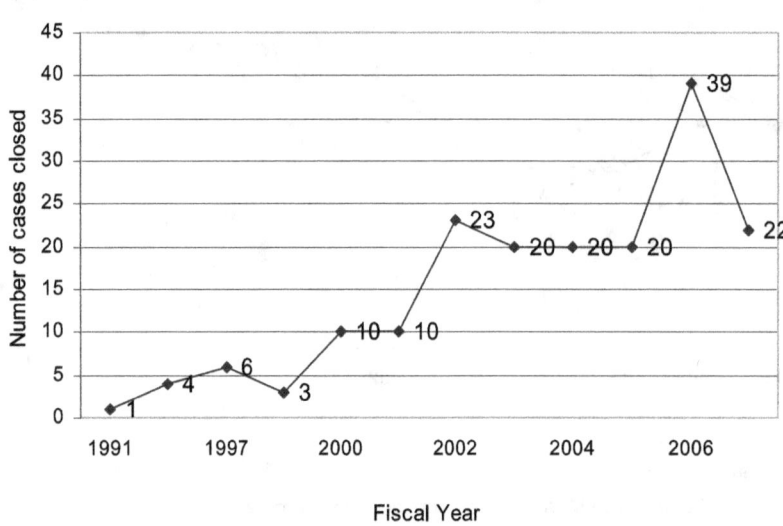

Fiscal Year

*Data is current through May 17, 2007.

Caption: In the 1990s the number of school desegregation cases dismissed pursuant to a finding of unitary status remained relatively low, reaching a crest in FY 1997 with 6 dismissals, compared to more recent years. The number effectively doubled between FY 2001 and FY 2002, from 10 to 23, and then doubled again between FY 2005 and FY 2006, from 20 to 39. Additionally, 22 dismissals occurred from the beginning of FY 2007 to May 17, 2007.

Source: Compiled by the U.S. Commission on Civil Rights from U.S. Department of Justice, Civil Rights Division, Response to U.S. Commission on Civil Rights' Interrogatories and Document Requests, Response to Interrogatory Request 2, May 17, 2007.

The number of school districts granted partial unitary status were 7 in FY 1997, 10 in FY 1998, 12 in FY 1999, 5 in FY 2000, and 2 in FY 2001.[76]

Summary

Since FY 2000, the DOJ has actively pursued the closure of school desegregation cases. While its school desegregation docket included 450 cases in recent years, as of May 2007 it numbers 266. The decrease in number of open cases coincides with an increase in EOS's budget and number of EOS staff.

---

[76] FY 2000 CRD Cong. Budget Submission, p. G-99; FY 2001 CRD Cong. Budget Submission, p. G-98; FY 2002 CRD Cong. Budget Submission, p. G-52; FY 2003 CRD Cong. Budget Submission, p. G-45.

CHAPTER 4: THE LEGAL STATUS OF SCHOOL DISTRICTS

In the decades after *Brown* ended legal discrimination in the nation's schools, the federal government, parents, and advocacy groups filed suits to ensure compliance. Over time, courts declared some of these districts unitary, ending judicial supervision; others remain under the scrutiny of the federal government and the legal system. In this chapter, the Commission on Civil Rights presents original research to identify the legal status of school districts in seven states. The chapter describes the frequency of unitary status among school districts and includes some historical information about when districts' were released from judicial supervision. It also examines differences in legal status according to district size.

Little consistent and reliable aggregate information exists today on the desegregation status of school districts nationally with regard to which districts are currently under court order, which were previously under court order but subsequently obtained unitary status, and which have never been subject to court supervision. The Commission has conducted a careful review of information to determine the status of all school districts in seven, mostly southern, states, representing most of the institutions under federal court supervision. The states are Alabama, Florida, Georgia, Louisiana, Mississippi, North Carolina, and South Carolina.

The states in question were selected based on a variety of factors. First, and most importantly, the selected states contain a sufficient number of school districts under existing or prior court orders to make useful comparisons between those that have obtained unitary status and those which remain under court supervision. Second, each of the states also has active school desegregation cases to which the United States remains a party.[1] Third, the states selected ensured that the study covered multiple federal judicial circuits and more than one state from any one circuit. Thus, the study includes all three states from the 11th Circuit (Alabama, Florida, and Georgia), two states from the 4th Circuit (North and South Carolina), and two states from the 5th Circuit (Louisiana and Mississippi).

A summary of the collected information appears in sections A through D. Details of school districts' desegregation status are reported in Appendices B through H. In addition, this section analyzes trends as to when districts received unitary status that may relate to the effects of case law or changes in federal policies on districts' legal status. The Commission sought to identify the years when the original desegregation cases were initiated,[2] as well as when unitary status was granted, if applicable. Information on the intent of officials in districts under court order and data on when and which districts obtained unitary status can help inform legal and policy debates.

Methodology for Determining Unitary Status

The U. S. Commission on Civil Rights compiled information on the legal status of the school districts of the seven states studied herein. The effort was comprehensive, examining all school districts in the selected states to determine whether or not they were under court order. The Commission first obtained

---

[1] *See* U.S. Department of Justice, Civil Rights Division, "Pending School Districts Operating Under Desegregation Cases to Which the United States is a Party," 2003; *see also* U.S. Department of Justice, Educational Opportunities Section, "Pending School Districts and States Operating Under Desegregation in Cases to Which the United States is a Party," Dec. 12, 2006.

[2] Because many courts revised desegregation orders over time, the years the lawsuits were initiated were used as the starting point for federal court supervision for the purposes of this study.

information from the following sources: (1) the U.S. Department of Education,[3] (2) the U.S. Department of Justice, particularly its list of open school desegregation cases, (3) public information databases,[4] (4) Lexis-Nexis searches, (5) state departments of education, and (6) the NAACP Legal Defense and Education Fund. The Commission assessed the desegregation status of each school district based on this information and wrote to each district asking school officials for confirmation.[5] The correspondence requested school districts to provide a copy of the court order granting unitary status, if applicable.

On the basis of its research, the Commission classified school districts into four categories—those with unitary status, those that remain under court jurisdiction, those that were never subject to court supervision because of segregation, and those with uncertain status. During this effort, the Commission identified the name of any relevant court case, the year the plaintiff initiated the case, and the year the court declared the district unitary. For districts remaining under court order, the Commission also solicited school officials' responses regarding their intent to pursue unitary status.[6] This information is found in Appendices B through H.

Commission staff further verified school districts with unitary status by obtaining and reviewing court orders and case docket sheets directly from courts using the Public Access to Court Electronic Records (PACER) database or calling court clerks and requesting that documents be faxed or mailed to the Commission.[7] In most instances, the Commission obtained both a final order granting unitary status and a docket sheet designating the case as closed.[8] The Commission did not attempt to identify whether school districts that received unitary status are subject to obligations that continue for a set number of years after the court issues the determination.[9] School districts that appear in this category were placed

---

[3] The U.S. Department of Education's (DOEd's) Office for Civil Rights (OCR) is tasked with ensuring that school districts receiving federal funds comply with nondiscrimination laws effected through Title VI of the Civil Rights Act of 1964 and subsequent legislation. OCR accomplishes this mandate in part through regulations that require previously segregated districts to enter into agreements to develop, implement, and routinely report strategies to integrate schools. The mandated reports are known as 441-B desegregation plans. In addition to reviewing 441-B documents, OCR investigates and works to resolve alleged Title VI violations. As a matter of jurisdictional prudence, OCR first determines whether any part of an alleged violation is addressed in previous federal court orders. *See* U.S. Department of Education, Office for Civil Rights, *OCR Case Resolution and Investigation Manual*, May 2005, <http://www.ed.gov/about/offices/list/ocr/docs/ocrcrm.html> (last accessed July 5, 2007). To this end, OCR maintains records of the litigation and statutory history of school districts with respect to segregation. The Commission acquired DOEd's compilation of school districts under court order.

[4] These include websites on school desegregation and internet search engines.

[5] In some instances, the school districts did not reply to Commission requests to verify this status. Thus, it is conceivable that there are court cases that Commission staff were unable to locate, when school officials did not confirm that the district was never subject to school desegregation litigation.

[6] In most instances, superintendents, not school boards, provided a statement of the district's intent.

[7] Of course, many of these cases are decades old and therefore some courts have chosen not to upload inactive or closed school desegregation cases to the Public Access to Court Electronic Records (PACER) database. In fact, staff learned through telephone conversations with court clerks in Mississippi that district courts have adopted the policy of not uploading school desegregation cases to PACER even when a case is on the active docket of the court. When staff members met such obstacles, they requested docket sheets and specific orders directly from the courts. In some instances, these items could not be located due to the documents' age or manner in which the courts archived these documents.

[8] In a limited number of instances, the Commission relied on other documents, such as settlement agreements, when staff could not obtain a final order or docket sheet from the court.

[9] Other researchers found variations in the meaning of unitary status or instances with "strings attached." Unitary status was sometimes a component of a broader consent decree or other agreement in which the district committed itself to certain practices for some period. For example, at least one agreement required districts to continue to operate their magnet school programs, mandating the state to continue such funding for years afterward. These authors suggest that unitary declarations do not always coincide with the end of court supervision. Thus, districts may not be free to assign students to neighborhood schools for years after achieving unitary status. *See* Charles T. Clotfelter, Helen

under court order and then subsequently granted unitary status for any possible combination of the six *Green* factors or even a factor not explicitly discussed in *Green*.

School districts classified by the Commission as still under court order include school districts that obtained partial unitary status as defined in *Freeman v. Pitts*.[10]

School districts the Commission categorized as nonlitigants either never operated a dual system or entered into voluntary desegregation plans with the U.S. Department of Education's Office for Civil Rights, or its predecessor, the U.S. Department of Health, Education, and Welfare's Office of Education.[11]

The Commission carefully reviewed its source information regarding desegregation litigation and assigned "uncertain" legal status to about a dozen school districts. The Commission found some information indicating that these school systems are a party to school desegregation litigation, but could not determine the current status of such litigation. Thus, these districts may still be under court order, may have obtained unitary status, or may have been dismissed from such litigation for other reasons.

Table 4.1
Number of School Districts Included in the Study by State

State	Districts subjected to the determination of unitary status	Districts included in analysis of desegregation measures
Alabama	131	125
Florida	67	67
Georgia	180	176
Louisiana	68	68
Mississippi	149	144
North Carolina	115	115
South Carolina	85	85
Total	795	780

Note: The included districts (1) are locally run (i.e., not state, federal, or university-affiliated efforts); (2) are recently under continuous operation (i.e., neither newly opened nor newly closed); (3) offer normal curriculum rather than being dedicated to special programs oriented toward particular careers or special needs. In addition, all districts included in the desegregation analyses have regular elementary schools and 2004/05 Department of Education racial and ethnic student enrollment data.

Caption: The Commission reviewed 131 districts in Alabama, 67 in Florida, 180 in Georgia, 68 in Louisiana, 149 in Mississippi, 115 in North Carolina, and 85 in South Carolina, for a total of 795 districts. The Commission included only 780 of these districts in the analysis of desegregation measures, omitting 6 in Alabama, 4 in Georgia, and 5 in Mississippi.

Source: Compiled by U.S. Commission on Civil Rights.

F. Ladd, Jacob L. Vigdor, all of Duke University, "Federal Oversight, Local Control and the Specter of 'Resegregation' in Southern Schools," January 2005, pp. 20–26 <http://www.s4.brown.edu/s4/colloquia/Fall05/PUBrowndraft20905.pdf> (last accessed Aug. 22, 2007). The Commission adopted the Department of Justice's approach in classifying school districts with such continuing obligations as closed matters and thus has designated such school systems as having obtained unitary status.

[10] *Freeman v. Pitts*, 503 U.S. 467, 491 (1992). For a discussion of this case, *see* Chapter 2.

[11] *See* Chapter 2, n. 64. The Commission classified school districts as nonlitigants when it found: (1) evidence that the school district was never subject to school desegregation litigation; or (2) a lack of any indication of court involvement because (a) the six resources identified above yielded no evidence of past or current litigation, and (b) the school districts did not provide a response to the Commission's initial direct inquiry to verify status.

The Commission gathered its information on school districts during the period from June 2006 to June 2007. It compiled the status of all school districts within the selected states, eliminating only those that were federally- or state-operated, recently (within the past three years) opened or closed, or directed toward special programs such as career-oriented curricula. The first column of table 4.1 shows the number of districts reviewed in each state. For example, the Commission reviewed 67 districts in Florida, 131 in Alabama, and 180 in Georgia. Altogether, the Commission sought the legal status on 795 school districts. The number of districts used for the analysis of desegregation in chapter 5—column 2 of the table—was a slightly smaller subset of those for which the Commission reviewed legal status.[12]

The Commission's extensive research, which examined multiple sources of information to determine unitary status, and its examination of school districts in states with large numbers of court orders is believed to make this effort the most accurate and comprehensive current record of the legal status of school districts.

A. The Commission's Results on Unitary Status Today

This section summarizes information from Appendices B through H, which show lists of unitary, court-supervised, and nonlitigant districts for each of the seven states. Tables 4.2 and 4.3 below show the numbers and percentages of districts by state according to the legal status identified in the Commission's research. The Commission's review of the status of 795 districts in seven states found that 193 had unitary status. As table 4.3 indicates, districts with unitary status represent 24.3 percent of those in the states the Commission reviewed.

---

[12] In addition to information on legal status, the chapter 5 analyses depend upon having districts' enrollment data by school and race/ethnicity. A fuller description of the criteria by which districts were included in the study's statistical analyses is presented in methodology sections in chapter 5 and appendix A.

Table 4.2
The Number of Districts with Unitary Status, Under Court Order, or Never Engaged in Litigation by State

State	Districts with Unitary Status	Districts Under Court Order	Uncertain Status*	Nonlitigant Districts	Total Districts Reviewed
Alabama	71	53		7	131
Florida	19	15		33	67
Georgia	33	76		71	180
Louisiana	16	43		9	68
Mississippi	24	71	1	53	149
North Carolina	12	15	12	76	115
South Carolina	18	14		53	85
Total	193	287	13	302	795

* Districts designated as uncertain are those for which the Commission found some information that they are or have been a party to school desegregation litigation, but could not determine the current status of such litigation. Thus, these districts may remain under court order, may have obtained unitary status, or may have gained a dismissal of the litigation against them for other reasons.

Caption: The Commission examined 795 districts and determined that 193 have unitary status: 71 in Alabama, 19 in Florida, 33 in Georgia, 16 in Louisiana, 24 in Mississippi, 12 in North Carolina, and 18 in South Carolina. Of the 287 districts operating under court order, the Commission determined that 53 are in Alabama, 15 in Florida, 76 in Georgia, 43 in Louisiana, 71 in Mississippi, 15 in North Carolina, and 14 in South Carolina. Of the 302 nonlitigant districts the Commission determined that 7 are in Alabama, 33 in Florida, 71 in Georgia, 9 in Louisiana, 53 in Mississippi, 76 in North Carolina, and 53 in South Carolina. The remaining 13 districts, 1 in Mississippi and 12 in North Carolina are of uncertain status.

Source: Compiled by U.S. Commission on Civil Rights.

Districts the Commission identified as remaining under court order totaled 287, representing 36.1 percent of those in the states the Commission reviewed. The Commission was unable to determine the current status of a dozen or more districts, which appear to have been the subject of litigation that may or may not have led to a court order and/or unitary status. These constitute less than 2 percent of those the Commission studied.

Table 4.3
The Percentages of Districts with Unitary Status, Under Court Order, or Never Engaged in Litigation by State

State	Districts with Unitary Status	Districts Under Court Order	Uncertain Status	Nonlitigant Districts	Total	Percent of Districts in All States
Alabama	54.2%	40.5%	0.0%	5.3%	100.0%	16.5%
Florida	28.4%	22.4%	0.0%	49.3%	100.0%	8.4%
Georgia	18.3%	42.2%	0.0%	39.4%	100.0%	22.6%
Louisiana	23.5%	63.2%	0.0%	13.2%	100.0%	8.6%
Mississippi	16.1%	47.7%	0.7%	35.6%	100.0%	18.7%
North Carolina	10.4%	13.0%	10.4%	66.1%	100.0%	14.5%
South Carolina	21.2%	16.5%	0.0%	62.4%	100.0%	10.7%
Combined states	24.3%	36.1%	1.6%	38.0%	100.0%	100.0%

Caption: **Comparing the districts of each state by legal status, Alabama shows a higher proportion of litigated districts and a higher proportion of districts with unitary status. Louisiana also demonstrates a high proportion of litigated districts, but with a higher proportion of districts under court order compared to the other states. North and South Carolina show higher proportions of nonlitigant districts compared to the other states and Florida shows a similar trend.**

Source: Compiled by U.S. Commission on Civil Rights.

Table 4.3 further shows that one state—Alabama—has a much larger proportion of districts with unitary status than others. More than half—54.2 percent—of Alabama's districts have unitary status. However, 40.5 percent remain under court order. A small number of districts in Alabama were not subject to court order.

In contrast, some states have relatively small proportions of districts with unitary status or under court order. The Commission's research suggests that nearly half or more of the districts in these states were never involved in litigation. For example, in Florida, a little more than a quarter—28.4 percent of districts—have unitary status and less than a quarter of them—22.4 percent—remain under court order. Nearly half—49.3 percent—of Florida districts were never involved in desegregation litigation according to the evidence the Commission compiled. North and South Carolina, like Florida, have relatively small proportions of districts with unitary status (10.4 and 21.2 percent, respectively) or remaining under court order (13.0 and 16.5 percent, respectively). The Commission did not find litigation involving 66.1 percent of districts in North Carolina and 62.4 percent of those in South Carolina.

Other states have large proportions of districts continuing under court order. Louisiana has the largest proportion of districts—63.2 percent—remaining under court order. Only 23.5 percent of the state's districts have unitary status. In Georgia and Mississippi, more than 40 percent of the districts remain under court order; only small proportions—18.3 and 16.1 percent respectively—have received unitary status.

B. Court Orders Imposed Since the Sixties

Most of the court orders have been in place since the 1960s and nearly all of them have been in place since at least the 1970s.[13] Of the 795 districts the Commission reviewed, 480 had been the subject of court orders. Tables 4.4 and 4.5 show that 386, or more than 80 percent of those under court order, came under such supervision in the 1960s. Another 85, or about 18 percent of districts' court orders, date from the 1970s. Only a few districts became the subject of court orders in decades since then—2 in the 1980s and 1 in the 1990s. A 1991 court order in Mississippi is the most recent one the Commission found.

Table 4.4
The Number of Districts Placed Under Court Order in Each Decade by State

State	Decade						Total Districts Ever Under Court Order
	1960s	1970s	1980s	1990s	2000s	Unknown	
Alabama	123	1	0	0	0	0	124
Florida	17	17	0	0	0	0	34
Georgia	101	6	0	0	0	2	109
Louisiana	49	9	1	0	0	0	59
Mississippi	57	32	1	1	0	4	95
North Carolina	17	10	0	0	0	0	27
South Carolina	22	10	0	0	0	0	32
Total	386	85	2	1	0	6	480

Caption: Of the districts in the study, 480 were ever subject to court orders. Three hundred and eighty-six of these districts were placed under court order in the 1960s: 123 in Alabama, 17 in Florida, 101 in Georgia, 49 in Louisiana, 57 in Mississippi, 17 in North Carolina, and 22 in South Carolina. Eighty-five of these districts were placed under court order in the 1970s: 1 in Alabama, 17 in Florida, 6 in Georgia, 9 in Louisiana, 32 in Mississippi, 10 in North Carolina, and 10 in South Carolina. The decades remain unknown for 6 districts. The Commission found no evidence to indicate that any districts were placed under court order in the 2000s.

Source: Compiled by U.S. Commission on Civil Rights.

Florida had the largest proportions of districts placed under court order in the 1970s—50.0 percent. A single district each in Louisiana and Mississippi were the subjects of court orders entered in the 1980s.

---

[13] Because many court orders were put in place early in the litigation process, the Commission derived the decade each district was placed under court order from the year the case was initiated.

Table 4.5
The Percentages of Districts Placed Under Court Order in Each Decade by State

State	Decade						Total
	1960s	1970s	1980s	1990s	2000s	Unknown	
Alabama	99.2%	0.8%	0.0%	0.0%	0.0%	0.0%	100.0%
Florida	50.0%	50.0%	0.0%	0.0%	0.0%	0.0%	100.0%
Georgia	92.7%	5.5%	0.0%	0.0%	0.0%	1.8%	100.0%
Louisiana	83.1%	15.3%	1.7%	0.0%	0.0%	0.0%	100.0%
Mississippi	60.0%	33.7%	1.1%	1.1%	0.0%	4.2%	100.0%
North Carolina	63.0%	37.0%	0.0%	0.0%	0.0%	0.0%	100.0%
South Carolina	68.8%	31.3%	0.0%	0.0%	0.0%	0.0%	100.0%
Combined states	80.4%	17.7%	0.4%	0.2%	0.0%	1.3%	100.0%

Caption: For each state included in the study, with the exception of Florida, 60.0 percent or more of the litigated districts were placed under court order in the 1960s. In Florida exactly 50.0 percent of litigated districts were placed under court order in the 1960s, and the remaining 50.0 percent in the 1970s. Compared to districts in other states, a much higher proportion of districts litigated in Alabama, Georgia, and Louisiana were placed under court order in the 1960s, 99.2 percent, 92.7 percent, and 83.1 percent respectively.

Source: Compiled by U.S. Commission on Civil Rights.

C. Obtaining Unitary Status Through the Decades

To supplement Department of Justice data in the previous chapter, this section analyzes the years in which districts obtained unitary status, noting the frequency with which courts released districts from court orders in various periods, particularly since 2000. The section also summarizes districts' reports of their contemporary efforts to resolve their desegregation cases.

Tables 4.6 and 4.7 show, for each state, the number and percentages of districts that have received unitary status across the decades. Of the 193 districts the Commission identified with unitary status, 121, or 62.7 percent, achieved that status since 2000. Only 32 districts gained unitary status during the 1970s and another 22 in the 1990s, representing 16.6 and 11.4 percent of the total, respectively. Efforts to obtain unitary status in the 1980s resulted in 17 attaining that goal during the decade, or 8.8 percent.

North Carolina is unlike other states in the timeframe during which its districts obtained unitary status. Its districts were most likely to obtain unitary status in the 1970s. Six, or half of those ultimately receiving the status, obtained it in that decade. Another 5 of the state's unitary districts, or 41.7 percent, received the status in the 1990s. The Commission was unable to identify any North Carolina district that gained unitary status in the 2000s.

Table 4.6
The Number of Districts Receiving Judicial Recognition of Unitary Status in Each Decade by State

State	Decade						Total Districts with Unitary Status
	1960s	1970s	1980s	1990s	2000s	Unknown	
Alabama	0	14	6	6	45	0	71
Florida	0	6	2	5	6	0	19
Georgia	0	2	2	4	25	0	33
Louisiana	0	3	1	0	11	1	16
Mississippi	0	1	3	2	18	0	24
North Carolina	0	6	1	5	0	0	12
South Carolina	0	0	2	0	16	0	18
Total	0	32	17	22	121	1	193

Caption: The majority of districts with unitary status, 121 of 193, received unitary status in the 2000s. No evidence was found to indicate that any districts received unitary status in the 1960s, though 1 district in Louisiana has an unknown date of unitary status. In the 1970s, 1980s, and 1990s, 32, 17, and 22 districts gained unitary status, respectively.

Source: Compiled by U.S. Commission on Civil Rights.

Nearly a third of Florida districts obtained unitary status in the 1970s, however an equal proportion of such Florida districts (31.6 percent) received unitary status in the 2000s. Similarly, 14 Alabama districts, or 19.7 percent of those with unitary status, gained it during the 1970s, but more than triple that number—45, or 63.4 percent,—obtained this status in the 2000s.

Table 4.7
The Percentages of Districts Receiving Unitary Status in Each Decade by State

State	Decade						Total Districts with Unitary Status
	1960s	1970s	1980s	1990s	2000s	Unknown	
Alabama	0.0%	19.7%	8.5%	8.5%	63.4%	0.0%	100.0%
Florida	0.0%	31.6%	10.5%	26.3%	31.6%	0.0%	100.0%
Georgia	0.0%	6.1%	6.1%	12.1%	75.8%	0.0%	100.0%
Louisiana	0.0%	18.8%	6.3%	0.0%	68.8%	6.3%	100.0%
Mississippi	0.0%	4.2%	12.5%	8.3%	75.0%	0.0%	100.0%
North Carolina	0.0%	50.0%	8.3%	41.7%	0.0%	0.0%	100.0%
South Carolina	0.0%	0.0%	11.1%	0.0%	88.9%	0.0%	100.0%
Combined states	0.0%	16.6%	8.8%	11.4%	62.7%	0.5%	100.0%

Caption: The majority of districts with unitary status, 62.7 percent, received unitary status in the 2000s, 11.4 percent in the 1990s, 8.8 percent in the 1980s, and 16.6 percent in the 1970s. In most states a high percentage—over 63.0 percent—of districts were granted unitary status in the 2000s. The exceptions are Florida, where less than 32.0 percent of districts gained unitary status in the 2000s, and North Carolina, where no districts gained unitary status in the 2000s.

Source: Compiled by U.S. Commission on Civil Rights.

For the 287 districts remaining under court order, tables 4.8 and 4.9 show whether or not the school systems are seeking unitary status. Approximately one quarter (75, or 26.1 percent) of the districts under court order reported to the Commission that they were currently seeking or planning to pursue unitary status. Some school officials indicated that the Department of Justice was involved in the effort.[14] Forty two percent (122) of the districts definitively stated that they were *not* pursuing unitary status. In another 12.9 percent (37) of the districts, administrators were equivocating on seeking unitary status. They were considering the advantages and disadvantages of the effort, uncertain about pursuing the status, or awaiting a Department of Justice initiative before acting on the matter. Nonresponding districts, which comprised 15.3 percent of those under court order, may include some that are undecided on a course of action.

Table 4.8
Current Efforts of Districts Under Court Order to Attain Unitary Status

State	Districts Currently Seeking or Planning to Seek Unitary Status	Districts Not Seeking Unitary Status	Districts with Disputed or Unclear Status	Districts Undecided About Seeking Unitary Status	Nonresponses or Unknown Intent	Total Districts Remaining Under Court Order
Alabama	22	14	6	8	3	53
Florida	4	8		3		15
Georgia	18	33		9	16	76
Louisiana	13	11	1	9	9	43
Mississippi	14	37		7	13	71
North Carolina	2	8	2	1	2	15
South Carolina	2	11			1	14
Total	75	122	9	37	44	287

Caption: The majority of all school districts currently under court order, 122 of 287, report that they do not plan to seek unitary status: 14 in Alabama, 8 in Florida, 33 in Georgia, 11 in Louisiana, 37 in Mississippi, 8 in North Carolina, and 11 in South Carolina. Only 75 districts report that they plan to seek, or are currently pursuing, unitary status: 22 in Alabama, 4 in Florida, 18 in Georgia, 13 in Louisiana, 14 in Mississippi, 2 in North Carolina, and 2 in South Carolina. Six districts in Alabama, 1 in Louisiana, and 2 in North Carolina dispute the Commission's determination of their legal status, maintaining that they have never been subject to a court order. A further 37 districts report that they are undecided about seeking unitary status, and another 44 districts did not respond to Commission inquiries regarding their intent.

Source: Compiled by U.S. Commission on Civil Rights.

In a few districts in Alabama, Louisiana, and North Carolina, school officials had a dispute or expressed confusion about whether the system had unitary status. In one instance, a district court had granted unitary status but the case was on appeal.

---

[14] *See* appendices B through H for more detailed information.

Table 4.9
Current Efforts of Districts Under Court Order to Attain Unitary Status as Percentages

State	Districts Currently Seeking or Planning to Seek Unitary Status	Districts Not Seeking Unitary Status	Districts with Disputed or Unclear Status	Districts Undecided About Seeking Unitary Status	Nonresponses or Unknown Intent	Total Districts Remaining Under Court Order
Alabama	41.5%	26.4%	11.3%	15.1%	5.7%	100.0%
Florida	26.7%	53.3%	0.0%	20.0%	0.0%	100.0%
Georgia	23.7%	43.4%	0.0%	11.8%	21.1%	100.0%
Louisiana	30.2%	25.6%	2.3%	20.9%	20.9%	100.0%
Mississippi	19.7%	52.1%	0.0%	9.9%	18.3%	100.0%
North Carolina	13.3%	53.3%	13.3%	6.7%	13.3%	100.0%
South Carolina	14.3%	78.6%	0.0%	0.0%	7.1%	100.0%
Combined states	26.1%	42.5%	3.1%	12.9%	15.3%	100.0%

Caption: Many of the school districts currently under court order, 42.5 percent, report that they do not plan to seek unitary status. Only 26.1 percent report that they plan to pursue, or are currently pursuing, unitary status. The remaining 31.3 percent of districts are either undecided about pursuing unitary status, dispute their status, have unclear status, or did not respond to Commission inquiries. In all states except Alabama, less than one third of the districts report that they are seeking or plan to seek unitary status. In two states, Alabama (26.4 percent) and Louisiana (25.6 percent), the percentage of districts not planning to seek unitary status is low. Most South Carolina districts (78.6 percent) are not seeking unitary status.

Source: Compiled by U.S. Commission on Civil Rights.

Table 4.9 shows that Alabama has the highest proportion of districts—41.5 percent—seeking, or planning to pursue, unitary status. In contrast, a little more than half of the districts in Florida and North Carolina are *not* seeking unitary status. Even more of Mississippi and South Carolina districts under court order (52.1 and 78.6 percent, respectively) are not attempting to obtain unitary status.

D. Obtaining Unitary Status and District Size

The districts the Commission reviewed vary greatly in the size of their student bodies. Approximately 75 percent of the districts (592) had enrollments of 1,000 to 9,999 students (including pre-kindergarten through high school). Nineteen percent (151) had enrollments of 10,000 to 99,999 students, while a small number of districts—1.4 percent (11)—have very large student bodies with enrollments over 100,000. Those with student bodies of less than 1,000 totaled 5 percent (40) of the districts reviewed.[15]

Table 4.10 displays districts' legal status by the size of their student enrollment. Most of the very large districts (7 out of 11) have unitary status. Small districts seldom had unitary status (10 out of 40). The districts with 1,000 to 9,999 students quite often remain under court order (231 out of 592).

---

[15] Percents are calculated from the totals in table 4.10, below.

Table 4.10
The Number of Districts with Unitary Status, Under Court Order, or Never Engaged in Litigation by School Size

District Size—Enrollment	Districts with Unitary Status	Districts Under Court Order	Uncertain Status*	Nonlitigant Districts	Total Districts Reviewed
Greater than 100,000	7	1	1	2	11
10,000 to 99,999	43	42	6	60	151
1,000 to 9,999	133	231	6	222	592
Less than 1,000	10	12		18	40
Unknown enrollment		1			1
Total	193	287	13	302	795

* Districts designated as uncertain are those for which the Commission found some information that they are or have been a party to school desegregation litigation, but could not determine the current status of such litigation. Thus, these districts may remain under court order, may have obtained unitary status, or may have gained a dismissal of the litigation against them for other reasons.

Caption: Most districts (592) have between 1,000 and 9,999 students. Of these, 133 districts are unitary, 231 are court supervised, and 222 remain nonlitigants. Districts with 10,000 to 99,999 students include 43 with unitary status, 42 under court order, and 60 nonlitigants. Fewer than a dozen districts in the study had enrollments of more than 100,000 pupils. Seven of these were unitary. The smallest districts, with less than 1,000 students, include 10 with unitary status, 12 subject to court supervision, and 18 never involved in litigation. Enrollment data were missing for one district.

Source: Compiled by U.S. Commission on Civil Rights.

The information in table 4.11 suggests that the largest districts are much more likely to have achieved judicial recognition of unitary status than the smallest districts. Of the districts ever under court order, table 4.11 shows that nearly sixty percent (59.7 percent) remain under supervision and 40.3 percent have obtained unitary status. However, among the largest districts 87.5 percent have obtained unitary status. Districts with enrollments of 10,000 to 99,999 students that were once under court order are about equally likely to have unitary status or remain under supervision. More than 60 percent of small districts (i.e., those with 1,000 to 9,999 students) and 54.5 percent of very small ones (with fewer than 1,000 pupils) remain under court order.

Table 4.11
The Percentages of Districts Ever Under Court Order Gaining Unitary Status by School Size

District Size— Enrollment	Districts with Unitary Status	Districts Under Court Order	Total
Greater than 100,000	87.5%	12.5%	100.0%
10,000 to 99,999	50.6%	49.4%	100.0%
1,000 to 9,999	36.5%	63.5%	100.0%
Less than 1,000	45.5%	54.5%	100.0%
Unknown enrollment	0.0%	100.0%	100.0%
Total	40.3%	59.7%	100.0%

Caption: For school districts ever subject to a court order, 87.5 percent of the largest litigated districts (over 100,000 students), 50.6 of the moderately large litigated districts (10,000 to 99,999), 36.5 percent of the moderately small litigated districts (1,000 to 9,999), and 45.5 percent of the smallest litigated districts (less than 1,000) gained unitary status.

Source: Compiled by U.S. Commission on Civil Rights.

To conclude, chapter 4 shows that nearly all cases were initiated by the 1970s. Substantially more school districts remain under court order as have obtained judicial recognition of their unitary status. Most of the unitary districts in this analysis obtained judicial recognition of that status since 2000. Whether districts have each type of legal status varies according to state and district size. For example, Louisiana has the largest proportion—more than 60 percent—of its districts remaining under court order; North and South Carolina have small proportions still under court order. Alabama has unitary status for more than 50 percent of its districts; North Carolina has the smallest proportion of unitary districts—about 10 percent—but the majority of its districts were never the subject of litigation. Finally, of the school districts ever under court order, nearly 90 percent of those with enrollments greater than 100,000 students have unitary status. In contrast, a majority of districts with fewer than 10,000 students remain under court order. Most districts remaining under court order are not seeking unitary status

CHAPTER 5: HOW THE LEGAL STATUS OF DISTRICTS RELATES TO THE RACIAL MIX OF STUDENTS

Some social scientists have suggested that school districts that have obtained unitary status lapse into racially concentrated schools.[1] In this chapter, the Commission on Civil Rights presents research regarding the racial/ethnic composition of students within school districts and explores to what extent obtaining unitary status is associated with changes in the racial mix of pupils assigned to schools. This effort uses measures of desegregation that examine whether racial/ethnic groups are evenly distributed across all the schools in a district. That is to say, they depict racial balance. The statistical analyses herein test (1) whether schools that obtain unitary status show less integration than districts remaining under court order, and (2) whether they are less integrated now than a decade ago (before case law clarified the criteria for attaining unitary status). These analyses are set forth in sections A and B that follow a description of the methodology for the research. The methodology section below explains how the Commission measured desegregation, its choices in the school districts it included in the analyses, and additional limitations of the statistical procedures.

Methodology for Analyzing the Effect of Unitary Status on Integration

The Commission combined information on unitary status with school data on the racial and ethnic composition of enrollment to perform an analysis of the effects of obtaining unitary status on levels of racial integration. The study design has many aspects that influence or constrain interpretations of the results—the measure of desegregation, the level of analysis (e.g., district versus metropolitan area), the school district size and structure, the chosen time frame, and the statistical representation of effects.

Measuring Desegregation

The research herein uses two desegregation measures—the dissimilarity index and the entropy index—to analyze the effects of unitary status.[2] Both indices measure whether students of different racial or ethnic groups are evenly spread among a district's schools. The dissimilarity index examines only two groups: blacks and whites. The entropy index includes other groups, such as Hispanics, Asian Americans, and Native Americans, in addition to African Americans and whites.

---

[1] *See, e.g.,* Gary Orfield, *Schools More Separate: Consequences of a Decade of Resegregation,* The Civil Rights Project, Harvard University, July 2001, pp. 4–5; NAACP Legal Defense and Educational Fund, Inc., Herschel Lee Johnson, ed., *2000 Annual Report,* (New York: NAACP, 2000) p. 8. *See also, Parents Involved in Cmty. Sch. v. Seattle Sch. Dist. No. 1,* 127 S. Ct. 2738, 2833 (Breyer, J., dissenting) ("[D]e facto resegregation is on the rise."); *but see,* 127 S. Ct. at 2769 (Thomas, J., concurring) ("At most, those statistics show a national trend toward classroom racial imbalance.").

[2] Descriptions of other measures of desegregation appear in appendix A. *Also see, e.g.,* Charles T. Clotfelter, Helen F. Ladd, Jacob L. Vigdor, all of Duke University, "Federal Oversight, Local Control and the Specter of 'Resegregation' in Southern Schools," January 2005 <http://www.s4.brown.edu/s4/colloquia/Fall05/PUBrowndraft20905.pdf> (last accessed Aug 22, 2007) (hereafter cited as Clotfelter, Ladd, and Vigdor, "Resegregation in Southern Schools"). The Commission preferred the dissimilarity index because, like the case law discussed herein, the measure focuses on the black/white balance of students and holds district administrators accountable for the aspect of desegregation they most directly control—the assignment of students to schools within the district. The entropy index is a multi-group counterpart to the dissimilarity index.

Dissimilarity Index

The dissimilarity index has a very long history of use in social science literature as a measure of residential segregation in addition to its more recent application to school desegregation. Its intuitive meaning contributes to its popularity. The dissimilarity index is the proportion of any one racial group of students that would have to switch schools to achieve perfect racial balance across the district.[3] Many experts like the measure because it holds school officials accountable for the aspect of desegregation over which they have most control, the assignment of pupils to schools. By mathematical definition, the index measures whether one particular racial/ethnic group is distributed across schools in a district in the same way as another group. Within its formula, the index holds the racial composition of the district fixed, but measures the extent to which students could be re-sorted among district schools, for example, through magnet school programs.[4]

Importantly, the dissimilarity index measures pupil assignment components of desegregation and not the effects of housing patterns that might result in racial clustering. In other words, the dissimilarity index does not reflect the district's racial composition, but only how evenly racial groups are spread across schools within the district. This aspect of the dissimilarity index is an advantage for examining the assignment of minority students to schools within the district. It is less helpful if the purpose is to represent the district's racial clustering relative to its external environment.[5]

Like most other measures of desegregation, the dissimilarity index contrasts only two groups.[6] In computing the index, one can contrast, for example, whites to nonwhites or whites to blacks. The Commission chose to compare concentrations of white and African American students because court-ordered desegregation primarily focused on integrating black and white students. Furthermore, in addition to maintaining the proper legal focus, this approach avoids the misleading impression that would otherwise arise where school systems appear less integrated because of the growth in nonblack minority populations.[7]

The dissimilarity index ranges in value from 0 to 1 so that it measures whether the proportion of African American students at each of the schools within a district is the same as the proportion of African Americans in the entire district.[8] High values of the index indicate that to achieve exact statistical racial balance among the district's schools, officials must reassign a greater number of pupils. Some researchers multiply the index, which is expressed as a proportion, by 100 to indicate the percent of

---

[3] *See* Clotfelter, Ladd, and Vigdor, "Resegregation in Southern Schools," p. 8.

[4] Byron F. Lutz, "Post *Brown vs. the Board of Education*: The Effects of the End of Court-Ordered Desegregation," Finance and Economics Discussion Series, Division of Research & Statistics and Monetary Affairs, Federal Reserve Board, Washington, D.C., 2005, p. 8 (hereafter cited as Lutz, "The Effects of the End of Court-Ordered Desegregation").

[5] In some circumstances, this aspect of the dissimilarity index (and other statistics that measure uniformity of the proportions of minority groups spread among schools) can be falsely interpreted to suggest that schools are more integrated than they are in fact. For example, if white flight leaves a school district nearly all black, but the few remaining whites are evenly spread across the district, the dissimilarity index may project a misleading impression that racial clustering has disappeared. Christine Rossell, "Using Multiple Criteria to Evaluate Public Policies: The Case of School Desegregation," *American Politics Quarterly,* April 1993, p. 172.

[6] Clotfelter, Ladd, and Vigdor, "Resegregation in Southern Schools," pp. 8–9.

[7] *See, e.g., ibid.,* pp. 12, 29, 33–34.

[8] *See* ibid., p. 8, footnote 5. The Commission's analysis contrasts African Americans and whites, substituting blacks—b_i and B—for

students that must change schools to achieve exact statistical racial balance. This analysis follows this practice.

One computes the index of dissimilarity (D), by summing over all the schools in the district:

$$D = 0.5 \sum |n_j/N - w_j/W| \, ,$$

where n_j is the number of nonwhite students in school j;

w_j is the number of white students in school j;

$N = \sum n_j$, the sum of nonwhite students in each of the districts' schools, that is, the total nonwhite enrollment in the district; and

$W = \sum w_j$, the sum of the number of white students in each of the district's schools, that is, the total white enrollment in the district.[9]

To compute the dissimilarity index for blacks and whites, one substitutes the number of African American pupils for the formula's number of nonwhite students, in essence including only those two groups in the computations. Following this formula, for each school district, one first finds the absolute value of the difference in the school's proportion of the district's African American students and its proportion of the district's white students. Then one sums the absolute values for all schools in the district and divides by two.

Entropy Index

While the dissimilarity index allows a comparison of the two racial groups that were the subject of original desegregation efforts (i.e., African Americans and whites), the entropy index determines the extent to which many groups are evenly distributed among schools in a district. It measures the average difference between a school's group proportions and those of the district.[10] The formula for the entropy index begins with the calculation of a diversity score (E) for the district, summing across the racial/ethnic groups (for $r = 1, \ldots , n$) and using natural logarithms:

$$E = \sum (P_r) \log[1/ P_r]$$

where P_r is a particular racial/ethnic group's proportion of the district population.

---

[9] *See* Clotfelter, Ladd, and Vigdor, "Resegregation in Southern Schools, p. 8; Lutz, "The Effects of the End of Court-Ordered Desegregation," 2005, p. 8.

[10] More technically, entropy, represented as "H," is the difference between the diversity of the system and the weighted average diversity of individual schools, each expressed as a fraction of the total diversity of the district. *See* John Iceland, Housing and Household Economic Statistics Division, U.S. Census Bureau, "Beyond Black and White: Metropolitan Residential Segregation in Multi-Ethnic America" (paper presented at the American Sociological Association meetings, Chicago, Illinois, August 16-19, 2002), pp. 9–10.

The score, E, is higher when the district is more diverse and ranges as high as the natural log of the number of groups used in the calculations. For example, with six racial/ethnic groups, the maximum diversity score is log 6 or 1.792, and occurs with equal representation, in other words, when each of the six groups comprises about 17 percent of the district.

Next, one must calculate the diversity score for each school (i) using a similar formula, summing over the racial/ethnic groups as before:

$$E_i = \sum (P_{ri}) \log[1/ P_{ri}]$$

> where P_{ri} is a particular racial/ethnic group's proportion of an individual school's enrollment.

The entropy index (H) is, in technical terms, an enrollment-weighted average deviation of each school's diversity score (E) from the district diversity score (E_i), expressed as a fraction of the district's total enrollment. H is a summation for each of the schools in a district (i = 1, ..., n).

$$\text{Entropy, or } H = \sum[(t_i)(E-E_i)/(E)(T)]$$

> where t_i is the total racial/ethnic enrollment of school i, and
>   T is the total district enrollment.

An entropy index of 0 indicates that a district's schools have the same composition as the system as a whole. The highest value of the index, 1, results when the district's schools contain only one group, a situation considered racially imbalanced.[11]

The statistical analyses using the dissimilarity and entropy indices are described in sections below. Summaries of districts' measures of desegregation appear in sections A and B below.

Level of Analysis

The Commission performed the analysis at the district level, computing the desegregation measures for districts based upon the racial/ethnic composition of their schools. This level of analysis facilitates the Commission's focus on court orders, the legal status of districts, and the assignment of pupils to schools within a district. Research on other aspects of desegregation sometimes requires the use of different levels of analysis which are not applied here. For example, the district level does not capture classroom assignments, which some argue isolate African American students from whites within schools; or residential area racial clustering sometimes attributed to school policies, such as mandatory pupil assignments that may have led to white flight. The district level analysis used here measures how students are assigned to schools within the parameters of the existing racial/ethnic composition of students within the district and represents the component of desegregation for which district administrators are most directly accountable.

---

[11] *See* ibid., p. 11.

Time Frame

The analysis first contrasts the desegregation measure for the various kinds of districts (those with unitary status, those under court order, and nonlitigants) for the most recent school year (see section A below). In addition, however, by calculating the dissimilarity index for a longer time frame, an analysis is also able to show whether or not, over time, integration waxes or wanes in districts, particularly those with unitary status. Section B presents an approach examining two time points. [12]

In section B, for each included school district, the analysis computes indices of desegregation not just for the most recent school year, but also for the 1992/93 school year. The 1992/93 school year is the first full school year following the *Dowell* decision. [13] Thus, the desegregation measure of the 1992/93 school year serves as a base to show whether integration in the most recent year for which data is available has increased or decreased relative to a decade or so ago.

Source of Data

To calculate measures of districts' desegregation, the Commission obtained schools' racial and ethnic enrollment from the Department of Education's "Common Core of Data." The most recent data available is for the 2004/05 school year and this is the year used in the analyses in sections A and B below. The Commission also obtained data for the 1992/93 school year and other years from the same source.

Districts in the state of Georgia lack racial/ethnic enrollment data for the 1992/93 (and earlier) school years in the source data. [14] The Commission substituted 1993/94 data for that state to complete the analysis.

Included School Districts

The Commission's analysis of desegregation drew upon the same district sample for which it reviewed unitary status in chapter 4. This effort eliminated only federally- or state-run districts, those recently opened or closed, or entities managing special, often career-oriented, programs. However, in this chapter, a few additional districts fell out of the analysis because they lacked racial and ethnic student enrollment data, preventing computation of the desegregation measures. Table 4.1, which appears in the earlier chapter, shows the number of districts forming the basis of the analyses of desegregation in column two—780.

---

[12] For convenience, the Commission describes the comparison and analyses of data from two points in time—the 1992/93 and 2004/05 schools years—as occurring "over time." There was no attempt to measure data for the intervening years.

[13] *Board of Ed. of Oklahoma City Public Schools, Independent Sch. Dist. No. 98, Oklahoma County, Okla. v. Dowell*, 498 U.S. 237 (1991).

[14] The U.S. Department of Education's National Center for Education Statistics collects school enrollment data and provides it to the public for analysis. In rare instances, states' racial/ethnic enrollment data is absent for one or more years. *See* <http://nces.ed.gov/ccd/pubschuniv.asp> (last accessed Apr. 30, 2007). Possible explanations for why such information is unavailable were not within the scope of the Commission's study.

In order to account for any inordinate effect on the results, the Commission treated some school systems differently in the analyses and presentation of desegregation measures. First, the Commission computed the desegregation measures (i.e., the dissimilarity and entropy indices) only for districts' "regular" elementary schools.[15] The Commission excluded vocational, special education, and alternative schools because they may have atypically constituted student bodies, perhaps including students from outside a district. Second, the Commission selected elementary schools as the best measure of a district's true level of integration. Elementary schools are typically more numerous and geographically distributed, while middle and high schools often combine rising students from several elementary schools. Thus, elementary schools serve as a better illustration of whether and to what degree racial imbalance exists among the schools within a district. Third, the Commission treated school districts with only one or two regular elementary schools separately, because the small numbers of schools offer administrative personnel little leeway in redistributing students among the facilities to achieve better racial balance. Accordingly, the Commission applies statistical models only to the sample of districts with three or more primary schools. Where appropriate, however, separate panels of tables show the results applicable to these smaller districts. Finally, separate results also appear for a few districts which have no African American students or no white students. In such instances, the proper value of the dissimilarity index is unclear.

The Commission included the maximum possible number of districts when it analyzed desegregation over time in section B. To carryout such analyses, however, one must first pair up districts' data from the two points of time to examine the changes. Matching districts from 1992/93 to 2004/05 resulted in little attrition (apart from the Georgia situation, handled as indicated), because the index of dissimilarity is based on districts, not individual schools. In more than a decade, numerous schools may close or open, but districts remain quite stable. The Commission did not impose any requirement of consistency in the schools comprising a district between matched school years for the very reason that one approach to effecting increased integration may be to close schools in racially clustered residential areas and open others on boundaries between racially identifiable communities. Notably, the analysis herein does not capture changes in desegregation for *individual* schools, but focuses on district increases and decreases.

Although the Commission did not require consistency in the schools comprising a district between matched school years, it did omit some additional districts in the section B analyses when it applied the selection criteria described above to the historical data forming the time trend. Details of the causes of attenuated cases are set forth in appendix A.

---

[15] In the Department of Education's Common Core Data (CCD), school "type" distinguishes "regular" schools from special education, vocational, and "other/alternative" schools. The Commission included as elementary schools any that the CCD designated as primary level. The CCD defines primary level as schools in which the lowest grade is pre-kindergarten through third and the highest grade is pre-kindergarten through eighth. Note that the database definitions classify schools with broader grade levels, for example third through ninth, as an "other" level. *See, e.g.,* U.S. Department of Education, National Center for Education Statistics (NCES), *CCD [Common Core of Data]: Documentation to the NCES Common Core of Data Public Elementary/Secondary School Universe Survey: School Year 2003–04,* February 2006, pp. A-4, A-6. In short, the Commission's analysis includes all "regular" primary-level schools. It does not include all elementary students because some primary pupils are in schools that mix primary, middle, and high school grade-levels. The Commission chose to avoid contaminating its results with the middle and high school students attending these more broadly-graded schools. See appendix A for additional information about such schools and the possible effects of excluding them on the analysis.

Statistical Analyses

The Commission combined information on unitary status with school data on the racial and ethnic composition of enrollment to perform an analysis of the effects of obtaining unitary status on levels of integration. To test the effect of unitary status, the analysis examines whether differences arise in school-level racial integration between districts which have obtained unitary status, those which remain under court supervision, and those that were never litigated. The sections present averages of measures of desegregation for the types of districts and use statistical procedures to determine whether any observed differences merit attention. A standard statistical method—analysis of variance (ANOVA)—formally tests whether any desegregation differences among the three groups of school districts are significant.[16]

To take into consideration other factors that may contribute to districts' inability to desegregate, such as district size, the Commission examined differences among the types of districts with respect to enrollment, number of schools, and the proportion of minority students. Toward this purpose, regression analysis provides a more complete explanation of differences in integration patterns among the three types of school districts. Such an approach will help determine, for example, whether large districts are less integrated in combination with other factors, such as when a district obtained judicial recognition of unitary status. Notably, regression analysis indicates when factors are associated with one another, although it does not resolve which factors are causes and which are effects.[17]

A. Differences in Integration Among Unitary, Court-Supervised, and Nonlitigant Districts

The Commission first examined whether the degree of desegregation of unitary districts differs from those under court order or from nonlitigants during the 2004/05 school year. This analysis addresses the issue of whether or not unitary districts today are less integrated than those continuing under court order or those whose racial balance was never litigated according to the Commission's research.

---

[16] Analysis of Variance (ANOVA) tests for significant differences between group averages, known as "means," when comparing more than two groups. When comparing only two groups, ANOVA yields results equivalent to the more widely understood t-test and similar to other tests of the differences between the means of two groups. *See* Hubert M. Blalock, Jr., *Social Statistics*, (New York: McGraw-Hill Book Co., 1972), pp. 317, 328–29.

[17] Multiple regression (or regression analysis) analyzes the relationship between several independent or predictor variables and a dependent variable, such as, the dissimilarity index or another desegregation measure. *See* appendix A and Blalock, *Social Statistics*, pp. 361–63.

The Dissimilarity Index and Legal Status

Results showing average dissimilarity indices by legal status, combining districts in all seven states, appear in table 5.1 below. The dissimilarity indices are transformed into percentages, ranging between zero and 100, rather than proportions. Results reveal that in the 2004/05 school year districts with unitary status appear, on average, less integrated than districts that were under court order or which were nonlitigants. On average, districts with unitary status had a dissimilarity index of 41.8 percent,[18] suggesting that school officials would need to reassign 41.8 percent of pupils to achieve a perfect balance of blacks and whites. Dissimilarity indices of districts under court order averaged 38.4 percent and those of nonlitigants averaged 32.4 percent. Despite the differences in averages, districts with each type of legal status show considerable range in their dissimilarity indices, for example from 3.9 to 92.8 percent for those with unitary status, suggesting that the groups overlap considerably in their results.

The districts' dissimilarity indices differ significantly by legal status, meaning that such differences are highly unlikely to occur by chance (i.e., the probability, p, of a random occurrence is less than one in 1,000 or "$p<.001$").[19] The average dissimilarity index of districts under court order, 38.4 percent, is significantly different from zero ($p<.001$). Not all such differences, however, are statistically significant. For example, unitary districts have higher average dissimilarity indices than districts under court supervision, but the difference between the two (41.8 versus 38.4 percent) is minimal. As a matter of statistical significance, the average dissimilarity index of unitary districts is no different than for districts under court supervision ($p<.098$, nonsignificant). On the other hand, the average dissimilarity index of nonlitigants is 6.0 percent lower than districts under court order. This effect *is* a statistically significant difference ($p<.001$), indicating that nonlitigant districts are more racially balanced than those under court supervision.[20]

Thus, the analysis of variance results show that black and white students are no more concentrated in districts with unitary status than in districts subject to court supervision, while districts never involved in litigation show a higher level of racial balance than either.

---

[18] Values appearing in this and other tables throughout the report are averages of the districts' indices. They are *not* weighted according to the number of students in the district, and therefore cannot be interpreted as an average national or (for table 5.2, below) state desegregation measure. In short, tables in this report display average desegregation measures from the districts' perspectives, not the students'.

[19] With legal status having a mean square effect of 2449.868 and mean square error of 300.901, the value of the applicable F-test is 8.142 with 3 and 492 degrees of freedom respectively. The value of the F-test indicates a very small probability (p) of mistaking a chance finding to be real. See appendix A for a lengthier explanation of analysis of variance and more detailed results. Statistical "models" using various factors (e.g., legal status, state, district size) to explain the different measures of desegregation are numbered consistently throughout appendix A's tables, whether containing analyses of variance or regression results. The effect of legal status on the dissimilarity index is model 1. *See* table A.5.

[20] *See* model 1 in appendix A, tables A.5 and A.6, for more details.

Table 5.1
Summary of Districts' Desegregation (the Dissimilarity Index) in the 2004/05 School Year by Unitary Status, Court Order, and Never Litigated

Legal Status	Number of Districts	Number of Elementary Schools	Dissimilarity Index for Blacks v. Whites		
			Average	Minimum	Maximum
COMBINED STATES					
Unitary Status	125	2,754	41.8%	3.9%	92.8%
Under Court Order	163	1,693	38.4%	0.8%	85.6%
Nonlitigants	197	1,825	32.4%	3.1%	78.4%
Uncertain Status	11	241	35.9%	19.3%	57.6%
Districts Excluded From the Analysis Because of Too Few Elementary Schools					
Unitary Status	*65*	*89*	*5.9%*	*0.0%*	*71.2%*
Under Court Order	*117*	*179*	*8.7%*	*0.0%*	*62.5%*
Nonlitigants	*97*	*151*	*6.9%*	*0.0%*	*52.5%*
Uncertain Status	*2*	*4*	*1.3%*	*0.4%*	*2.1%*
Districts Excluded Because of 0% Black or 0% White Enrollment					
Nonlitigants	*3*	*3*	*50.0%*	*50.0%*	*50.0%*

Caption: Districts with unitary status have a higher average dissimilarity index for blacks versus whites, 41.8 percent, when compared to districts still under court order, 38.4 percent, and nonlitigant districts, 32.4 percent. By this measure of desegregation, white and black students are distributed less evenly in districts subject to court order when compared to nonlitigants, and districts that obtain unitary status have even more concentrated black and white student populations.

Source: Compiled by U.S. Commission on Civil Rights.

Table 5.1 also shows districts that the Commission treated separately in the analysis. A considerable number of districts contain only one or two regular elementary schools and have dissimilarity indices near zero. Because administrators in such districts lack school alternatives to which to assign pupils, the Commission included only districts with three or more regular elementary schools in the main analysis shown in the top panel of the table. Summing information in table 5.1 shows that of the 780 districts included in the 2004/05 school year analysis, 36.0 percent (281) had only one or two regular elementary schools. In addition, a few school districts had student bodies with either no African American or no white pupils. The Commission excluded these districts because of ambiguity in whether their dissimilarity index should be zero or a greater value. Table 5.1 shows three such districts and assigns their dissimilarity index as 50 percent. Each of them was a nonlitigant with a single regular elementary school. In short, the unusual values of the dissimilarity indices generated by the special circumstances of the districts in the lower sections of table 5.1 have not influenced the statistical results.

Table 5.2 shows the average dissimilarity indices according to the decade in which the districts obtained unitary status. The information from table 5.1 is repeated here for nonlitigants and districts under court order to ease comparisons.

Table 5.2
Districts' Desegregation (the Dissimilarity Index) in the 2004/05 School Year by Decade District Obtained Unitary Status (Including Districts with Other Legal Statuses)

Legal Status	Decade Obtained Unitary Status	Number of Districts	Number of Elementary Schools	Dissimilarity Index for Blacks v. Whites		
				Average	Minimum	Maximum
COMBINED STATES						
Unitary Status	2000s	66	1,089	35.6%	3.9%	77.8%
	1990s	20	781	51.4%	11.3%	82.4%
	1980s	12	179	42.5%	27.5%	60.2%
	1970s	26	690	49.7%	8.8%	92.8%
	unknown	1	15	46.5%	46.5%	46.5%
	Total	125	2,754	41.8%	3.9%	92.8%
Under Court Order		163	1,693	38.4%	0.8%	85.6%
Nonlitigants		197	1,825	32.4%	3.1%	78.4%
Uncertain Status		11	241	35.9%	19.3%	57.6%

Caption: More districts received unitary status in the 2000s than all prior decades. These 66 districts have a lower average dissimilarity index, 35.6 percent, for blacks versus whites than any other grouping of litigated districts. Districts that received unitary status in the 1990s, 1980s, and 1970s have higher average dissimilarity indices, 51.4, 42.5, and 49.7 percent, respectively. As table 5.1 showed, districts under court order have an even lower average dissimilarity index of 38.4 percent, and nonlitigants average below that—32.4 percent.

Source: Compiled by U.S. Commission on Civil Rights.

Districts that obtained unitary status in the 2000s have dissimilarity indices that average 35.6 percent. Dissimilarity indices for districts that obtained release from court supervision in earlier decades are higher—49.7 percent for those gaining it in the 1970s, 42.5 percent for those in the 1980s, and 51.4 percent for those in the 1990s. Thus, the lower dissimilarity indices of districts that obtained unitary status in the 2000s suggest that the systems are less racially concentrated than districts that obtained unitary status in earlier decades.

Analysis of variance indicates that in addition to legal status, the decade in which districts attained unitary status explains a statistically significant amount of variation in the dissimilarity index (p<.001).[21] The effect arises from the difference between districts obtaining unitary status in the 2000s compared with those receiving unitary recognition in earlier decades. The dissimilarity indices of districts receiving unitary recognition in the 1970s, 1980s, and 1990s do not differ among themselves, but they differ from systems pronounced unitary since 2000.[22] In short, the analysis of variance confirms a finding that districts obtaining unitary status in the 2000s are less racially concentrated than districts that gained the status earlier.

State Differences in the Dissimilarity Index and Legal Status

State control of educational systems could give rise to differences that might affect districts' dissimilarity indices. These differences might include such factors as the extent of school funding, local political leadership, the nature of federal enforcement efforts, or the adoption of alternative desegregation policies. Table 5.3 shows the average dissimilarity indices for each state by legal status. Statistical analysis indicates that state differences in the average 2004/05 dissimilarity indices explain a significant amount of variation.[23] Yet, even by state, the average dissimilarity indices of districts under court order still differ significantly from zero (p<.001). Furthermore, indices of *unitary* districts are significantly higher on average than districts under court order (p=.045). In taking account of state differences, however, the average dissimilarity indices of *nonlitigants* do *not* differ from districts under court order (p=.177, nonsignificant).[24] Differences among states are indicated below, not all of which follow this general pattern.

In Louisiana, school districts with unitary status would need to reassign, on average, slightly less than half—48.3 percent—of their students to achieve exact statistical racial balance. Districts under court order need to reassign, on average, 50.1 percent of students to do so. As is similar to some other states, the dissimilarity indices of districts under court order range between near fully integrated, at 5.3 percent, to highly racially concentrated, at 81.4 percent. The dissimilarity indices of Louisiana are statistically higher than each of the six other states in the analysis (p<.005 in each instance).[25]

---

[21] The mean square effect is 1910.741; the mean square error is 291.020. With 7 and 488 degrees of freedom, F=6.566, p<.001. The effects of legal status and the decade of receiving unitary status on the dissimilarity index appears in model 13 of appendix A. *See* table A.5.

[22] See appendix A, table A.5 for regression analyses showing that receiving unitary status in the 2000s explains a statistically significant amount of variation in districts' dissimilarity index (i.e., the difference in explained variance between models 21 and 9, p<.001). However, distinguishing among districts that received unitary recognition in the 1970s, 1980s, and 1990s does not further increase the explained variation (the difference between models 17 and 21, p=.711, nonsignificant).

[23] A regression model using legal status to explain district differences in the dissimilarity index yields an R^2 of 0.107 (i.e., the amount of explained variation is 10.7 percent). The R^2 of a model explaining the dissimilarity index with only legal status is 0.047 (or 4.7 percent). The increase of 6.0 percent in explained variance as a result of including state is statistically significant (the F test for the change (or "F-change") equals 5.432, with 6 and 486 degrees of freedom, p<.001). *See* appendix A, table A.7, the differences in models 5 and 1.

[24] *See* appendix A, tables A.5 and A.6, model 5.

[25] Because state differences are not the focus of this report, details of the specific state contrasts are not shown.

Table 5.3
Summaries by State of Districts' Desegregation (the Dissimilarity Index) in the 2004/05 School Year by Unitary Status, Court Order, and Never Litigated

State	Legal Status	Number of Districts	Number of Elementary Schools	Dissimilarity Index for Blacks v. Whites		
				Average	Minimum	Maximum
ALABAMA						
	Unitary Status	44	359	40.0%	3.9%	80.5%
	Under Court Order	33	269	39.7%	9.4%	85.6%
	Nonlitigants	2	9	27.5%	12.0%	43.0%
	Districts Excluded From the Analysis Because of Too Few Elementary Schools					
	Unitary Status	*25*	*34*	*10.6%*	*0.0%*	*71.2%*
	Under Court Order	*17*	*27*	*5.6%*	*0.0%*	*28.5%*
	Nonlitigants	*4*	*6*	*15.7%*	*0.0%*	*52.5%*
FLORIDA						
	Unitary Status	19	1,316	47.4%	19.7%	77.4%
	Under Court Order	12	275	30.3%	6.7%	57.6%
	Nonlitigants	28	273	34.7%	12.5%	76.2%
	Districts Excluded From the Analysis Because of Too Few Elementary Schools					
	Under Court Order	*3*	*4*	*4.8%*	*0.0%*	*14.4%*
	Nonlitigants	*5*	*7*	*7.8%*	*0.0%*	*36.8%*
GEORGIA						
	Unitary Status	12	348	44.3%	6.6%	92.8%
	Under Court Order	39	283	29.2%	2.3%	75.5%
	Nonlitigants	45	485	31.6%	3.1%	72.2%
	Districts Excluded From the Analysis Because of Too Few Elementary Schools					
	Unitary Status	*20*	*28*	*3.2%*	*0.0%*	*37.9%*
	Under Court Order	*36*	*50*	*2.5%*	*0.0%*	*38.2%*
	Nonlitigants	*22*	*37*	*8.3%*	*0.0%*	*45.2%*
	Districts Excluded Because of 0% Black or 0% White Enrollment					
	Nonlitigants	*2*	*2*	*50.0%*	*50.0%*	*50.0%*
LOUISIANA						
	Unitary Status	14	227	48.3%	11.6%	60.4%
	Under Court Order	35	499	50.1%	5.3%	81.4%
	Nonlitigants	5	31	44.7%	13.0%	66.2%
	Districts Excluded From the Analysis Because of Too Few Elementary Schools					
	Unitary Status	*2*	*3*	*4.2%*	*0.0%*	*8.4%*
	Under Court Order	*8*	*14*	*27.0%*	*0.0%*	*62.5%*
	Nonlitigants	*4*	*8*	*12.7%*	*0.1%*	*36.4%*

Continued

Table 5.3 (continued)
Summaries by State of Districts' Desegregation (the Dissimilarity Index) in the 2004/05 School Year by Unitary Status, Court Order, and Never Litigated

State	Legal Status	Number of Districts	Number of Elementary Schools	Dissimilarity Index for Blacks v. Whites		
				Average	Minimum	Maximum
MISSISSIPPI						
	Unitary Status	13	72	38.2%	11.7%	59.2%
	Under Court Order	22	136	44.1%	0.8%	78.6%
	Nonlitigants	20	107	33.1%	8.5%	78.4%
	Districts Excluded From the Analysis Because of Too Few Elementary Schools					
	Unitary Status	*11*	*14*	*2.7%*	*0.0%*	*16.0%*
	Under Court Order	*46*	*73*	*11.3%*	*0.0%*	*59.8%*
	Nonlitigants	*30*	*41*	*5.8%*	*0.0%*	*46.9%*
	Uncertain Status	*1*	*2*	*0.4%*	*0.4%*	*0.4%*
	Districts Excluded Because of 0% Black or 0% White Enrollment					
	Nonlitigants	*1*	*1*	*50.0%*	*50.0%*	*50.0%*
NORTH CAROLINA						
	Unitary Status	12	311	44.5%	28.3%	59.1%
	Under Court Order	14	165	35.9%	21.9%	48.7%
	Nonlitigants	58	528	31.1%	3.3%	57.4%
	Uncertain Status	11	241	35.9%	19.3%	57.6%
	Districts Excluded From the Analysis Because of Too Few Elementary Schools					
	Under Court Order	*1*	*2*	*3.6%*	*3.6%*	*3.6%*
	Nonlitigants	*18*	*29*	*5.2%*	*0.0%*	*27.9%*
	Uncertain Status	*1*	*2*	*2.1%*	*2.1%*	*2.1%*
SOUTH CAROLINA						
	Unitary Status	11	121	30.1%	15.3%	37.7%
	Under Court Order	8	66	27.5%	15.1%	37.8%
	Nonlitigants	39	392	32.1%	5.6%	66.4%
	Districts Excluded From the Analysis Because of Too Few Elementary Schools					
	Unitary Status	*7*	*10*	*2.2%*	*0.0%*	*11.6%*
	Under Court Order	*6*	*9*	*13.2%*	*0.0%*	*50.2%*
	Nonlitigants	*14*	*23*	*4.9%*	*0.0%*	*33.7%*

Caption: In Alabama, unitary districts would need to reassign 40 percent of their students to achieve racial balance. Florida unitary districts would necessarily transfer 47.4 percent of their students, while court-supervised districts would need to move 30.3 percent. Georgia unitary districts could do with shifting 44.3 percent of their students, while districts under court order would need to reassign 29.2 percent. Louisiana unitary districts would need to move approximately half of their students. Mississippi's unitary districts could do with transferring 38.2 percent of their students. North Carolina school systems would need to reassign 44.5 percent of students in unitary districts, and 35.9 percent of those in districts under court order. South Carolina districts would need to shift 30.1 percent of students in unitary districts, and 27.5 percent of students in court ordered districts.

Source: Compiled by U.S. Commission on Civil Rights.

As in Louisiana, in Mississippi and Alabama, the average dissimilarity indices of districts with unitary status are equal to or less than the averages of districts under court order. The average dissimilarity index is 44.1 percent for Mississippi districts remaining under court order and 38.2 for those with unitary status. Perhaps more importantly, the results for Mississippi are statistically different from Louisiana, Georgia, and South Carolina ($p<.05$ in every instance). In Alabama, districts with unitary status and those under court order average approximately 40 percent on the index. Alabama's indices differ statistically from those of Louisiana but not indices of other analyzed states ($p<.001$ for Louisiana; $p>.100$ for all other states, nonsignificant).

In Georgia, North and South Carolina, and Florida, district averages on the dissimilarity indices are greater for districts with unitary status than those under court order. (See table 5.3.) For example, in Georgia, 29.2 percent of students in districts under court order would have to be reassigned to achieve perfect racial balance of the system's elementary schools. For districts with unitary status, school officials would need to move 44.3 percent to other schools. Georgia's dissimilarity indices are statistically lower than Mississippi's and Louisiana's ($p<.05$ and $p<.001$, respectively). South Carolina's dissimilarity indices, at 30.1 percent for unitary systems, and 27.5 percent for districts under court order, are also significantly lower than Mississippi's ($p<.05$) and Louisiana's ($p<.001$). North Carolina's dissimilarity indices are 44.5 percent for districts with unitary status and 35.9 percent for those still under court order. North Carolina's average dissimilarity indices differ statistically only from those of Louisiana ($p<.001$). Florida's indices—47.4 percent and 30.3 percent for districts with unitary status and court supervision, respectively—also differ significantly from the high values of Louisiana ($p<.005$).

To summarize, an analysis of the dissimilarity indices by state reveals many significant differences. For example, districts in Louisiana, whether unitary or under court jurisdiction, would need to reassign significantly higher proportions of students to achieve racial balance throughout their school systems than in other states. At the same time, some states show greater differences in the average dissimilarity indices of districts with different types of legal status. Districts under court order and those with unitary status averaged nearly the same on their dissimilarity indices, for example, in Alabama, but were vastly different in Georgia.

White Student Enrollment Related to the Dissimilarity Index and Legal Status

The dissimilarity index is conceptually independent of the percent of white students in the district. The formula of the index treats a district's proportion of white students as a *given*, a basis from which it measures the extent to which the percent of such students in each district school varies. In other words, by mathematical definition, a large or small *district* proportion of white students does not affect the size of the dissimilarity index; however, large *and* small proportions of white students *in schools within the district* do.

Table 5.4
Districts' Desegregation (the Dissimilarity Index) in the 2004/05 School Year by District's Percent White Enrollment and Legal Status

Districts' Percent White Enrollment	Legal Status	Number of Districts	Number of Elementary Schools	Dissimilarity Index for Blacks v. Whites		
				Average	Minimum	Maximum
COMBINED STATES						
Less than 25 percent	Unitary Status	26	656	54.2%	16.9%	92.8%
	Under Court Order	27	333	51.3%	11.9%	85.6%
	Nonlitigants	8	71	36.9%	8.5%	66.4%
	Uncertain Status	1	23	43.5%	43.5%	43.5%
25 percent or more, but less than 50 percent	Unitary Status	35	1,068	42.4%	4.1%	76.7%
	Under Court Order	39	499	41.2%	0.8%	78.6%
	Nonlitigants	43	487	34.0%	3.1%	78.4%
	Uncertain Status	4	63	39.5%	19.4%	57.6%
50 percent or more, but less than 75 percent	Unitary Status	43	814	36.5%	3.9%	57.8%
	Under Court Order	62	537	33.8%	4.2%	71.0%
	Nonlitigants	60	642	30.7%	3.3%	66.2%
	Uncertain Status	5	151	34.8%	31.0%	45.5%
75 percent or more	Unitary Status	21	216	36.4%	10.0%	59.8%
	Under Court Order	35	324	33.4%	2.3%	79.6%
	Nonlitigants	86	625	32.4%	3.9%	76.2%
	Uncertain Status	1	4	19.3%	19.3%	19.3%
Total	Unitary Status	125	2,754	41.8%	3.9%	92.8%
	Under Court Order	163	1,693	38.4%	0.8%	85.6%
	Nonlitigants	197	1,825	32.4%	3.1%	78.4%
	Uncertain Status	11	241	35.9%	19.3%	57.6%

Note: For a breakout of the districts excluded from this analysis because they had only one or two elementary schools or zero percent white or black students, see appendix A, table A.2.

Caption: The average dissimilarity indices for districts with low white enrollment are higher than the indices for districts with high white enrollment. For districts with less than 25 percent white enrollment, the average dissimilarity index is 54.2 percent for those with unitary status and 51.3 percent for those under court order. Districts with white enrollments between 25 and 50 percent show an average dissimilarity index of 42.4 percent for unitary districts, and 41.2 percent for districts under court order. Districts with 50 to 75 percent white enrollment have an average dissimilarity index of 36.5 percent for unitary districts and 33.8 percent for districts under court order. In districts with 75 percent or more white enrollment, the average dissimilarity indices are 36.4 and 33.4 percent respectively for those with unitary status and those under court order.

Source: Compiled by U.S. Commission on Civil Rights.

Despite this conceptual independence of the district's percent of white students and the dissimilarity index, table 5.4 demonstrates that the two factors are *empirically* related. Results in the table suggest that districts with smaller proportions of white students have greater concentrations of those students in some of the district's schools rather than others. For districts whose enrollments are less than 25 percent white, the average dissimilarity index is 54.2 percent for those with unitary status and 51.3 percent for those under court order suggesting that school officials would need to reassign more than half of all students to achieve perfect racial balance. For districts with between 25 and 50 percent white students, the dissimilarity indices are 42.4 percent for unitary systems and 41.2 percent for those under court order. For majority white districts with 50 to 75 percent white enrollment, the average dissimilarity indices are 36.4 percent for unitary districts and 33.4 percent for court-supervised ones. Finally, the districts in which student enrollment was 75 percent or more white had average dissimilarity indices that nearly matched those with lesser concentrated but still majority white enrollments—36.4 and 33.4 percent respectively for those with unitary status and those under court order. The statistical significance of the percentage of white students within a district is examined in the next section along with the effects of district size.

District Size Related to the Dissimilarity Index and Legal Status

Chapter 4 showed that gaining unitary status is related to district size, measured by the number of enrolled students.[26] Table 5.5 shows the average dissimilarity index of districts according to district size and legal status. Larger school districts have higher average dissimilarity indices regardless of their legal status. Of the 11 school districts with enrollments of 100,000 or more, the seven with unitary status had an average dissimilarity index of 58.8 percent; the one under court order had a dissimilarity index of 57.6 percent; and the two that were nonlitigants had indices averaging 50.6 percent. Of districts with 10,000 to 99,999 students, districts with unitary status averaged 47.6 percent, those under court order 43.7 percent, and nonlitigants 35.5 percent. Of those with student bodies ranging 1,000 to 9,999, districts with unitary status averaged 36.9 percent on the dissimilarity index; those remaining under court supervision averaged 36.4 percent; and nonlitigants averaged 30.8 percent. Thus, the largest districts have higher dissimilarity indices no matter what their status, and vice versa with smaller districts.[27]

---

[26] The Commission considered the number of schools as an alternative measure of district size. However, the district's enrollment and its number of schools were very highly correlated (.969, or, when representing both variables in logarithms, .940), suggesting that the two measures would yield similar results. Thus, the analysis represents size using only the district's enrollment.

[27] A handful of school systems for which Commission staff were unable to determine legal status do not follow any particular trend in dissimilarity indices with regard to district size.

Table 5.5
Districts' Desegregation (the Dissimilarity Index) in the 2004/05 School Year by District Size and Legal Status

District Size	Legal Status	Number of Districts	Number of Elementary Schools	Dissimilarity Index for Blacks v. Whites		
				Average	Minimum	Maximum
COMBINED STATES						
Greater than 100,000	Unitary Status	7	938	58.8%	46.1%	77.4%
	Under Court Order	1	121	57.6%	57.6%	57.6%
	Nonlitigants	2	128	50.6%	45.1%	56.1%
	Uncertain Status	1	84	33.2%	33.2%	33.2%
10,000 to 99,999	Unitary Status	43	1,417	47.6%	15.3%	92.8%
	Under Court Order	42	929	43.7%	12.2%	81.4%
	Nonlitigants	60	942	35.5%	11.4%	66.4%
	Uncertain Status	6	130	40.3%	31.0%	57.6%
1,000 to 9,999	Unitary Status	75	399	36.9%	3.9%	80.5%
	Under Court Order	120	643	36.4%	0.8%	85.6%
	Nonlitigants	135	755	30.8%	3.1%	78.4%
	Uncertain Status	4	27	30.0%	19.3%	52.9%
Total	Unitary Status	125	2,754	41.8%	3.9%	92.8%
	Under Court Order	163	1,693	38.4%	0.8%	85.6%
	Nonlitigants	197	1,825	32.4%	3.1%	78.4%
	Uncertain Status	11	241	35.9%	19.3%	57.6%

Note: For a breakout of the districts excluded from this analysis because they had only one or two elementary schools or zero percent white or black students, see appendix A, table A.3.

Caption: Of the 11 largest school districts (greater than 100,000 students), those with unitary status had an average dissimilarity index of 58.8 percent; those under court order had a dissimilarity index of 57.6 percent; and the nonlitigants had indices averaging 50.6 percent. Of the next largest districts (10,000 to 99,999 students), those with unitary status had an average index of 47.6 percent, those under court order 43.7 percent, and nonlitigants 35.5 percent. Districts with 1,000 to 9,999 pupils and unitary status averaged 36.9 percent on the dissimilarity index; those remaining under court supervision 36.4 percent; and nonlitigants 30.8 percent.

Source: Compiled by U.S. Commission on Civil Rights.

Notably, the Commission's threshold of requiring three or more elementary schools excluded all districts with fewer than 1,000 students from the main analysis. Furthermore, all of the districts excluded through the application of the three-or-more-elementary-schools criteria had fewer than 10,000 students.[28] Thus, very small districts and many small ones are not present in the analysis.

---

[28] See appendix A, table A.3 for detailed information about the sizes and dissimilarity indices of the excluded districts.

In its effort to better understand how legal status (whether unitary, under court jurisdiction, or nonlitigant) affects districts' levels of integration, the Commission performed an analysis of covariance (ANCOVA)[29] of the dissimilarity index, using district size, the percent of the enrollment that is white, state (i.e., Alabama, Georgia, etc.), legal status, and the decade of attaining unitary status to explain differences among the school systems. For this exercise, district size and the district's percent of whites are expressed with a full range of variation rather than split into the categories displayed in tables 5.4 and 5.5. For size, the analysis uses base 10 logs of the number of enrolled students, which yield increments that correspond to the categories in table 5.5.[30]

The analysis of covariance including district size, the percentage of white students, and other factors is statistically significant (p<.001), indicating differences between groups.[31] However, the significant differences are *only partly* because of the districts' legal status. Taking into account the effects of district size and these other factors, the amount of the dissimilarity index attributable to districts *having court supervision* is not statistically different from zero (p=.142, nonsignificant). The average dissimilarity index of nonlitigants is also indistinguishable from the average index of school systems under court jurisdiction (p=.544, nonsignificant). However, having unitary status results in a statistically significant increase of 7.2 percent in the dissimilarity index (p=.033), an effect that is countered with a statistically significant average 11.3 percent *decrease* in the index for districts that received unitary recognition in 2000 or thereafter (p=.002). In addition, the effects of district size and percent white are highly significant (t=6.547, p<.001; and t= -5.337, p<001).[32] These latter effects indicate that the larger the district's size and the lower its percent white enrollment, the higher its dissimilarity index. However, although the district's legal status appears to matter in this analysis, further study below reveals that the other factors—receiving unitary status in 2000 or thereafter, district size, and the district's proportion of white students—are more important.

---

[29] Analysis of covariance is similar to analysis of variance. An analysis of variance uses variables that one can only divide into groups or categories (e.g., race, ethnicity, gender, and legal status) to explain the dependent variable (i.e., the desegregation measure in this study). In addition to categorical variables, an analysis of covariance includes one or more "continuous" explanatory factors. A "continuous" variable is one with values expressed in numbers where increments or decreases are meaningful. Examples of continuous variables include temperature, age, or percentages.

[30] Using the base 10 logarithms assigns district size values as follows: Districts with 0 to 1,000 students have a base 10 log ranging from 0 to 3; those with 1,000 to 10,000 receive values of 3 to 4; those with 10,000 to 100,000, 4 to 5; and those with 100,000, 5 to 6. The use of logarithms transforms enrollment figures such that small increments in the number of students are more important for smaller school districts than for larger systems. This transformation makes the progression from small to large districts more linear, a desirable property to meet statistical requirements for performing a regression analysis.

[31] The mean square effect is 2728.933; the mean square error is 238.456. With 15 and 480 degrees of freedom, F=11.444, p<.001. *See* model 17 in appendix A, table A.5.

[32] *See* model 17 in appendix A. In particular, table A.8, shows more analyses of covariance for the districts' size and percent white enrollment. Significant differences also occur between the states in this model.

To demonstrate the potency of legal status along with district size in another manner, the Commission performed a series of regressions.[33] Together district size (the base 10 log of enrollment) and the district's percent of white students explain 14.4 percent of the variation in districts' dissimilarity indices.[34] Adding state to the regression equation increases the explained variation to 24.1 percent (a 9.7 percent increase, statistically significant at p<.001).[35] In contrast, the legal status of districts does not explain any significant additional variation beyond that captured in size, percentage of white student population, and state. With legal status along with size, percent white, and state, the explained variance (R^2) in the dissimilarity index was 24.2 percent, but the increase of 0.1 percent because of adding legal status was insignificant (p=.897).[36]

The results are slightly more complex, however. The effect of unitary status becomes statistically different from court supervision when the explanatory factors distinguish districts receiving unitary recognition before and after the year 2000. Including the 2000 distinction along with all of the earlier named factors (size, percent white, state, and legal status) increased the R^2 to 26.1 percent (an increase of 1.9 percent that *is* statistically significant, p=.001). The effects of this regression model indicate that having unitary status increases the dissimilarity index 6.1 percent (p<.05) and receiving the status after the year 2000 decreases the index by 10.2 percent (p=.001), tendencies evident in table 5.2.[37]

These findings indicate that upon deeper analyses, whether the district is under court supervision or a nonlitigant is not uniquely related to the system's dissimilarity index. A district's state, size, and percentage of white student population account for considerable variation in its dissimilarity index. Most dissimilarity index differences by legal status that are evident in table 5.1 and ensuing charts arise because unitary, court supervised, and nonlitigant districts vary by size, percent white, and state.

A finding that the dissimilarity indices *are* related to whether the district attained unitary status in the most recent decade (the 2000s) may have a simple explanation: that the districts granted unitary status since the year 2000 properly deserved that designation.

A More Diverse Measure of Desegregation and Legal Status

All of the previous analyses have used the dissimilarity index as the measure of desegregation. As noted earlier, the dissimilarity index represents only two racial/ethic groups: African Americans and whites. Entropy is another measure of desegregation that represents the racial/ethnic balance among a district's schools, but it does so for any number of multiple groups. In simple terms, it summarizes the difference in the proportion of each minority group in each school compared to the proportion of the same group in the district as a whole. Smaller differences represent greater integration. As with the dissimilarity index,

---

[33] Social scientists often have difficulty determining underlying causes of a phenomenon when explanatory factors are interrelated. Each regression yields a statistic known as R-square (R^2) that represents the amount of variation factors such as district size and legal status explain in the dependent variable (i.e., the dissimilarity index, in this example). To determine whether one factor is a good substitute for another, one can perform a regression analysis using that factor to explain the dependent variable; then perform a second regression with both factors in the statistical equation. The increase in the R^2 from the "model" using just one factor to the second one including an additional factor reveals the unique contribution of the second factor to explaining the dependent variable.

[34] *See* appendix A, table A.7, model 25.

[35] *See* appendix A, table A.7, model 29.

[36] *See* appendix A, table A.7, model 33.

[37] *See* model 21 in the results in appendix A and table A.9.

the entropy index ranges between 0 and 1, but is multiplied by 100 to range from 0 to 100 herein. Such values are thereby easily interpreted as the percent of students that must change schools to achieve exact statistical racial balance in the district.

Table 5.6 shows the average entropy indices for districts with unitary status, those under court order, and nonlitigants. In addition, it displays average entropy indices for districts with unitary status according to the decade in which the districts received judicial recognition for that status. *The entropy indices suggest that, factoring in Hispanic, Asian American, Native American, and other ethnic groups, districts are much more integrated than the dissimilarity indices indicated.* Districts with unitary status average 16.1 percent on the entropy index, suggesting that on average, school officials need only reassign 16.1 percent of students to achieve perfect racial/ethnic balance among their system's schools. Districts under court order could achieve full statistical integration by moving, on average, 14.6 percent of students. On average, only 10 percent of pupils require reassignment among nonlitigants.

Table 5.6
Summary of Districts' Entropy Index in the 2004/05 School Year by Unitary Status, Court Order, and Never Litigated

Legal Status	Decade Obtained Unitary Status	Number of Districts	Number of Elementary Regular Schools	Entropy		
				Average	Minimum	Maximum
COMBINED STATES						
Unitary Status	2000s	66	1,089	12.2%	0.8%	37.8%
	1990s	20	781	21.5%	3.1%	48.7%
	1980s	12	179	16.8%	5.9%	33.1%
	1970s	26	690	21.3%	2.5%	54.1%
	unknown	1	15	25.5%	25.5%	25.5%
	Total	125	2,754	16.1%	0.8%	54.1%
Under Court Order		163	1,693	14.6%	0.4%	45.4%
Nonlitigants		197	1,825	10.0%	0.7%	46.8%
Uncertain Status		11	241	12.8%	2.9%	26.9%
Districts Excluded From the Analysis Because of Too Few Elementary Schools						
Unitary Status		65	89	1.1%	0.0%	22.5%
Under Court Order		117	179	2.4%	0.0%	29.3%
Nonlitigants		97	151	1.3%	0.0%	13.6%
Uncertain Status		2	4	0.2%	0.0%	0.4%
Districts Excluded Because of 0% Black or 0% White Enrollment						
Nonlitigants		3	3	0.0%	0.0%	0.0%

Caption: Districts with unitary status have a higher average entropy index, 16.1 percent, compared to districts that are still under court order or are nonlitigants, 14.6 and 10.0 percent respectively. Districts which received unitary status in the decades before 2000 have higher average entropy indices compared to districts that received unitary status in the 2000s, which average only 12.2 percent.

Source: Compiled by U.S. Commission on Civil Rights.

An analysis of variance of the entropy indices by legal status reveals statistically significant differences depending upon legal status (p<.001).[38] The 14.6 average entropy index of school districts under court jurisdiction is significantly different from zero (p<.001). Furthermore, nonlitigants have a significantly lower average entropy index (by 4.5 percent) than districts under the jurisdiction of courts (i.e., 14.6 minus 4.5 is 10.0 with rounding error, the average in table 5.6) (p<.001). However, with an average entropy index that is only 1.57 percent higher than districts under court jurisdiction, the degree of integration of unitary systems is indistinguishable from their supervised counterparts (p=.181, nonsignificant).[39]

As with the dissimilarity index, the level of the entropy index appears related to the decade in which a district received judicial recognition for unitary status. Table 5.6 shows that districts receiving unitary status in the year 2000 or after are less racially clustered, with, on average, entropy indices of only 12.2 percent. Districts that received unitary status in earlier decades have entropy indices suggesting that averages of 16.8 to 21.5 percent would need to be reassigned to evenly distribute racial groups within the district. Analysis of variance of the entropy index, adding both legal status and the decade of unitary status, shows statistically significant differences among groups (p<.001).[40] The dissimilarity indices of districts receiving unitary recognition in the 1970s, 1980s, and 1990s do not differ; those of systems becoming unitary in the 2000 decade are different compared to earlier decades.[41] Districts obtaining unitary status in the 2000s are less racially concentrated than districts recognized as unitary earlier.

The difference in meaning of the entropy and dissimilarity indices is subtle. The entropy measure suggests that of districts that gained unitary status in the 1970s through the 1990s, approximately one-fifth of students from the multiple racial/ethnic groups would require reassignment to achieve precise racial/ethnic balance. Parallel dissimilarity indices in table 5.2 indicate that school administrators would have to reassign averages of 42 to 52 percent of African American or white students to accomplish that end. These are not inconsistent results because the majority of the fifth of students that would need to be reassigned to achieve multi-group racial balance could be African Americans or whites.

---

[38] With the 2004/05 entropy index , the analysis of variance mean square effect is 1115.844, and the mean square error is 97.304. The F-test is 11.468 with 3 and 492 degrees of freedom. The result is highly significant, p<.001. *See* appendix A, table A.5, model 2.

[39] *See* appendix A, table A.6, model 2.

[40] The mean square effect is 816.949; the mean square error is 93.243. With 7 and 488 degrees of freedom, F=8.762, p<.001. *See* appendix A, table A.5, model 14.

[41] The average entropy index of districts that received unitary status since 2000 differs from that of school systems recognized as unitary in the 1970s and 1990s (p<.001), but is not significantly different from the level of those obtaining the status in the 1980s (p=.131), likely because the latter group contains too few districts (only 12) for a statistically significant result. Details of the group contrasts are not presented. Note, however, that the regression results in appendix A (table A.7) show that adding a distinction of districts obtaining unitary status since 2000 explains a significant amount of variation in the entropy indices (subtracting the variation in model 10 from model 22), but adding three more subgroupings for those receiving the status in the 1970s, 1980s, and 1990s does not (subtracting variation in model 22 from model 18).

The Commission also carried out an analysis of covariance of the entropy index with all of the other factors—district size (the base 10 log of student enrollment), the percent of the enrollment that is white, state (i.e., Alabama, Georgia, etc.), legal status, and the decade of attaining unitary status—to explain differences among the school systems. The results are statistically significant (p<.001), indicating differences between groups.[42] The entropy index of districts having court supervision is essentially zero (i.e., insignificantly different from zero, p=.355) when taking into account the effects of district size, percent white, and state. The average entropy indices of nonlitigants are no different from those of systems under court jurisdiction (p=.781, nonsignificant). The average entropy index of districts with unitary status is 4.7 percent higher than that of districts under court order, a statistically significant (p=.01), but small amount.[43] The effects of district size and percent white on the entropy index are highly significant (t=6.712, p<.001; and t= -7.501, p<001),[44] as are those of states.[45] *As with the other desegregation measure, the larger the district's size and the lower its percent white enrollment, the higher its entropy. The small effect of districts having unitary status proves to be unimportant in the analysis below, although receiving unitary status in 2000 or thereafter does matter.*

As before, the Commission performed additional regressions to reveal the explanatory value of legal status along with district size and other potent variables. District size (the base 10 log of enrollment) and percent of white students explain 18.9 percent of the variation in districts' entropy indices;[46] adding state increases the explained variation to 33.5 percent (a statistically significant increase of 14.7 percent, p<.001).[47] The legal status of districts explains no additional variation (i.e., the increase is 0.000, p=.956, insignificant) after district size, percent white, and state.[48] However, using legal status and an indication of districts that received unitary status in the 2000s leads to a statistically significant increase in explained variance (2.5 percent, p<.001, for an R^2 = 36.1 percent) and a significant effect of having unitary status.[49] Thus, relative to the entropy index anticipated upon the basis of size, percent white, and states, districts with unitary status would need to reassign 3.7 percent more students (p=.005) than those under court order. Those that received their status in the 2000s would need to reassign 6.7 percent fewer students to achieve perfect racial balance across schools than those declared unitary sooner.[50]

---

[42] The mean square effect is 1237.338; the mean square error is 68.044. With 15 and 480 degrees of freedom, F=18.184, p<.001. *See* appendix A, table A.5, model 18.

[43] *See* appendix A, table A.6, model 18.

[44] *See* appendix A, table A.8, model 18.

[45] The effects of states on the entropy index is most evident in the increase in the indices' variation explained when the model includes state identifiers in addition to other factors such as district's size and its percent of white enrollment. *See* appendix A, table A.7, the difference between model 30 and model 26, where, for example, the increase in R^2 = 14.7 percent (p<.001).

[46] *See* appendix A, table A.7, model 26.

[47] *See* appendix A, table A.7, the difference between models 30 and 26.

[48] *See* appendix A, table A.7, the difference between models 34, and 30.

[49] *See* appendix A, table A.7, the differences in models 22 and 10 (where model 10 is the same as model 34). *See also* table A.6, model 22.

[50] *See* appendix A. tables A.6 and A. 9, model 22.

These findings confirm that a district's state, size, and percent white account for considerable variation in this desegregation measure, the entropy index. Most differences in entropy indices among unitary, court-supervised, and nonlitigant districts result from variations in size, percent white, and state that are related to legal status, but not the desegregation measure. Again, the districts attaining unitary status in the most recent decade, the 2000s, show lower entropy indices, a finding which may result from the careful selection of those school systems for release from court supervision.

B. Effects of Unitary Status on Changes in Integration Over Time

The second part of the Commission's statistical analysis examines unitary, court-supervised, and nonlitigant school districts and changes in desegregation levels in 1992/93 and 2004/05. While the static 2004/05 analysis above shows the degree of integration each type of district has currently achieved, looking at each district at these two points in time will indicate whether current desegregation is an improvement over, or backsliding from, past efforts. For those who believe that judicial recognition of unitary status has led to diminished racial balance in schools since the early 1990s, this analysis will reveal support for, or contradictions to, underlying assumptions that districts with unitary status are less integrated in 2004/05 than they were in 1992/93; that districts under court order have maintained levels of integration over the decade; and that nonlitigated districts remain unaffected by emphases on achieving racial/ethnic diversity.

This approach takes the difference between a district's index of dissimilarity in the 2004/05 and 1992/93 school years. It then determines whether the three groups of school districts—those with unitary, court-supervised, or nonlitigant status—differ in the change in segregation over time. With respect to these changes in districts' degree of integration, the analysis parallels that of the previous section. It presents averages for the types of districts, uses ANOVA to test the significance of the differences, and provides a fuller explanation of the effects of other factors, such as school size, using covariance and regression analyses. Finally, the section presents an analysis using the entropy index as an alternative measure of desegregation that better represents racial balance among all groups—Hispanics, Asian Americans, and Native Americans, as well as African Americans and whites.

Changes Over Time in the Dissimilarity Index and Legal Status

Table 5.7 presents averages of 2004/05 and 1992/93 levels of integration, measured using the index of dissimilarity, and the over time change for districts with unitary status, those under court order, and nonlitigants. As before, the dissimilarity indices have been multiplied by 100 so that they range from 0 to 100 and can be interpreted most readily as the percent of students that would have to be reassigned to another school to achieve perfect racial balance in the district. Lower values on the index of dissimilarity represent greater integration; higher values suggest that the district is further from racial balance.

The dissimilarity indices in table 5.7 for the 2004/05 school year differ slightly from those presented in table 5.1 because of districts that (1) did not match entities in 1992/93, as may occur when a district was formed more recently, and (2) had fewer than three regular elementary schools in 1992/93 even though they had three or more in 2004/05. Compared to the unmatched 2004 results using the dissimilarity index in table 5.1, table 5.7 includes only 23 fewer districts because of the requirement that they have three or more regular elementary schools in both years.[51] With the minor sample attrition from the named causes, the average 2004/05 dissimilarity index for districts with unitary status increased from 41.8 to 43.0 percent.

Note further that the Department of Education's Common Core of Data did not contain any enrollment data for districts in the state of Georgia in the 1992/93 school year. The Commission substituted 1993/94 data for that state in this analysis.

The results in table 5.7 suggest that districts with unitary status or under court order are slightly less integrated in the 2004/05 school year than they were a decade or so earlier. The average dissimilarity index for districts with unitary status was 39.5 percent in 1992/93 (or 1993/94 in Georgia) and increased to an average of 43.0 percent in 2004/05, with the difference indicating that an additional 3.5 percent of students would have to be assigned to other schools to achieve perfect racial balance today. For districts under court order, the dissimilarity indices averaged 35.6 percent in 1992/93 (or 1993/94) and increased by 2.8 percent to 38.5 percent (with rounding error) in 2004/05. Districts the Commission identified as nonlitigants are slightly more integrated in 2004/05 than in 1992/93. The average of their dissimilarity indices decreased from 33.6 to 32.7 percent.

In addition to averages of the dissimilarity index, table 5.7 shows a range of values for districts with each type of legal status. The minimum and maximum values of the difference suggests that individual districts' dissimilarity indices decreased as much as 58.3 percent for nonlitigants, 55.6 percent for those under court order, and 33.7 percent for those with unitary status. At the same time, other individual districts had dissimilarity indices that increased as much as 51.8 percent for nonlitigants, 53.7 percent for those with unitary status, and 71.1 percent for those under court order.

---

[51] Table 5.1 excludes 281 districts because with too few regular elementary schools. Table 5.7 excludes 304. *See* appendix A, table A.1.

Table 5.7
Summary of Districts' Desegregation (the Dissimilarity Index) in the 2004/05 School Year Compared to 1992/93 (or 1993/94) by Unitary Status, Court Order, and Never Litigated

Legal Status	Number of Matched Districts	Number of Elementary Schools		2004 Dissimilarity Index for Blacks v. Whites			1992 (or 1993*) Dissimilarity Index for Blacks v. Whites			Difference Between 2004 and 1992 (or 1993*) Dissimilarity Indices		
		2004	1992 (or 1993)*	Average	Minimum	Maximum	Average	Minimum	Maximum	Average	Minimum	Maximum
COMBINED STATES												
Unitary Status	114	2,715	2,294	43.0%	3.9%	92.8%	39.5%	2.9%	85.2%	3.5%	-33.7%	53.7%
Under Court Order	149	1,636	1,517	38.5%	0.8%	85.6%	35.6%	2.5%	91.4%	2.8%	-55.6%	71.1%
Nonlitigants	175	1,745	1,490	32.7%	3.1%	78.4%	33.6%	2.2%	87.0%	-0.9%	-58.3%	51.8%
Uncertain Status	11	241	189	35.9%	19.3%	57.6%	30.7%	7.4%	51.4%	5.2%	-7.8%	37.3%
Districts Excluded From the Analysis Because of Too Few Elementary Schools												
Unitary Status	*72*	*119*	*119*	*8.8%*	*0.0%*	*71.2%*	*8.9%*	*0.0%*	*56.3%*	*-0.2%*	*-44.1%*	*59.8%*
Under Court Order	*123*	*211*	*231*	*11.5%*	*0.0%*	*78.6%*	*12.8%*	*0.0%*	*77.6%*	*-1.3%*	*-48.3%*	*78.6%*
Nonlitigants	*107*	*200*	*178*	*10.2%*	*0.0%*	*76.2%*	*9.2%*	*0.0%*	*56.8%*	*1.0%*	*-56.8%*	*46.7%*
Uncertain Status	*2*	*4*	*3*	*1.3%*	*0.4%*	*2.1%*	*7.2%*	*0.0%*	*14.5%*	*-6.0%*	*-12.4%*	*0.4%*
Districts Excluded Because of 0% Black or 00% White Enrollment												
Unitary Status	*2*	*6*	*6*	*34.7%*	*16.4%*	*53.0%*	*50.0%*	*50.0%*	*50.0%*	*-15.3%*	*-33.6%*	*3.0%*
Under Court Order	*2*	*16*	*7*	*60.2%*	*40.8%*	*79.6%*	*50.0%*	*50.0%*	*50.0%*	*10.2%*	*-9.2%*	*29.6%*
Nonlitigants	*10*	*21*	*18*	*28.9%*	*0.0%*	*52.5%*	*50.0%*	*50.0%*	*50.0%*	*-21.1%*	*-50.0%*	*2.5%*

*Enrollment data was not available for the state of Georgia in the 1992/93 school year. Data from the 1993/94 school year were substituted.

Caption: Litigated districts are slightly less integrated in the 2004/05 school year than they were in the early 1990s. Districts with unitary status experienced a 3.5 percent increase in the average of their dissimilarity indices, while districts under court order experienced an increase of 2.8 percent. Nonlitigant districts experienced almost a 1 percent decrease in their average index.

Source: Compiled by U.S. Commission on Civil Rights.

An analysis of variance of the change in dissimilarity index between 1992/93 (or, for Georgia, 1993/94) and 2004/05 indicates the existence of significant differences among districts according to their legal status ($p<.001$).[52] These differences arise from districts under court order, with dissimilarity indices that increased, on average, 2.8 across the period (an amount significantly greater than zero, $p<.05$); and nonlitigants, with a 3.7 decrease that contrasts to the rise among court supervised districts (significant at $p<.05$). The dissimilarity indices of unitary districts increased across the years, but the rise was not statistically greater than that of districts under court supervision ($p=.685$, nonsignificant.).[53]

Earlier analyses indicated that the decade in which districts received their unitary status was also important. Including the decade in the analysis of variance also produced statistically significant differences between groups in the change over time in the dissimilarity index ($p<.001$).[54] The result derives from the differences in the desegregation measure between districts obtaining unitary status before and after the year 2000. Obtaining unitary status after the year 2000 is associated with a

---

[52] The mean square effect is 613.478; the mean square error is 194.497. The F-test is 3.154, $p<.025$, statistically significant. *See* appendix A, table A.5, model 3.

[53] *See* appendix A, table A.6, model 3.

[54] The mean square effect of legal status and decade of legal status is 777.685; the mean square error is 188.090. The F-test is 4.135, $p<.001$. *See* appendix A, table A.5, model 15.

statistically significant lowering of the dissimilarity index over time than for districts declared unitary in the earlier decades (e.g., 9.9 percent below that of districts becoming unitary before 2000) (p<.001).[55]

Differences in the Dissimilarity Index Over Time by State and Legal Status

The Commission also examined whether the changes over time in districts' dissimilarity indices varied among the seven states in its study. Analysis of variance indicates statistically significant differences among states in how their dissimilarity indices changed from the early 1990s to the mid 2000s by legal status (p<.05).[56] With state differences taken into account, districts under court order manifested a statistically significant increase in average dissimilarity index from more than a decade ago to the 2004/05 school year.[57] But the changes evident among unitary districts or nonlitigants are not statistically different from the increase of those under court order.[58] In other words, all districts increased essentially the same amount, regardless of legal status.

Looking at the differences among states, the parameters of the analysis reveal that Alabama, Mississippi, and North Carolina are not statistically different among themselves or from other states. However, Louisiana and Florida had significantly larger increases in districts' dissimilarity indices over time than Georgia (p=.001 and p<.05, respectively). Louisiana also had significantly larger increases across the period than South Carolina (p<.05).[59]

The results of the dissimilarity index trends by legal status, however, are much more complex than the statistically significant effects with legal status or state. Table 5.8 presents figures for each of the seven states. In South Carolina, interestingly, unitary districts with three or more regular elementary schools appear slightly *more integrated* on average today than in the 1992/93 school year. The dissimilarity indices average 30.4 percent in 2004/05 compared to 36.2 percent in 1992/93, representing a 5.7 percent increase in integration. North Carolina's districts with unitary status became much less integrated by 2004/05, with the average dissimilarity index rising from 29.0 percent in 1992/93 to 44.5 percent in 2004/05. Unitary districts in most other states became slightly less integrated over time with the average of their dissimilarity indices increasing 1.8 percent in Alabama and Georgia, approximately 4.4 percent in Louisiana, or 6.3 percent in Florida. Unitary districts in Mississippi maintained the racial balance of the earlier year with an increase of a mere 0.7 percent.

---

[55] *See* appendix A, tables A.5 and A,9, model 23, and table A.7, panels E and F, models 19 and 23.

[56] An analysis of variance of overtime changes in the dissimilarity indices with legal status and state as explanatory factors produces a mean square effect of 472.909 and a mean square error of 191.652. With 9 and 439 degrees of freedom F=2.468, p=.009. *See* appendix A, table A.5, model 7.

[57] The effect parameter (i.e., the unstandardized coefficient) for districts under court order testing the difference from zero is +6.912, p=.001). *See* appendix A, table A.6, model 7.

[58] The effect parameters of unitary and nonlitigant districts, testing the difference from the coefficient for districts under court order (i.e., +6.912) are both nonsignificant, p=.782 and p=.127, respectively. *See* appendix A, table A.6, model 7.

[59] The extensive number of parameters to show all of the contrasts between the seven states are not shown in the report because state differences are only of general interest.

Only two states' districts under court order became, on average, more integrated between 1992/93 and 2004/05. For example, the average dissimilarity index of districts under court order in Mississippi decreased 3.3 percent, from 45.5 to 42.2 percent, between the years. The average of those under court order in South Carolina decreased from 31.0 to 28.9 percent, a 2.0 percent increase in integration (with rounding error). However, in four other states, districts under court order became *less* integrated from the early 1990s to the present. The averages of their dissimilarity indices increased 1.3, 2.9, 5.0, and 7.0 percent in Georgia, North Carolina, Alabama, and Louisiana, respectively. The average dissimilarity index of Florida's districts under court order was nearly stable, with only a 0.7 percent increase.

Districts the Commission identified as nonlitigants increased their integration from more than a decade ago to the 2004/05 school year in two states—Georgia and North Carolina. Georgia's nonlitigant districts had an average dissimilarity index of 37.8 percent in 1993/94 and 31.1 percent in 2004/05, indicating that 6.7 percent fewer students need reassignment to achieve a perfect racial balance of African American and white students in the more recent year. In North Carolina, 3.0 percent fewer students would have required reassignment in 2004/05 as a result of the dissimilarity index dropping from 34.7 percent in 1992/93 to 31.7 percent in the recent year. Four states—South Carolina, Florida, Mississippi, and Louisiana—show average decreases in integration among nonlitigants of 1.4, 3.5, 4.9, and 11.9 percent, respectively, from 1992/93 to 2004/05. In the seventh state the Commission studied—Alabama—the only districts that escaped litigation were small, with fewer than three regular elementary schools.[60]

---

[60] Table 5.8 indicates that four Alabama districts that the Commission identified as nonlitigants had only 7 or 8 regular elementary schools between them in either the 2004/05 or 1992/93 school years. An additional nonlitigant district had no African American enrollees in 1992/93 and only two regular elementary schools.

Table 5.8
Summary by State of Districts' Desegregation (the Dissimilarity Index) in the 2004/05 School Year Compared to 1992/93 (or 1993/94) by Unitary Status, Court Order, and Never Litigated

State	Legal Status	Number of Matched Districts	Number of Elementary Schools		2004 Dissimilarity Index for Blacks v. Whites			1992 (or 1993*) Dissimilarity Index for Blacks v. Whites			Difference Between 2004 and 1992 (or 1993*) Dissimilarity Indices		
			2004	1992 (or 1993)*	Average	Minimum	Maximum	Average	Minimum	Maximum	Average	Minimum	Maximum
ALABAMA													
	Unitary Status	35	326	319	41.8%	3.9%	80.5%	40.1%	4.5%	77.8%	1.8%	-33.1%	53.7%
	Under Court Order	31	252	238	39.1%	9.4%	85.6%	34.1%	2.9%	67.5%	5.0%	-55.6%	71.1%
	Nonlitigants	0	0	0									
Districts Excluded From the Analysis Because of Too Few Elementary Schools													
	Unitary Status	*31*	*60*	*54*	*15.8%*	*0.0%*	*71.2%*	*11.5%*	*0.0%*	*56.3%*	*4.3%*	*-44.1%*	*59.8%*
	Under Court Order	*17*	*30*	*35*	*6.6%*	*0.0%*	*28.5%*	*13.3%*	*0.0%*	*48.5%*	*-6.7%*	*-48.3%*	*8.4%*
	Nonlitigants	*4*	*7*	*8*	*13.3%*	*0.0%*	*43.0%*	*22.9%*	*0.0%*	*50.0%*	*-9.6%*	*-31.4%*	*0.0%*
Districts Excluded Because of 0% Black or 0% White Enrollment													
	Unitary Status	*2*	*6*	*6*	*34.7%*	*16.4%*	*53.0%*	*50.0%*	*50.0%*	*50.0%*	*-15.3%*	*-33.6%*	*3.0%*
	Under Court Order	*1*	*13*	*3*	*79.6%*	*79.6%*	*79.6%*	*50.0%*	*50.0%*	*50.0%*	*29.6%*	*29.6%*	*29.6%*
	Nonlitigants	*1*	*2*	*2*	*52.5%*	*52.5%*	*52.5%*	*50.0%*	*50.0%*	*50.0%*	*2.5%*	*2.5%*	*2.5%*
FLORIDA													
	Unitary Status	19	1,316	1,035	47.4%	19.7%	77.4%	41.1%	11.0%	71.7%	6.3%	-11.1%	30.5%
	Under Court Order	12	275	200	30.3%	6.7%	57.6%	29.6%	8.3%	63.7%	0.7%	-21.1%	9.3%
	Nonlitigants	23	258	193	34.1%	12.5%	60.1%	30.6%	9.4%	63.4%	3.5%	-16.8%	24.3%
Districts Excluded From the Analysis Because of Too Few Elementary Schools													
	Under Court Order	*3*	*4*	*5*	*4.8%*	*0.0%*	*14.4%*	*9.8%*	*0.0%*	*29.4%*	*-5.0%*	*-15.0%*	*0.0%*
	Nonlitigants	*10*	*22*	*16*	*22.7%*	*0.0%*	*76.2%*	*16.7%*	*0.0%*	*50.4%*	*6.0%*	*-9.5%*	*29.0%*
GEORGIA													
	Unitary Status	11	345	306	47.8%	11.3%	92.8%	46.0%	16.2%	85.2%	1.8%	-33.7%	25.2%
	Under Court Order	34	265	255	30.3%	2.3%	75.5%	29.0%	2.5%	65.0%	1.3%	-43.9%	19.3%
	Nonlitigants	38	459	367	31.1%	3.1%	67.6%	37.8%	3.5%	87.0%	-6.7%	-58.3%	22.9%
Districts Excluded From the Analysis Because of Too Few Elementary Schools													
	Unitary Status	*20*	*29*	*28*	*3.1%*	*0.0%*	*37.9%*	*2.6%*	*0.0%*	*26.6%*	*0.5%*	*-5.4%*	*11.3%*
	Under Court Order	*39*	*64*	*70*	*5.0%*	*0.0%*	*38.2%*	*6.8%*	*0.0%*	*61.5%*	*-1.8%*	*-41.7%*	*36.2%*
	Nonlitigants	*27*	*58*	*49*	*13.8%*	*0.0%*	*72.2%*	*9.4%*	*0.0%*	*42.2%*	*4.4%*	*-15.4%*	*46.7%*
Districts Excluded Because of 0% Black or 0% White Enrollment													
	Nonlitigants	*4*	*7*	*4*	*37.1%*	*13.9%*	*50.0%*	*50.0%*	*50.0%*	*50.0%*	*-17.1%*	*-36.1%*	*0.0%*
LOUISIANA													
	Unitary Status	14	227	221	48.3%	11.6%	60.4%	43.9%	2.9%	63.1%	4.4%	-20.5%	13.8%
	Under Court Order	34	495	483	50.0%	5.3%	81.4%	42.9%	5.2%	76.2%	7.0%	-14.6%	33.3%
	Nonlitigants	5	31	29	44.7%	13.0%	66.2%	32.8%	9.3%	61.7%	11.9%	3.7%	26.8%
Districts Excluded From the Analysis Because of Too Few Elementary Schools													
	Unitary Status	*2*	*3*	*3*	*4.2%*	*0.0%*	*8.4%*	*14.5%*	*0.0%*	*28.9%*	*-10.3%*	*-20.5%*	*0.0%*
	Under Court Order	*8*	*17*	*19*	*34.1%*	*0.0%*	*62.5%*	*28.9%*	*0.0%*	*75.3%*	*5.2%*	*-14.7%*	*25.2%*
	Nonlitigants	*2*	*4*	*5*	*23.5%*	*10.5%*	*36.4%*	*11.3%*	*7.3%*	*15.3%*	*12.2%*	*3.2%*	*21.1%*

Continued

Table 5.8 (continued)
Summary by State of Districts' Desegregation (the Dissimilarity Index) in the 2004/05 School Year
Compared to 1992/93 (or 1993/94) by Unitary Status, Court Order, and Never Litigated

State	Legal Status	Number of Matched Districts	Number of Elementary Schools		2004 Dissimilarity Index for Blacks v. Whites			1992 (or 1993*) Dissimilarity Index for Blacks v. Whites			Difference Between 2004 and 1992 (or 1993*) Dissimilarity Indices		
			2004	1992 (or 1993)*	Average	Minimum	Maximum	Average	Minimum	Maximum	Average	Minimum	Maximum
MISSISSIPPI													
	Unitary Status	13	72	63	38.2%	11.7%	59.2%	37.5%	11.0%	67.5%	0.7%	-33.3%	41.5%
	Under Court Order	17	121	132	42.2%	0.8%	74.7%	45.5%	5.3%	91.4%	-3.3%	-22.0%	13.8%
	Nonlitigants	17	96	83	34.6%	13.8%	78.4%	29.6%	4.9%	74.5%	4.9%	-20.5%	51.8%
Districts Excluded From the Analysis Because of Too Few Elementary Schools													
	Unitary Status	*11*	*14*	*22*	*2.7%*	*0.0%*	*16.0%*	*11.0%*	*0.0%*	*34.2%*	*-8.3%*	*-34.2%*	*4.7%*
	Under Court Order	*48*	*82*	*86*	*15.1%*	*0.0%*	*78.6%*	*13.6%*	*0.0%*	*77.6%*	*1.4%*	*-41.1%*	*78.6%*
	Nonlitigants	*30*	*45*	*45*	*6.2%*	*0.0%*	*46.9%*	*8.6%*	*0.0%*	*56.8%*	*-2.5%*	*-56.8%*	*14.2%*
	Uncertain Status	*1*	*2*	*1*	*0.4%*	*0.4%*	*0.4%*	*0.0%*	*0.0%*	*0.0%*	*0.4%*	*0.4%*	*0.4%*
Districts Excluded From the Analysis Because of Too Few Elementary Schools													
	Under Court Order	*1*	*3*	*4*	*40.8%*	*40.8%*	*40.8%*	*50.0%*	*50.0%*	*50.0%*	*-9.2%*	*-9.2%*	*-9.2%*
	Nonlitigants	*4*	*8*	*5*	*28.0%*	*0.0%*	*50.0%*	*50.0%*	*50.0%*	*50.0%*	*-22.0%*	*-50.0%*	*0.0%*
NORTH CAROLINA													
	Unitary Status	12	311	229	44.5%	28.3%	59.1%	29.0%	18.8%	48.7%	15.6%	-1.0%	29.5%
	Under Court Order	14	165	148	35.9%	21.9%	48.7%	33.0%	8.7%	64.1%	2.9%	-17.8%	20.2%
	Nonlitigants	56	521	470	31.7%	3.9%	57.4%	34.7%	2.2%	64.8%	-3.0%	-39.4%	14.3%
	Uncertain Status	11	241	189	35.9%	19.3%	57.6%	30.7%	7.4%	51.4%	5.2%	-7.8%	37.3%
Districts Excluded From the Analysis Because of Too Few Elementary Schools													
	Under Court Order	*1*	*2*	*2*	*3.6%*	*3.6%*	*3.6%*	*31.3%*	*31.3%*	*31.3%*	*-27.7%*	*-27.7%*	*-27.7%*
	Nonlitigants	*18*	*31*	*32*	*5.4%*	*0.0%*	*27.9%*	*6.4%*	*0.0%*	*24.2%*	*-1.0%*	*-24.1%*	*23.4%*
	Uncertain Status	*1*	*2*	*2*	*2.1%*	*2.1%*	*2.1%*	*14.5%*	*14.5%*	*14.5%*	*-12.4%*	*-12.4%*	*-12.4%*
Districts Excluded Because of 0% Black or 0% White Enrollment													
	Nonlitigants	*2*	*5*	*7*	*13.1%*	*0.0%*	*26.1%*	*50.0%*	*50.0%*	*50.0%*	*-36.9%*	*-50.0%*	*-23.9%*
SOUTH CAROLINA													
	Unitary Status	10	118	121	30.4%	15.3%	37.7%	36.2%	11.8%	58.4%	-5.7%	-28.6%	14.3%
	Under Court Order	7	63	61	28.9%	15.1%	37.8%	31.0%	11.6%	49.3%	-2.0%	-26.6%	11.6%
	Nonlitigants	36	380	348	32.7%	5.6%	66.4%	31.3%	7.4%	59.3%	1.4%	-15.3%	26.9%
Districts Excluded From the Analysis Because of Too Few Elementary Schools													
	Unitary Status	*8*	*13*	*12*	*5.3%*	*0.0%*	*27.0%*	*10.5%*	*0.0%*	*48.7%*	*-5.2%*	*-26.4%*	*11.6%*
	Under Court Order	*7*	*12*	*14*	*13.9%*	*0.0%*	*50.2%*	*19.3%*	*0.0%*	*42.4%*	*-5.4%*	*-24.8%*	*12.4%*
	Nonlitigants	*16*	*33*	*23*	*6.9%*	*0.0%*	*31.7%*	*4.8%*	*0.0%*	*27.0%*	*2.1%*	*-9.6%*	*20.8%*

*Enrollment data was not available for the state of Georgia in the 1992/93 school year. Data from the 1993/94 school year were substituted.

Caption: From the early 1990s to the 2004/05 school year, the average dissimilarity indices of unitary districts increased in Alabama, Florida, Georgia, Louisiana, Mississippi, and North Carolina by 1.8 percent, 6.3 percent, 1.8 percent, 4.4 percent, 0.7 percent, and 15.6 percent respectively. Unitary districts in South Carolina had a decrease of 5.7 percent. Districts under court order experienced increases in their average dissimilarity indices in Alabama, Florida, Georgia, Louisiana, and North Carolina by 5.0 percent, 0.7 percent, 1.3 percent, 7.0 percent, and 2.9 percent respectively. Court supervised districts in Mississippi and South Carolina show decreases of 3.3 and 2.0 percent, respectively. The average dissimilarity indices of nonlitigant districts increased in Florida, Louisiana, Mississippi, and South Carolina by 3.5 percent, 11.9 percent, 4.9 percent, 1.4 percent, respectively. In Georgia and North Carolina nonlitigant districts show decreases in average dissimilarity indices, by 6.7 percent and 3.0 percent, respectively.

Source: Compiled by U.S. Commission on Civil Rights.

In brief, the table shows that certain states had large increases over time in the average dissimilarity indices for unitary districts, and others had large changes for nonlitigants. At the same time, in South Carolina, the average of dissimilarity indices decreased in districts with unitary status, while in Georgia the averages decreased for nonlitigants. Such complexities are called "interactions" of the state and legal status factors, because the data trends are contrary to the pattern of increases or decreases observed with just the state variable, or only the legal status designation. The Commission did not compute the analysis of variance to test for the statistical significance of these interactions. However, the results suggest that researchers should pursue why the states' average dissimilarity indices vary so unexpectedly according to legal status.

Changes Over Time in the Entropy Index and Legal Status

Rapid growth in other minority groups, particularly the extraordinary influx of Hispanics, has transformed the demographics of schools over the past three decades.[61] Derived from schools' black/white racial balance, the dissimilarity index may not reveal any effect of this demographic transformation on the racial/ethnic concentration of students in district schools. Using an alternative measure of desegregation, the entropy index, indicates whether the apparent pattern of change in integration among African Americans and whites from the 1992/93 school year to the 2004/05 school year occurs when one considers other minority groups as well. Table 5.9 presents the entropy index showing 2004/05 versus 1992/93 changes in desegregation for districts by legal status.

---

[61] *See, e.g.,* Sam Dillon, "U.S. Data Show Rapid Minority Growth in School Rolls," *New York Times*, June 1, 2007, p. A21; National Center for Education Statistics, *The Condition of Education 2007*, Commissioner's Statement, June 2007, pp. iv–v.

Table 5.9
Summary of Districts' Desegregation (the Entropy Index) in the 2004/05 School Year Compared to 1992/93 (or 1993/94) by Unitary Status, Court Order, and Never Litigated

Legal Status	Number of Matched Districts	Number of Elementary Schools		2004 Entropy Index			1992 (or 1993*) Entropy Index			Difference Between 2004 and 1992 (or 1993*) Entropy Indices		
		2004	1992 (or 1993)*	Average	Minimum	Maximum	Average	Minimum	Maximum	Average	Minimum	Maximum
COMBINED STATES												
Unitary Status	114	2,715	2,294	16.9%	0.9%	54.1%	17.2%	0.5%	53.8%	-0.3%	-27.5%	21.1%
Under Court Order	149	1,636	1,517	14.8%	0.4%	43.1%	15.2%	0.1%	68.6%	-0.4%	-34.6%	24.3%
Nonlitigants	175	1,745	1,490	10.5%	0.7%	46.8%	11.3%	0.2%	51.1%	-0.8%	-38.8%	34.8%
Uncertain Status	11	241	189	12.8%	2.9%	26.9%	12.7%	1.9%	30.6%	0.1%	-7.8%	17.2%
Districts Excluded From the Analysis Because of Too Few Elementary Schools												
Unitary Status	*72*	*119*	*119*	*2.2%*	*0.0%*	*33.1%*	*2.7%*	*0.0%*	*33.1%*	*-0.5%*	*-31.3%*	*19.5%*
Under Court Order	*123*	*211*	*231*	*3.4%*	*0.0%*	*45.4%*	*4.6%*	*0.0%*	*46.2%*	*-1.2%*	*-34.4%*	*45.4%*
Nonlitigants	*107*	*200*	*178*	*2.1%*	*0.0%*	*34.2%*	*2.2%*	*0.0%*	*21.6%*	*-0.1%*	*-20.0%*	*12.6%*
Uncertain Status	*2*	*4*	*3*	*0.2%*	*0.0%*	*0.4%*	*1.4%*	*0.0%*	*2.8%*	*-1.2%*	*-2.4%*	*0.0%*
Districts Excluded Because of 0% Black or 0% White Enrollment												
Unitary Status	*2*	*6*	*6*	*3.7%*	*2.5%*	*4.8%*	*6.5%*	*5.3%*	*7.7%*	*-2.8%*	*-2.9%*	*-2.8%*
Under Court Order	*2*	*16*	*7*	*10.7%*	*6.5%*	*14.9%*	*18.3%*	*16.2%*	*20.4%*	*-7.6%*	*-9.7%*	*-5.4%*
Nonlitigants	*10*	*21*	*18*	*2.7%*	*0.0%*	*7.1%*	*2.7%*	*0.0%*	*19.1%*	*0.0%*	*-15.3%*	*7.1%*

*Enrollment data was not available for the state of Georgia in the 1992/93 school year. Data from the 1993/94 school year were substituted.

Caption: District integration, measured by the average entropy index, changed by less than 1 percent from the early 1990s to the 2004/05 school year. Unitary, court-supervised, and nonlitigant districts included in the study show average increases of 0.3, 0.4, and 0.8 percent, respectively. However, the largest increases in integration of school systems were 27.5, 34.6, and 38.8 percent for unitary, court-supervised, and nonlitigant districts, respectively, and the largest increases in racial concentration were 21.1, 24.3, and 34.8, respectively for districts with the three types of legal status.

Source: Compiled by U.S. Commission on Civil Rights.

As with the dissimilarity index in the earlier table 5.7, table 5.9 shows averages of the desegregation measure for districts with unitary status, those under court order, and those never involved in litigation. The entropy indices are multiplied by 100 to range from 0 to 100 and facilitate their interpretation as the percent of students that must be reassigned to other schools to achieve exact statistical racial balance in the district. Lower entropy values suggest greater integration; higher levels indicate that the district is further from racial balance. Also, as noted earlier, the 2004/05 school year results in table 5.9 differ slightly from entropy indices presented in table 5.6 because of district attrition. Because of this, the average 2004/05 entropy indices increase slightly, for example, from 16.1 percent in table 5.6 to 16.9 percent in table 5.9 for districts with unitary status, and from 10.0 to 10.5 percent for nonlitigants. Note further that, as before, the decade-long comparisons uses 1993/94 enrollment data for the state of Georgia because 1992/93 information is unavailable.

Earlier results in table 5.7 used the dissimilarity index and suggested that levels of integration of blacks and whites diminished between the earlier year and 2004/05 for districts under court order or with judicial recognition of their unitary status. In contrast, table 5.9 suggests districts' integration, measured by the entropy index, remained much the same. The average district change in the entropy indices from 1992/93 (or 1993/94) to 2004/05 decreased 0.3 percent for districts with unitary status; 0.4 percent for those under court order; and 0.8 percent for nonlitigants. An analysis of variance reveals that the changes over time are not significant.[62] The decrease in average entropy for districts under court order is not different from zero (p=.536, nonsignificant). The other two groups—unitary districts and nonlitigants—have average entropy indices that are statistically the same as systems remaining under court order (i.e., their differences are nonsignificant with p=.922 and p=.646, respectively).[63] These results indicate that similar proportions of African American, white, Hispanic, Asian American, and Native American students would need to be reassigned in 2004/05 as in the earlier year to achieve perfect statistical racial balance. Again, the results do not necessarily contradict the earlier results with the dissimilarity indices. The finding with the dissimilarity index suggests that perhaps slightly more African American and white students would have to be reassigned in 2004/05 than earlier to achieve strict parity; however the proportions of them together with other minorities that must move to achieve balance is essentially the same in both years in the context of all the groups.

Other statistical analyses indicate that neither state,[64] nor state in combination with district size (the log base 10 of student enrollment) and percent white in the school system[65] are related to any differences by legal status of changes over time in the entropy index. However, small statistically significant differences emerge when the analysis distinguishes districts receiving unitary status in the 2000s from those obtaining that status in earlier decades.[66] Unitary districts have an average entropy index that increases 3.1 percent more than court-supervised systems in 2004/05 compared to 1992/93. However, the entropy index of unitary districts that received recognition of that status during the 2000s averages 6.3 percent lower than those declared unitary sooner.[67]

---

[62] The mean square effect and error are 8.143 and 58.383 respectively. With 3 and 445 degrees of freedom, F=0.139, p=.936, nonsignificant. *See* appendix A, table A.5, model 4.

[63] *See* appendix A, table A.6, model 4.

[64] In the analysis of variance using legal status and state to explain differences in the entropy index between 1992/93 (or 1993/94) and 2004/05, the mean square effect and error are 75.242 and 57.694, respectively. With 9 and 439 degrees of freedom, F=1.304, p=.232, nonsignificant. *See* appendix A, table A.5, model 8.

[65] Including legal status, state, district size (the base 10 log of student enrollment) and the percent white, the analysis of variance of the changes from 1992/93 to 2004/05 in the entropy index yields a mean square effect and error of 71.041 and 57.720, respectively. F= 1.231 with 11 and 437 degrees of freedom, p=.264, nonsignificant. *See* appendix A, table A.5, model 12.

[66] The mean square effect is 154.234; the mean square error is 55.400. F=2.784, with 12 and 436 degrees of freedom respectively, p=.001. *See* appendix A, table A.5, model 24. Note that this analysis only distinguishes receiving unitary status before and after 2000. An analysis using the 1970s, 1980s, and 1990s in addition to the 2000s increased the explained variance only 1.0 percent, a nonsignificant amount (i.e., the change in F=1.502, the degrees of freedom for the change are 3 and 433; p=.213). *See* appendix A, table A.7, panel E, showing the difference between explained variance in models 20 and 24. Also see models 16 and 20 in table A.5.

[67] See appendix A, table A.6, model 24, with an effect parameter for unitary districts 3.143 greater than court supervised districts (p=.010, statistically significant); and table A.9, model 24, with -6.342 for districts recognized as unitary in the 2000s (p<.001, statistically significant).

Conclusion

To conclude, in chapter 5, the Commission explored the relationship between legal status and the racial/ethnic concentration of students in districts' schools. To do so, the Commission measured the concentration using current data as well as changes over time. The Commission then analyzed this data using the dissimilarity index and the entropy index. Both indices represent how evenly spread groups are among a district's schools. The former, in this study, characterizes the distribution of African Americans and whites; the latter that of blacks, whites, Hispanics, Asian Americans, and Native Americans.

The largely parallel analyses with these measures indicate the following: Simplistically, in districts under court order, African Americans and whites are not evenly spread among district schools; unitary districts are equally, but *not* more, racially concentrated than those under court order; and nonlitigant districts are less racially concentrated. Variation in the racial balance of students in districts schools seems to arise from differences in other factors—district size, the district's percent of white student enrollment, and the state in which the district is located. Large districts and those with smaller proportions of white enrollment have greater racial/ethnic concentration than smaller districts or those with more than, say, 25 percent white enrollment. Some apparent differences in indices by legal status arise because unitary, court supervised, and nonlitigant districts vary by size, percent of white enrollment, and state. For example, districts with unitary status tend to be larger, and thereby have higher concentrations of racial/ethnic pupils.

When size, white enrollment, and state are allowed to explain district's differences in desegregation measures, significant effects of legal status occur indicating that districts which received unitary status since the year 2000 have lower concentrations of racial/ethnic groups than those granted that status in earlier years. A significant decade effect occurred using each of the four desegregation formulae. It may occur because districts recognized as unitary in recent years deserved that status. Thus, in whatever way the Department of Justice affects the process of districts' obtaining unitary status, its efforts since the year 2000 appear appropriate.

Using entropy, rather than the dissimilarity index, greatly reduces the magnitude of the proportions of students that school officials would need to reassign to achieve perfect racial balance among district schools. Thus, factoring in Hispanics, Asian Americans, and Native Americans, together with blacks and whites, suggests that districts are much more integrated than the dissimilarity indices suggested. The effects by legal status of measuring integration with entropy remain largely the same.

Looking at changes in desegregation indices over time did not reveal dramatic increases in racial concentrations of students in districts with unitary status. The dissimilarity indices of both unitary districts and those under court supervision increased over time, but the index of the former was not significantly greater than that of the latter. Thus, for example, using the dissimilarity index, school officials in schools that are under court order would need to reassign 2.8 percent more students in the recent year to achieve racial balance than they did more than a decade ago. According to the entropy index, however, the racial concentrations of students in district schools did not change at all over time except when distinguishing between districts that obtained unitary status before and after 2000.

CHAPTER 6: THE COMMISSION'S FINDINGS AND RECOMMENDATIONS

Findings

1. For decades following the Civil War, harsh state-sponsored schemes of segregation in public schools were pervasive in certain areas of the United States.

2. In 1954, in the case of *Brown v. Board of Education of Topeka*, 347 U.S. 483 (1954), the Supreme Court held that *de jure* desegregation was unconstitutional and that the doctrine of "separate but equal" has no place in education.

3. In 1957, President Eisenhower signed the Civil Rights Act of 1957, which created the U.S. Commission on Civil Rights.

4. From its inception, the Commission has studied and issued reports on the harms of school segregation.

5. Following *Brown*, many lawsuits were instituted against segregated school districts, especially in the South. As a result, many of these districts were placed under judicial supervision.

6. In *Green v. County School Board of New Kent County*, 391 U.S. 430 (1968), the Supreme Court provided the standards that courts employ in supervising segregated school districts.

7. In some instances, school boards closed schools rather than integrate. In others, court orders to desegregate were met with massive resistance, open hostility, and violence. At times, intervention by federal troops was necessary to quell violence and enforce the law.

8. In part to address this situation, Congress passed the Civil Rights Act of 1964 and the Elementary and Secondary Education Act of 1965.

9. This federal intervention was necessary to address persistent constitutional violations in the segregated school districts. Historically, schools had been run by elected local officials. Judicial supervision, however, subordinated local school authorities to an unelected authority.

10. Many of these court orders have remained in place for several decades. Of the districts placed under court order, 80 percent were placed under court jurisdiction in the 1960s, 18 percent came under court jurisdiction in the 1970s, and only 1 percent fell under court jurisdiction in the 1980s and 1990s.

11. The demographics of the nation's school-aged children have changed dramatically. In the 1960s, more than four of every five students were white. By 2005, only 58 percent of the student population was white, while Hispanic students comprised 20 percent, Black students comprised 16 percent, and Asian students comprised 4 percent.

12. In *Board of Education of Oklahoma City Public Schools v. Dowell*, 498 U.S. 237 (1991), and *Freeman v. Pitts*, 503 U.S. 467 (1992), the Supreme Court clarified the means by which school districts might obtain unitary status and be relieved from judicial oversight. In these decisions, the Court ruled that a declaration of unitary status (and relief from judicial supervision) as to one

or more aspects of school administration is appropriate when a school district demonstrates that it has complied with a judicial desegregation order since it was entered and the vestiges of past discrimination are eliminated. The Court also stressed the importance of returning school districts to local control.

13. Despite these decisions, the Department of Justice reported that, as of 2000, approximately 430 school districts remained under court order.

14. In recent years, the Department of Justice has increased its efforts to assist qualified school districts in obtaining unitary status. According to DOJ's records, from FY 2000 to the present, the Department's docket of elementary and secondary school desegregation cases has been reduced from approximately 430 cases to 266 cases.

15. The Commission's review of seven, mostly southern states, indicates that only about 37 percent of unitary districts obtained that status over the previous three decades (1970s-1990s). Thus, more than half of the school districts that have achieved unitary status have done so since 2000.

16. Of the districts the Commission surveyed, just over a quarter of those districts remaining under court order are seeking or planning to pursue unitary status. Many of the remaining districts are undecided.

17. The Commission's review indicates that as of June 2007:

    a. In Alabama, 71 school districts have been declared unitary, 53 school districts remain under court order, and 7 school districts have never been subject to litigation.

    b. In Florida, 19 school districts have been declared unitary, 15 school districts remain under court order, and 33 school districts have never been subject to litigation.

    c. In Georgia, 33 school districts have been declared unitary, 76 school districts remain under court order, and 71 school districts have never been subject to litigation.

    d. In Louisiana, 16 school districts have been declared unitary, 43 school districts remain under court order, and 9 school districts have never been subject to litigation.

    e. In Mississippi, 24 school districts have been declared unitary, 71 school districts remain under court order, and 53 school districts have never been subject to litigation.

    f. In North Carolina, 12 school districts have been declared unitary, 15 school districts remain under court order, and 76 school districts have never been subject to litigation.

    g. In South Carolina, 18 school districts have been declared unitary, 14 school districts remain under court order, and 53 school districts have never been subject to litigation.

18. There are significant differences between the states studied. For example, Louisiana's overall dissimilarity index, which measures the level of balance between black and white student populations, is substantially higher than that of the other states.[1] At the same time, other states' desegregation measures vary by legal status. For example, in Alabama, districts under court supervision and those with unitary status exhibited nearly the same levels of racial balance (as determined by use of the dissimilarity index). In Georgia, by contrast, unitary and court-supervised districts had very different levels of racial balance.

19. Larger districts are much more likely to seek and obtain a finding of unitary status than smaller districts. Nearly 90 percent of the very large districts (more than 100,000 students) have obtained unitary status. About 50 percent of moderately sized districts (10,000 to 99,999 students) have obtained unitary status. Less than half of small districts (1,000 to 9,999 students) and very small districts (less than 1,000 students) have obtained unitary status.

20. Although larger school districts are more likely to obtain unitary status, they exhibit higher average levels of racial clustering regardless of whether they remain under court order. Districts with the largest student populations (enrollments of 100,000 or more) would have to shift 50 percent or more of their 2004/05 students to obtain perfectly equal racial balance. This would be so regardless of whether the district was under judicial supervision, had obtained unitary status, or had never been subject to a court order.

21. On the other hand, smaller districts (1,000 to 9,999 students) are less likely to obtain judicial recognition of unitary status, yet exhibit significantly less racial clustering. On average, these schools would have to shift a smaller percentage of students, less than 37 percent for each legal category, to obtain perfect racial balance. Thus, many smaller school districts are currently under judicial supervision despite the fact that they have higher rates of integration than larger districts that have already obtained unitary status.

22. The analyses show that districts which have achieved unitary status exhibit no greater levels of racial concentration than districts still under court supervision, while districts that have never been under court supervision have lower levels of racial clustering. Indeed, when other factors are considered, such as the size of a district's student population, the percentage of white student enrollment, and the state in which the district is located, legal status does not explain variation in the levels of racial balance. Larger districts and systems with small proportions of white enrollment tend to have greater racial clustering of students among their schools. Districts that have achieved unitary status may demonstrate greater racial concentration, on average, because they are larger and have smaller proportions of white students.

---

[1] The dissimilarity index is defined in chapter 5.

23. When other racial or ethnic groups, such as Hispanics, Asian Americans, and Native Americans are taken into consideration, the analysis indicates that, on average, districts are much more integrated than a simple black-white comparison (using the dissimilarity index) would indicate. For example, using a strictly black-white measure of balance, 42 percent of students in unitary districts would need to be reassigned to achieve a hypothetical racial balance. The same analysis, taking into consideration additional racial and ethnic groups, would require only a 16 percent change in student population for unitary districts.

24. In addition, changes over time (from the early 1990s to 2004/05) showed *no overall increases or decreases* in racial balance, when other racial and ethnic groups were included in the analysis. This result is the same for unitary districts, those with court supervision, as well as nonlitigants. Thus, whether districts had high or low balance in 2004/05, their degree of integration was essentially the same as in the early 1990s.

25. Looking at differences in integration from the early 1990s to 2004/05, the results suggest that fears of substantial increases in levels of racial concentration arising from districts obtaining unitary status are unfounded. The average dissimilarity indices of *both* unitary districts *and* those under court order increased slightly during that period. The magnitude of this increase, although statistically significant, is small, and the racial concentration for both unitary districts and those under court order were statistically equivalent.

26. Districts that have obtained unitary status since 2000 are more integrated, on average, than those districts that obtained unitary status in the 1970s, 1980s, and 1990s. This is true using either an exclusively black-white measure of balance or a measure of balance that takes into consideration other racial and ethnic groups.

27. Comparing school year data from circa 1992/93 to 2004/05, districts that were never involved in desegregation litigation experienced a minor change in racial balance, becoming slightly more integrated. The average levels of the balance between white and black student populations of such districts decreased by almost 1.0 percent.

Recommendations

1. The Department of Justice should continue its active review of all school districts that have been under federal court supervision to determine whether they qualify for unitary status or whether more work must be done.

2. The Department of Justice should increase its efforts to ensure that school districts comply with existing court orders and that they address the various factors established in *Green v. County School Board of New Kent County*, 391 U.S. 430 (1968).

3. The Department of Justice should continue to provide guidance to assist small or moderately-sized school districts to qualify for and obtain unitary status as appropriate during its case review process.

4. Social scientists, academics, and relevant government agencies should pursue underlying explanations for differences in measured desegregation among the states. By way of example, researchers might explore whether state differences arise from district autonomy; state law, policy, and guidance; or federal processing of unitary status matters.

5. Social scientists, academics, and relevant government agencies should try to identify why large school districts tend to have greater racial concentrations of students by race than are found among smaller districts.

6. State Boards of Education should undertake a review of their school districts subject to federal court supervision to determine the reasons why they have been unable to achieve or unwilling to seek unitary status. Additionally, states and school districts should seek to remove any extrajudicial barriers to unitary status.

APPENDIX A: METHODOLOGICAL ISSUES AND DETAILED STATISTICAL RESULTS

Detailed explanations of some aspects of the methodology of the Commission's study appear below along with parameters of the analyses of variance and regressions presented in chapter 5. First, a section describes alternative measures of desegregation to the dissimilarity index the Commission used, indicating similarities and differences, the advantages and disadvantages, and the computational formulae. A second section explains the number of school districts included in the Commission's review of unitary status and each part of its statistical analyses. Another section provides an analysis of 2004 data that uses a larger sample of schools from the selected states. The final section presents detailed statistical models for the analyses.

Measures of Segregation

The choice in how to measure the segregation of students is fundamental to any research on that topic. The Commission chose the dissimilarity index to best reflect the measurement courts use to hold school officials accountable for the assignment of African American and white pupils to district schools. In addition, the Commission analyzed the entropy measure, because it represents the even distribution of multiple racial and ethnic groups among a district's schools in the same manner in which the dissimilarity index does for just blacks and whites.

The Commission recognizes that researchers have used a variety of formulae to measure school segregation and address purposes that are often broader than this report. The discussion below provides insight into the perceived weaknesses of some measures, efforts to overcome such disadvantages, and the importance of applying the correct measure to the problem at hand.

The authors of a recent paper identify two general types of segregation yardsticks—measures of racial isolation and of racial imbalance.[1] Sections below describe common variants and advantages and disadvantages of each type.

Measures of Racial Isolation

Measures of isolation capture the extent to which black students are in schools primarily with other minority students, in effect "isolated" from other groups such as non-Hispanic white students. One widely used measure of racial isolation is the percentage of black students in schools that are 90 to 100 percent *nonwhite*. The measure emphasizes the isolation of black students from white students, and may have worked well in the past because of the application of the Supreme Court's *Brown v. Board of Education* decision to that group or the race's predominance in the South.[2] As the nation's population became more diverse, however, researchers have developed new measures of desegregation.

---

[1] Charles T. Clotfelter, Helen F. Ladd, and Jacob L. Vigdor, all of Duke University, "Federal Oversight, Local Control, and the Specter of 'Resegregation' in Southern Schools," January 2005, pp. 5–11 <http://www.s4.brown.edu/s4/colloquia/Fall05/PUBrowndraft20905.pdf> (last accessed Aug 22, 2007) (hereafter cited as Clotfelter, Ladd, and Vigdor, "Resegregation in Southern Schools").

[2] Ibid., pp. 5–6.

Recognizing recent rapid growth in Hispanic and other nonwhite enrollments, an alternative measure of isolation is the percentage of black students in schools that are 90 to 100 percent *black*. Such a measure represents the extent to which black students are concentrated in schools with students like themselves. In other words, it indicates whether black pupils are isolated from a diverse environment, not necessarily a Caucasian one. Notably, this measure produces the same values as the first formulation in schools without Hispanic or other non-black minority students and diverges in districts with growing numbers of Hispanic pupils.[3]

A third isolation measure, called an exposure rate of black students to black students, is an average of schools' percentages of black students, with each percentage weighted by the number of African American students in that school. It represents the proportion of African American students that the typical black pupil encounters in school. The exposure rate indicates how isolated blacks pupils are from students of other races.[4]

A weakness of measures of isolation is that they are sensitive to the rapid change in the racial composition of the school age population. As the number of white students decreases nationally, measures of racial isolation, such as those indicated above, would increase, regardless of school policies or judicial enforcement. As summed up in one study:

As a consequence of the increasing racial diversification of American schools, this particular measure of racial isolation [the proportion of blacks attending 90 to 100 percent nonwhite schools] may have lost much of its meaning as a measure of racial segregation.[5]

Moreover, such measures would seem to hold school officials accountable for housing patterns over which they have no control. School officials view such measures as unfair because the policy makers wish to be accountable only for the enrollment patterns over which they have more control (potentially *de jure* segregation) and not for a heavily minority population among students in the district (most likely

---

[3] Ibid., p. 6.

[4] Summing over all the schools in the district, the formula for the exposure rate (E) of black students to black students is:

$$E_{(\text{blacks to blacks})} = [\sum B_j \, b_j \,] / \sum B_j \text{, where}$$

B_j is the number of black students in school j; and

b_j is school j's percentage of black students.

See ibid., p. 6.

Alternatively, if one were to calculate the proportion of the *district's* black students who are in each school, that is,

$$p_j = B_j / \sum B_j,$$

$$E_{(\text{blacks to blacks})} = \sum p_j \, b_j.$$

In short, the exposure rate is a district sum of the percentage of black students in each school weighted by the proportion of the district's black students who are in that school. (Also, if the number of non-black students in a school is defined as N_j, then

$$b_j = B_j / [B_j + N_j]$$

$$E_{(\text{blacks to blacks})} = [\sum B_j \, B_j / [B_j + N_j]] / \sum B_j .)$$

[5] Clotfelter, Ladd, and Vigdor, "Resegregation in Southern Schools," p. 34.

de facto segregation).[6] For these reasons, the Commission's study did not use measures of racial isolation.

Measures of Racial Imbalance

Indices of racial imbalance are not a function of the school district's racial composition. They measure the extent to which students of a particular race are unevenly distributed across schools within the district. By such measures, schools are fully segregated if members of the racial group attend schools that have only members of that race. The measures show full integration when all of the district's schools have the same racial composition.[7]

The Commission's research identified three common measures of racial imbalance, each of which can target any racial group or nonwhites, and has a range from zero, representing full integration, to one, representing segregation. The measures are: a "gap-based segregation index," the dissimilarity index, and an entropy index.[8] The latter two are used in the research herein.

The gap-based segregation index is an exposure rate corrected to remove any effect of the district's racial composition. To measure the balance between white and nonwhite students the gap index calculates the exposure rate of whites to nonwhites, that is, the nonwhite percentage in the typical white student's class or school. However, when a district's schools are racially balanced, such an exposure rate's maximum value is the percentage of its nonwhite students.

---

[6] *See* ibid., pp. 6–7.

[7] *See* ibid., p. 7.

[8] *See* ibid., pp. 7–9.

The gap index converts this value to zero, representing fully balanced, and allows departures from this situation to range as high as one for fully segregated.[9]

The dissimilarity index indicates the proportion of any one racial group of students that would have to switch schools to achieve racial balance across the district.[10] Some have criticized the dissimilarity index and other racial balance measures: "…[I]f almost all whites leave a school system, but the remaining few are evenly distributed across schools, racial balance will be perfect and the plan will be judged a success, although there are almost no whites left."[11] But residential patterns with racial concentrations may bear no relationship to the actions of school officials or other governmental authorities. Thus, measures of balance such as the dissimilarity index remain a viable means of representing how evenly blacks (or other minorities) and the educational system's *existing whites* are spread among schools *within* a district.

Unlike the other measures of segregation above, the entropy index reflects differences in racial balance among multiple groups. Both the gap-based and dissimilarity formulae divide the relevant population into two groups for contrast.[12] However, the entropy index determines the extent to which many groups are evenly distributed among organizational units such as schools in a district. It measures the average difference between a school's group proportions and that of the district.[13] An entropy index of 0 indicates that a district's schools have the same composition as the system as a whole. The highest value

---

[9] Summing over all the schools in the district, the formula for the exposure rate of white students to nonwhite students is:

$$E_{(\text{whites to nonwhites})} = [\ \Sigma\ W_j\ p_j\ ]\ /\ \Sigma\ W_j\ , \text{ where}$$

W_j is the number of white students in school j; and

p_j is school j's percentage of *nonwhite* students.

The formula for the gap-based segregation index, S, measuring imbalance for district k is:

$$S_k = (p_k - E_{(\text{whites to nonwhites})})/p_k \text{ or } 1 - E_{(\text{whites to nonwhites})})/p_k\ , \text{ where}$$

p_k is the district k's proportion of nonwhite students.

Used in more detailed studies of racial imbalance, the authors note that the gap-based index is easily decomposed into segregation between and within schools. *See* ibid., pp. 7–8.

[10] Summing over all the schools in the district, the index of dissimilarity (D) is defined as:

$$D = 1/2\ \Sigma\ |n_j/N - w_j/W|, \text{ where}$$

n_j is the number of nonwhite students in school j;

w_j is the number of white students in school j;

$N = \Sigma n_j$ or the total nonwhite enrollment in the district; and

$W = \Sigma w_j$ is the total white enrollment in the district.

See ibid., p. 8, footnote 5.

[11] Christine Rossell, "Using Multiple Criteria to Evaluate Public Policies: The Case of School Desegregation," *American Politics Quarterly,* April 1993, p. 172.

[12] People who are not members of either group are omitted. *See* Clotfelter, Ladd, and Vigdor, "Resegregation in Southern Schools," pp. 8–9.

[13] More technically, entropy, represented as "H," is the difference between the diversity (entropy) of the system and the weighted average diversity of individual schools, expressed as a fraction of the total diversity (entropy) of the district. *See* John Iceland, Housing and Household Economic Statistics Division, U.S. Census Bureau, "Beyond Black and White: Metropolitan Residential Segregation in Multi-Ethnic America" (paper presented at the American Sociological Association meetings, Chicago, Illinois, August 16-19, 2002), pp. 9–10.

of the index, 1, results when the district's schools contain only one group, a situation considered most segregated.[14]

The measures of balance are suited for the Commission's analyses because they describe pupil assignment within districts for which school authorities are directly accountable. Although the concentration of racial minorities in some school districts and not others is also a subject meriting intense attention and research, the underlying causes of it appear to arise from myriad sources that one cannot necessarily attribute to school officials.

Studies may also perform other levels of analysis, looking, for example, at integration of classrooms or curriculum within schools; or, more broadly, of metropolitan or suburban areas.[15] Again, such subjects merit attention but are beyond the scope of the Commission's study.

School Districts Included or Excluded from the Study

The Commission's study consists of three subsets of analyses each of which is based on a slightly different group of school districts. This section explains differences in the number of districts in each analysis. Part 1 consists of the unitary status information the Commission identified and presented in chapter 4. Part 2 refers to the statistical analyses of desegregation measures in chapter 5 and is further divided into 2A, the static analysis of desegregation measures in the 2004/05 school year; and 2B, the overtime differences between desegregation measures in 1992/93 (or, for Georgia, 1993/94) and 2004/05.

---

[14] The formula for the entropy index begins with the calculation of a diversity score (E) for the district summing across the racial/ethnic groups (for $r = 1, \ldots , n$) and using natural logarithms:

$$E = \sum (P_r) \log[1/ P_r]$$

where P_r is a particular racial/ethnic group's proportion of the district population.

The score, E, is higher when the district is more diverse and ranges as high as the natural log of the number of groups used in the calculations. For example, with six racial/ethnic groups, the maximum diversity score is log 6 or 1.792, and occurs with equal representation, in other words, when each of the six groups comprises about 17 percent of the district.

Next, one must calculate the diversity score for each school (i) using a similar formula, summing over the racial/ethnic groups as before:

$$E_i = \sum (P_{ri}) \log[1/ P_{ri}]$$

where P_{ri} is a particular racial/ethnic group's proportion of an individual school's enrollment.

The entropy index (H) is the weighted average deviation of each school's diversity score from the district diversity score, expressed as a fraction of the district's total enrollment. H is a summation for each of the schools in a district ($i = 1, \ldots, n$).

Entropy, or $H = \sum[(t_i)(E-E_i)/(E)(T)]$

where t_i is the total racial/ethnic enrollment of school i, and

   T is the total district enrollment.

See Iceland, "Beyond Black and White," p. 11.

[15] For an example of recent research on residential segregation *see* ibid.

The Determination of Unitary Status

Within the selected states, the Commission comprehensively pursued information on *all* school districts' unitary or other legal status (part 1). Nonetheless, the Commission identified several types of districts that were inappropriate for a study focusing on the desegregation of locally-run elementary schools. Thus, the Commission eliminated districts that were state- or federally-run; newly opened or closed; and devoted to special programs such as career-oriented curricula. Table A.1 shows that the Commission's efforts to determine legal status included 795 districts. The districts were spread across the seven states with the largest number, 180, in Georgia, and the smallest, 67, in Florida.

The 2004/05 School Year Analysis of Desegregation Measures

The statistical analyses in chapter 5 used all possible school districts from the Commission's efforts to determine legal status. First, the Commission computed the index of dissimilarity for districts' regular elementary schools. Because younger pupils are apt to attend schools that are more local, elementary schools yield the best measure of a district's integration or lack thereof. Middle and high schools often combine rising students from several elementary schools and because of the increased mix of pupils from their broader geographic coverage, they may have a reduced value of the index of dissimilarity for the district as a whole.

In carrying out the necessary computations, the Commission found that some districts did not have elementary schools. Rather, in such districts, primary-level pupils attend schools along with students in higher grades. The Commission's case base of 795 districts dropped to 780 because of their lack of regular elementary schools or of enrollment data. See table A.1. A later analysis in this appendix explains the difficulties in using the broadly-graded schools of these districts and illustrates some of their potential effects on the results.

The Commission also eliminated school districts with only one or two regular elementary schools, because the small numbers of schools offer administrative personnel little leeway in redistributing students among the facilities to achieve better racial balance.[16] This criterion excluded 281 of the 780 districts.

---

[16] Of course, many smaller districts have only a single middle or high school facility attended by all students. Had the Commission chosen to study integration in middle and high schools, it would have had to eliminate many such institutions from the analysis.

Table A.1
Number of School Districts Included in the Study by State

		ALABAMA	FLORIDA	GEORGIA	LOUSIANA	MISSISSIPPI	NORTH CAROLINA	SOUTH CAROLINA	TOTAL
Part I*	Districts subjected to the determination of unitary status	131	67	180	68	149	115	85	795
Part 2*	Districts with desegregation indices for regular elementary schools	125	67	176	68	144	115	85	780
Part 2A	Analysis of school year 2004/05	79	59	96	54	55	95	58	496
	Districts excluded because of too few regular elementary schools	*46*	*8*	*78*	*14*	*88*	*20*	*27*	*281*
	Districts excluded because of 0% white or 0% African American enrollment	*0*	*0*	*2*	*0*	*1*	*0*	*0*	*3*
	Total exclusions from part 2A	*46*	*8*	*80*	*14*	*89*	*20*	*27*	*284*
Part 2B	Analysis contrasting school year 2004/05 with 1992/93	66	54	83	53	47	93	53	449
	Districts from 2004/05 that failed to match 1992/93 (or 1993/94 in Georgia) districts	*3*	*0*	*4*	*3*	*2*	*0*	*1*	*13*
	Districts excluded because of too few regular elementary schools in either 2004/05 or 1992/93 (or 1993/94 in Georgia)	*52*	*13*	*86*	*12*	*90*	*20*	*31*	*304*
	Districts excluded because of 0% white or 0% African American enrollment	*4*	*0*	*3*	*0*	*5*	*2*	*0*	*14*
	Total exclusions from Part 2B	*59*	*13*	*93*	*15*	*97*	*22*	*32*	*331*

*Districts were excluded from all analyses because they were (1) state- or federally-run; (2) newly opened or newly closed; (3) special programs such as career-oriented curricula; or (4) a combination of these. In addition, the Commission eliminated districts that lacked elementary schools, enrollment data, or racial and ethnic information on students from analyses involving the desegregation indices.

Caption: Of the 795 districts subject to a determination of unitary status, 780 are candidates for inclusion in the analyses of the desegregation indices. Of the districts omitted from the analyses of the desegregation indices for the 2004/05 school year, 281 are omitted for having too few regular elementary schools and 3 are omitted for having no white or no African American enrollment. For the analyses comparing the 2004/05 and 1992/93 school years, 13 districts were omitted because they failed to match with 1992/93 districts, 304 districts were omitted for having too few regular elementary schools in either 2004/05 or 1992/93, and 14 districts were omitted for having no white or no black students.

Source: Compiled by U.S. Commission on Civil Rights.

In addition, the Commission identified three schools that had zero white enrollment or zero African American enrollment. The dissimilarity index could assume different extreme values depending on the treatment of zero divided by zero for these cases. Because of the undefined value of the dissimilarity index, the Commission separated these three cases from the main analyses. Table A-1 shows that the analysis of desegregation in the 2004/05 school year included 496 districts with a total of 284 districts that did not meet the criteria for inclusion.

Several of the tables in chapter 5 display districts that did not meet the inclusion criteria according to legal status, state, and other factors (e.g., tables 5.1, 5.3, 5.6). Data from tables 5.4 and 5.5 are repeated below with the information on the excluded districts because it was not presented in the earlier chapter. The reader may use this information to calculate average district dissimilarity indices that would have resulted had these school systems been included in the analyses. Table A.2, corresponding to table 5.4, contains the dissimilarity indices of the excluded districts according to the percent of their white enrollment. Table A.3, corresponding to table 5.5, shows dissimilarity indices of the excluded systems by their district enrollment. Notably, all of the excluded school systems had district enrollments of less than 10,000 students. Indeed, the Commission's threshold of requiring three or more elementary schools excluded all districts with fewer than 1,000 students from the main analysis.

Table A.2
The Excluded School Systems: Districts' Desegregation (the Dissimilarity Index) in the 2004/05 School Year by District's Percent White Enrollment and Legal Status

Districts' Percent White Enrollment	Legal Status	Number of Districts	Number of Elementary Schools	Dissimilarity Index for Blacks v. Whites		
				Average	Minimum	Maximum
COMBINED STATES						
Districts Excluded From the Analysis Because of Too Few Elementary Schools						
Less than 25 percent	Unitary Status	20	27	10.4%	0.0%	71.2%
	Under Court Order	36	54	10.6%	0.0%	62.5%
	Nonlitigants	19	25	7.0%	0.0%	36.8%
	Uncertain Status	1	2	0.4%	0.4%	0.4%
25 percent or more, but less than 50 percent	Unitary Status	15	21	6.8%	0.0%	48.1%
	Under Court Order	30	51	11.8%	0.0%	59.8%
	Nonlitigants	17	26	5.0%	0.0%	45.2%
50 percent or more, but less than 75 percent	Unitary Status	24	33	2.8%	0.0%	33.2%
	Under Court Order	38	54	4.1%	0.0%	37.9%
	Nonlitigants	29	51	5.1%	0.0%	46.9%
	Uncertain Status	1	2	2.1%	2.1%	2.1%
75 percent or more	Unitary Status	6	8	0.7%	0.0%	2.5%
	Under Court Order	13	20	9.8%	0.0%	54.5%
	Nonlitigants	32	49	9.5%	0.0%	52.5%
Total	Unitary Status	65	89	5.9%	0.0%	71.2%
	Under Court Order	117	179	8.7%	0.0%	62.5%
	Nonlitigants	97	151	6.9%	0.0%	52.5%
	Uncertain Status	2	4	1.3%	0.4%	2.1%
Districts Excluded Because of 0% Black or 0% White Enrollment						
Less than 25 percent	Nonlitigants	1	1	50.0%	50.0%	50.0%
75 percent or more	Nonlitigants	2	2	50.0%	50.0%	50.0%
Total	Nonlitigants	3	3	50.0%	50.0%	50.0%

Caption: The average dissimilarity index for the total number of districts excluded for having too few schools is 5.9 for unitary districts, 8.7 for districts under court order, and 6.9 for nonlitigant districts. Those with less than 25 percent white enrollment have an average dissimilarity index of 10.4 percent for unitary districts, 10.6 percent for those under court order, and 7.0 percent for nonlitigants. Districts with white enrollments between 25 and 50 percent have an average dissimilarity index of 6.8 percent for unitary districts, 11.8 percent for districts under court order, and 5.0 percent for nonlitigants. Those with 50 to 75 percent white enrollment have an average dissimilarity index of 2.8 percent for unitary districts, 4.1 percent for districts under court order, and 5.1 for nonlitigants. Those with 75 percent or more white enrollment show average dissimilarity indices of 0.7 percent for unitary districts, 9.8 percent, and 9.5 percent, respectively. The three districts excluded for having no white or black student enrollment have assigned values of 50 percent for their dissimilarity indices.

Source: Compiled by U.S. Commission on Civil Rights.

Table A.3
The Excluded School Systems: Districts' Desegregation (the Dissimilarity Index) in the 2004/05 School Year by District Size and Legal Status

District Size	Legal Status	Number of Districts	Number of Elementary Schools	Dissimilarity Index for Blacks v. Whites		
				Average	Minimum	Maximum
COMBINED STATES						
Districts Excluded From the Analysis Because of Too Few Elementary Schools						
1,000 to 9,999	*Unitary Status*	*56*	*79*	*6.7%*	*0.0%*	*71.2%*
	Under Court Order	*107*	*168*	*9.0%*	*0.0%*	*62.5%*
	Nonlitigants	*84*	*137*	*7.6%*	*0.0%*	*52.5%*
	Uncertain Status	*2*	*4*	*1.3%*	*0.4%*	*2.1%*
Less than 1,000	*Unitary Status*	*9*	*10*	*0.9%*	*0.0%*	*8.4%*
	Under Court Order	*10*	*11*	*5.6%*	*0.0%*	*56.0%*
	Nonlitigants	*13*	*14*	*2.6%*	*0.0%*	*33.7%*
Total	*Unitary Status*	*65*	*89*	*5.9%*	*0.0%*	*71.2%*
	Under Court Order	*117*	*179*	*8.7%*	*0.0%*	*62.5%*
	Nonlitigants	*97*	*151*	*6.9%*	*0.0%*	*52.5%*
	Uncertain Status	*2*	*4*	*1.3%*	*0.4%*	*2.1%*
Districts Excluded Because of 0% Black or 0% White Enrollment						
1,000 to 9,999	*Nonlitigants*	*2*	*2*	*50.0%*	*50.0%*	*50.0%*
Less than 1,000	*Nonlitigants*	*1*	*1*	*50.0%*	*50.0%*	*50.0%*
Total	*Nonlitigants*	*3*	*3*	*50.0%*	*50.0%*	*50.0%*

Caption: **All of the districts excluded from the analysis for having too few elementary schools had enrollments of less than 9,999 students. The average dissimilarity index for districts with at least 1,000 students was 6.7 percent for unitary districts, 9.0 percent for districts under court order, and 7.6 percent for nonlitigants. Districts with less than 1,000 students had lower average dissimilarity indices—0.9 percent, 5.6 percent, and 2.6 percent, for unitary, court-supervised, and nonlitigant systems, respectively.**

Source: Compiled by U.S. Commission on Civil Rights.

Changes in Desegregation Measures from 1992/93 to 2004/05

When the Commission analyzed districts' trends in desegregation at two points in time, the number of districts was necessarily smaller. First, the Commission matched enrollment data from the 2004/05 school year to data from the 1992/1993 school year. Over time, schools may have closed and other schools opened. The Commission, however, did not require a one-to-one match of schools for its analysis, because the process of opening and closing schools could constitute an effective strategy to bring about greater integration. Nonetheless, the Commission was unable to match some districts' enrollment data from the two school years. Notably, the source data—the Department of Education's Common Core of Data (CCD)—lacked enrollment data for all of the state of Georgia's districts in 1992/93. The Commission substituted 1993/94 enrollment data for districts in this state. After this modification to the study design, the Commission could not match enrollment data from the early 1990s for 13 districts that, as a result, it omitted from the analysis. (See table A.1.)

The Commission also applied the same criteria of the static 2004/05 analysis to avoid using desegregation measures with undefined or extreme values. It excluded districts with only one or two regular elementary schools whether in 2004/05 or 1992/93 (or, for Georgia, 1993/94). Table A.1 shows that the Commission omitted 304 districts for having too few regular elementary schools, 23 more than met this criteria for 2004/05. The Commission omitted 14 districts because they had zero African American or zero white enrollment in 2004/05 or 1992/93 (or, for Georgia, 1993/94), an additional 11 districts compared with the analyses of just the most recent year of data.

In all, the Commission's analyses of the two time points included 449 districts, ranging from 47 school systems in Mississippi to 93 in North Carolina. The 331 omitted districts were mostly those with only one or two regular elementary schools.

Analyses of Schools With Grades Extending Beyond the Primary Years

The Commission's analysis of the relation between legal status and desegregation is based on districts' primary schools. The CCD defines primary level as schools in which the lowest grade is pre-kindergarten through third and the highest grade is pre-kindergarten through eighth. The database definitions classify schools with broader grade levels, for example third through ninth, as an "other" level.[17] Thus, the Commission's analysis includes the primary-level schools, but not all elementary students, because some primary pupils are in schools that mix primary, middle, and high school grade-levels. The Commission chose to avoid contaminating its results with the middle and high school students attending these more broadly-graded schools. This section contains some results indicating the effect of excluding pupils in the broadly-graded schools from the analysis.

The 2004/05 CCD data include sufficient detail to separately calculate the racial composition of the elementary-level students in schools with broad grade ranges. On the other hand, the 1992/93 CCD data do not distinguish the racial/ethnic composition of elementary pupils from that of the school's middle or high school students. Because of the inability to compute the racial/ethnic balance for elementary students in such schools throughout all analyses, the Commission elected to omit the broadly graded schools. Nonetheless, the detailed data in the 2004/05 year allow a comparison of desegregation results for elementary school students between samples of districts with and without the broadly graded schools.

---

[17] *See, e.g.,* U.S. Department of Education, National Center for Education Statistics (NCES), *CCD [Common Core of Data]: Documentation to the NCES Common Core of Data Public Elementary/Secondary School Universe Survey: School Year 2003–04,* February 2006, pp. A-4, A-6.

The Commission's analysis of the dissimilarity index includes 780 districts and 6,939 schools as presented in chapter 5 of this report. As discussed in this appendix, there are 194 districts with "other" level schools that have elementary grades in them. Including the "other" level schools with elementary grades in them affects the computed desegregation measures of 116 districts already in the Commission's analysis; it also adds another 40 districts to the analyses. Of the 40 additional districts, 34 have only 1 or 2 regular elementary schools but surpass this criterion when counting the broadly-graded facilities. The Commission also collected legal status for six districts that have *no* regular elementary schools, but have 3 or more schools with extended grade ranges. These six districts are present in the chapter 4 tables and absent from chapter 5 analyses, but included in the results below.

Table A.4 shows the average dissimilarity index of districts by legal status using this larger sample of school systems. The dissimilarity indices are calculated using the racial enrollment of only elementary-level students.

Table A.4
Summary of Districts' Desegregation (the Dissimilarity Index) in the 2004/05 School Year by Unitary Status, Court Order, and Never Litigated, Including Schools With Broad Grade Ranges

State	Legal Status	Number of Districts	Number of Elementary Schools	Dissimilarity Index for Blacks v. Whites		
				Average	Minimum	Maximum
COMBINED STATES						
	Unitary Status	132	2,915	42.4%	3.9%	92.8%
	Under Court Order	186	1,877	39.7%	0.8%	85.6%
	Nonlitigants	207	1,946	32.7%	2.5%	78.4%
	Uncertain Status	11	242	35.9%	19.3%	57.6%
Districts Excluded From the Analysis Because of Too Few Elementary Schools						
	Unitary Status	*61*	*83*	*5.3%*	*0.0%*	*71.2%*
	Under Court Order	*100*	*153*	*8.2%*	*0.0%*	*76.4%*
	Nonlitigants	*91*	*140*	*6.8%*	*0.0%*	*66.2%*
	Uncertain Status	*2*	*4*	*1.3%*	*0.4%*	*2.1%*
Districts Excluded Because of 0% Black or 0% White Enrollment						
	Nonlitigants	*3*	*3*	*50.0%*	*50.0%*	*50.0%*

Caption: The average dissimilarity indices of school systems when schools with broad grade ranges are included in the analysis are: 42.4 percent for the 132 districts with unitary status; 39.7 percent for the 186 districts still under court order; and 32.7 for the 207 districts not subject to litigation. The districts with uncertain status have a dissimilarity index of 35.9 percent. Fewer districts have only one or two elementary schools and are thereby excluded from the analysis.

Source: Compiled by U.S. Commission on Civil Rights.

Compared to the results in chapter 5, including the schools with broad grade ranges increases the number of schools and districts in the main analysis as already noted. However, the average dissimilarity indices of unitary, court-supervised, and nonlitigant districts changes very little. The average for unitary districts increased from 41.8 percent table 5.1 to 42.4 percent in table A.4. The average of districts under court order increased from 38.4 to 39.7 percent. The average dissimilarity index of districts that were not subject to litigation increased from 32.4 percent to 32.7 percent. With the larger sample, districts with unitary status continue to have a slightly higher average dissimilarity index compared to court-supervised districts. Districts that were not subject to litigation still have a lower average dissimilarity index compared to those under court order.

In short, the Commission's study of districts' desegregation measures could be more likely to identify small differences as statistically significant with the larger sample obtained by including schools with irregular grade ranges. The 2004/05 dissimilarity indices suggest, however, that differences according to legal status would remain much the same, if the database enabled the Commission to include these unusual schools in the analysis. Any analyses of differences in racial balance over time, however, are precluded by the inability to determine the racial composition of elementary level pupils in these schools without introducing bias of a potentially different racial balance among middle and/or high school students.

Districts that Obtained Unitary Status After the 2004/05 School Year

The Commission was able to obtain information on unitary status that is more recent than the data available on school enrollment. Specifically, the Commission identified districts that received recognition of unitary status as recent as June 2007, while school enrollment figures are available only through the 2004/05 school year. To achieve the greatest currency, the Commission elected to include districts for which the recognition of unitary status is very recent in the study results. The racial/ethnic balance of such districts may have changed since the 2004/05 school year. Regression analyses, similar to those presented later in this appendix, did not show any significant increases in explained variation in the desegregation measures related to districts receiving unitary status specifically in 2006 and 2007.[18] Thus, the Commission found no indication that its treatment of these districts had detrimental effects on the results.

---

[18] When added to the most comprehensive regression models depicted in table A.7 below, the increase in explained variance for having obtained unitary recognition after 2005 was between 0.0 and 0.4 percent for each desegregation measure (all nonsignificant). The effect parameters for obtaining recognition after 2005 were also insignificant in models with each of the four desegregation measures.

Detailed Statistical Results of Integration and Legal Status

Chapter 5 presented brief results indicating the statistical significance of the relationships between measures of desegregation, legal status, and a few other factors such as district size. The section below gives detailed analyses of variance and regressions supporting that chapter.

ANOVA results: General differences among groups of districts in racial/ethnic concentration

The Commission's analyses present four measures of the concentrations of minority students in schools within districts—(1) the dissimilarity index (which represents African Americans and whites) in the 2004/05 school year; (2) the change in the dissimilarity index from 1992/93 (or, in Georgia, 1993/94) to 2004/05; (3) the entropy index (which represents multiple racial/ethnic groups) for 2004/05; and (4) the change in the entropy index of 1992/93 (or 1993/94) versus 2004/05. Panel A of table A.5 presents the analysis of variance results using legal status to explain differences in each of the desegregation measures (numbered 1, 2, 3, and 4), referred to as the "dependent variables."

The first three lines of the analyses in panel A are statistically significant. That is, they show large "mean square *effects*" (i.e., differences from the overall average level of desegregation that are associated with the type of legal status) relative to the size of the "mean square *error*" (i.e., variations from the average desegregation level that seem random or unrelated to the type of legal status). The F-test is a ratio of mean square effects to mean square errors and elucidates the probability that a result would occur by chance in some small proportion of instances. The first three F-tests in table A.5 are far greater than 2.000, a threshold above which results are typically statistically significant at the "$p < .05$" level, implying that chance occurrences happen in fewer than five out of 100 instances.[19] The results for these three analyses are highly significant with probability levels (p-levels) of .000 to .025 indicating that false observations of such differences in the desegregation measures by legal status might appear in less than one in 1,000 occurrences.

---

[19] Statistical significance also depends upon the degrees of freedom. The degrees of freedom express the number of variables used to explain variation in the dependent variable and the amount of data available for estimating the effects of the explanatory factors. The two components of the degrees of freedom sum to the number of cases minus one.

Table A.5
ANOVA results: Explaining districts' desegregation with legal status and other factors

Model	The desegregation measure and explanatory factors in the analysis	Number of districts in the analysis	Mean square Effect	Mean Square error	Error degrees of freedom	F-test	Significance (p-level)
Panel A: Only legal status as an explanatory factor							
1	Dissimilarity index in 2004/05 school year	496	2449.868	300.901	3, 492	8.142	.000*
2	Entropy index in 2004/05 school year	496	1115.844	97.304	3, 492	11.468	.000*
3	Change in dissimilarity index from 1992/93 (or 1993/94) to 2004/05	449	613.478	194.497	3, 445	3.154	.025*
4	Change in entropy index from 1992/93 (or 1993/94) to 2004/05	449	8.143	58.383	3, 445	0.139	.936
Panel B: Legal status and state							
5	Dissimilarity index in 2004/05 school year	496	1850.333	285.473	9, 486	6.482	.000*
6	Entropy index in 2004/05 school year	496	968.637	87.455	9, 486	11.076	.000*
7	Change in dissimilarity index from 1992/93 (or 1993/94) to 2004/05	449	472.909	191.652	9, 439	2.468	.009*
8	Change in entropy index from 1992/93 (or 1993/94) to 2004/05	449	75.242	57.694	9, 439	1.304	.232
Panel C: Legal status, state, the log (base 10) of the district's enrollment, and district's percent of white students							
9	Dissimilarity index in 2004/05 school year	496	3420.975	243.310	11, 484	14.060	.000*
10	Entropy index in 2004/05 school year	496	1563.016	70.305	11, 484	22.232	.000*
11	Change in dissimilarity index from 1992/93 (or 1993/94) to 2004/05	449	668.324	185.446	11, 437	3.604	.000*
12	Change in entropy index from 1992/93 (or 1993/94) to 2004/05	449	71.041	57.720	11, 437	1.231	.264
Panel D: Legal status and decade of unitary status							
13	Dissimilarity index in 2004/05 school year	496	1910.741	291.020	7, 488	6.566	.000*
14	Entropy index in 2004/05 school year	496	816.949	93.243	7, 488	8.762	.000*
15	Change in dissimilarity index from 1992/93 (or 1993/94) to 2004/05	449	777.685	188.090	7, 441	4.135	.000*
16	Change in entropy index from 1992/93 (or 1993/94) to 2004/05	449	179.955	56.112	7, 441	3.207	.003*
Panel E: Legal status, decade of unitary status, state, the log (base 10) of the district's enrollment, and district's percent of white students							
17	Dissimilarity index in 2004/05 school year	496	2728.933	238.456	15, 480	11.444	.000*
18	Entropy index in 2004/05 school year	496	1237.338	68.044	15, 480	18.184	.000*
19	Change in dissimilarity index from 1992/93 (or 1993/94) to 2004/05	449	694.749	180.070	15, 433	3.858	.000*
20	Change in entropy index from 1992/93 (or 1993/94) to 2004/05	449	139.972	55.209	15, 433	2.535	.001*
Panel F: Legal status, whether the district obtained unitary status before or after 2000, state, the log (base 10) of the district's enrollment, and district's percent of white students							
21	Dissimilarity index in 2004/05 school year	496	3383.792	237.655	12, 483	14.238	.000*
22	Entropy index in 2004/05 school year	496	1539.776	67.792	12, 483	22.713	.000*
23	Change in dissimilarity index from 1992/93 (or 1993/94) to 2004/05	449	831.738	179.841	12, 436	4.625	.000*
24	Change in entropy index from 1992/93 (or 1993/94) to 2004/05	449	154.234	55.400	12, 436	2.784	.001*

* Indicates significance at the 0.05 level.

Caption: ANOVA results using only legal status, legal status and the state in which the district is located, and ANCOVA using legal status, state, size of the district, and percent white enrollment produce statistically significant group differences on all measures of desegregation except for the over time change in the entropy index. Similar ANOVA and ANCOVA distinguishing the decades in which districts obtained recognition of unitary status produces statistically significant group differences on all four of the desegregation measures.

Source: Compiled by U.S. Commission on Civil Rights.

Other panels in table A.5 show analysis of variance of the four desegregation measures using legal status and additional explanatory factors. Panel B shows the results using legal status and the state in which the district is located for each of the desegregation measures (models numbered 5, 6, 7, and 8). Panel C presents an analysis of covariance[20] of each of the desegregation measures (models numbered 9, 10, 11, 12) using legal status, state, district size (the base 10 log of the district's enrollment), and the district's percent of students who are white. Panels B and C show results similar to panel A: the groups articulated through the explanatory variables differ significantly in integration expressed by the first three desegregation measures, but not by changes in the entropy index over time.

Panels D, E, and F show similar analysis of variance and covariance distinguishing the decade in which districts obtained recognition of unitary status. Panel D is an analysis of variance of each of the dependent variables with legal status and the decade of unitary status as explanatory factors. Panel E is an analysis of covariance explaining the four measures of desegregation with legal status, the decade effect, state, the district's size (number of students in base 10 logs), and the district's percent of white students. Panel F shows analyses of covariance of the four dependent variables similar to those in Panel E, except that the decade effect distinguishes between districts that received unitary status before and after 2000, rather than during the 1970s, 1980s, 1990s, and 2000s. Adding an effect of the decade in which districts received unitary status produces analysis of variance (and covariance) with statistically significant group differences among districts in panels D, E, and F, *on all four* of the desegregation measures.

Significant F-tests are general indicators that the levels of the desegregation measures vary by group, e.g., between districts with unitary status, those under court jurisdiction, and nonlitigants, or alternatively between school systems by state or another factor in the analysis. The analyses of variance F-tests do not identify which groups are different. The following sections will present parameters that contrast districts by type of legal status and other factors.

---

[20] In contrast to analysis of variance, an analysis of covariance includes some explanatory variables that are not divided into groups or categories but rather expressed on a scale where higher and lower values have inherent meaning. The number of students enrolled in a district and the district's percent of students who are white are the scaled variables, called "covariates," in these analyses, with the former transformed into logarithms.

Levels of Racial/Ethnic Concentration by Legal Status

Table A.6 presents contrasts among the groups of districts based upon their legal status. The table has six panels with "models" of the various desegregation measures and explanatory factors that correspond by number to those listed in table A.3. The analysis tested the desegregation measure of districts under court order to determine if this average (identified as the "unstandardized coefficient" in the "court order" column) is statistically different from zero (where zero corresponds to perfect racial/ethnic balance among schools in the district). The design then compares unitary districts and those that were not subject to desegregation litigation to school systems under court order to determine whether each of the two groups differs from the base value of court-supervised districts. The "unstandardized coefficients" for these latter two groups represent the difference between their average desegregation measure and that of the court-supervised group. The table also includes t-tests,[21] and corresponding p-levels, which evaluate significance for the difference between (1) the first group and zero; or (2) the latter two groups and the court-supervised districts.

Table A.6 shows that the average desegregation level of court-supervised districts is statistically greater than zero when measured by the (1) 2004/05 dissimilarity index; (2) 2004/05 entropy index; and (3) change in dissimilarity from the early 1990s to 2004/05. It is *not* statistically significant when measured by the (4) change in entropy from the early 1990s to 2004/05. The same statistical effects, both significant and insignificant, emerge in models explaining the variation in the average court-supervised districts' desegregation using just legal status (panel A), or legal status and the state in which the district is located (panel B), or legal status and the decade in which other districts in the analysis received unitary status (panel D).

When the analysis includes additional factors such as district size and the district's percent of students who are white, in combination with state (panels C, E, and F), the average desegregation level of districts under court order is no longer statistically different from zero for any of the four measures of racial/ethnic balance. Such findings suggest that these other factors—state differences and district size and white enrollment—determine the level of desegregation among court-supervised districts.

Looking at districts that were not involved in litigation, their racial concentration level is significantly lower than that of court-supervised districts for three desegregation measures in models using explanatory variables of just legal status (panel A), or legal status and the decade in which other districts received unitary status (panel D). In fact, however, allowing variations among states reduces the effect of legal status in two models: In panel B, the only statistically significant effect of nonlitigant districts is when using state and legal status to explain the average 2004/05 entropy index (model 6). When district size, the percent of white enrollment, and state are explanatory factors (panels C, E, and F), none of the four desegregation measures show statistically significant results. Thus, nonlitigant districts do not differ from those under court order when differences in district size and the district's percent of white enrollment are allowed to explain variations in the desegregation measures. Indeed, the average change over time in the entropy index for nonlitigant districts does *not* differ statistically from court-supervised districts in any model (models 4, 8, 12, 16, 20, and 24).

---

[21] The F-tests presented in table A.5 were appropriate for testing significance with multiple groups. The corresponding t-tests in table A.6 are an appropriate test for evaluating differences between *two* groups or one group and a specified value such as zero.

Table A.6
ANOVA results: Legal status contrasts in various models explaining districts' desegregation

Model	Contrasting districts under court order to zero (i.e., the constant)			Unitary districts to those under court order			Nonlitigants to districts under court order		
	Unstandarized coefficient	t-test	Significance (p-level)	Unstandarized coefficient	t-test	Significance (p-level)	Unstandarized coefficient	t-test	Significance (p-level)
Panel A: Only legal status as an explanatory factor									
1	38.410	28.270	.000*	3.421	1.659	.098	-5.976	-3.254	.001*
2	14.556	18.839	.000*	1.570	1.339	.181	-4.526	-4.333	.000*
3	2.816	2.465	.014*	0.704	0.406	.685	-3.678	-2.366	.018*
4	-0.387	-0.619	.536	0.093	0.098	.922	-0.391	-0.459	.646
Panel B: Legal status and state (based upon Louisiana)									
5	48.325	20.248	.000*	4.159	2.008	.045*	-2.700	-1.352	.177
6	22.356	16.924	.000*	2.313	2.018	.044*	-2.310	-2.089	.037*
7	6.912	3.488	.001*	0.488	0.277	.782	-2.659	-1.527	.127
8	2.081	1.914	.056	0.094	0.097	.923	0.258	0.270	.787
Panel C: Legal status, state, the log (base 10) of the district's enrollment, and district's percent of white students									
9	7.965	1.045	.297	0.478	0.245	.807	0.892	0.467	.640
10	1.865	0.455	.649	0.039	0.037	.970	0.207	0.202	.840
11	7.865	1.112	.267	-0.756	-0.424	.672	-0.977	-0.555	.579
12	2.226	0.564	.573	-0.135	-0.136	.892	0.566	0.576	.565
Panel D: Legal status and decade of unitary status									
13	38.410	28.746	.000*	11.295	3.135	.002*	-5.976	-3.308	.001*
14	14.556	19.245	.000*	6.717	3.294	.001*	-4.526	-4.427	.000*
15	2.816	2.507	.013*	4.708	1.615	.107	-3.678	-2.406	.017*
16	-0.387	-0.631	.528	3.355	2.108	.036*	-0.391	-0.469	.640
Panel E: Legal status, decade of unitary status, state, the log (base 10) of the district's enrollment, and district's percent of white students									
17	11.193	1.469	.142	7.226	2.136	.033*	1.038	0.549	.583
18	3.766	0.926	.355	4.654	2.575	.010*	0.282	0.279	.781
19	11.184	1.592	.112	3.192	1.079	.281	-0.804	-0.463	.644
20	4.467	1.148	.252	3.347	2.044	.042*	0.680	0.707	.480
Panel F: Legal status, whether the district obtained unitary status before or after 2000, state, the log (base 10) of the district's enrollment, and district's percent of white students									
21	10.442	1.380	.168	6.090	2.437	.015*	1.004	0.532	.595
22	3.492	0.864	.388	3.726	2.792	.005*	0.280	0.278	.781
23	10.213	1.461	.145	4.385	1.983	.048*	-0.832	-0.479	.632
24	3.724	0.960	.338	3.143	2.561	.010*	0.659	0.685	.494

* Indicates significance at the 0.05 level.

Caption: When district size and white enrollment are explanatory factors, districts under court order cease to show desegregation averages that are statistically significant from zero for any of the measures of racial and ethnic balance; nor do nonlitigant districts differ significantly from court order districts. When the analyses distinguish the decades in which districts obtain recognition of unitary status, the unitary districts show significantly higher imbalance than court-supervised school systems on several measures of desegregation.

Source: Compiled by U.S. Commission on Civil Rights.

Unitary districts do not differ statistically in their 2004/05 dissimilarity index from that of systems under court order when viewing results by legal status (panel A, model 1). However, districts with unitary status differ significantly in desegregation level from court-supervised ones on three of the four measures when the analyses distinguish among districts that obtained recognition of the unitary status in different decades—the 1970s, 1980s, 1990s, and 2000s (see panel D, models 13, 14, and 16). The three statistically significant differences remain even when other factors, such as the district's size and white enrollment, are included (panel E, models 17, 18, and 20). When the analysis uses a more simple distinction between obtaining unitary status before or since 2000 (panel F), legal status has a statistically significant effect on all four desegregation measures. Thus, when distinguishing districts that became unitary since the year 2000, significant differences do occur between court-supervised and unitary districts, but further analysis below suggests that they may be unimportant relative to district variations in size and the percent of white enrollment.

Regression analyses

The Commission carried out many regression analyses[22] to demonstrate the amount of variance relevant factors explain in the four measures of desegregation. Table A.7 shows the proportion of the total variance in each of the desegregation measures that variables such as legal status, state, district size, and the district's percent of white enrollment explain when used singly or in combination. This proportion of explained variance is called "R-square."[23] Social scientists sometimes prefer an "adjusted R-square" that corrects for a tendency of the R-square to over estimate the explained variance when one is using more than one explanatory variable.[24] The table shows both. In many instances, table A.7 also shows the difference in the R-square between two regression models where one analysis uses more factors to

---

[22] Multiple regression (or regression analysis) analyzes the relationship between several independent or predictor variables and a dependent variable (i.e., the dissimilarity index or another desegregation measure). Regression techniques can discern relationships, but do not resolve the direction of any causal effects among explanatory factors. For example, see Hubert M. Blalock, Jr., *Social Statistics*, (New York: McGraw-Hill Book Company, 1972), pp. 361–63.

The form of the statistical procedure applied herein analyzes the multivariate relationship of a few factors, designated as "predictors:" (1) a measure of district size—district enrollment, (2) the percentage of white students, and (3) district desegregation status (i.e., unitary, under court order, etc.). Regression analysis uses the predictors to explain the "dependent" variable—the 2004/05 school year index of dissimilarity (or another measure of desegregation) or any change in the desegregation measure between the 1992/93 school year and 2004/05.

For chapter 5's section A analyses of the dissimilarity and entropy indices, the regression model is:

$$[\tilde{Y}_{I04j}] = \alpha_j + \beta_{1j}X_{1j} + \beta_{2j}X_{2j} + \beta_{3j}D_{3j} + \beta_{4j}D_{4j} + \varepsilon_j$$

where $\tilde{Y}_{I04j}$ is the index of dissimilarity or another desegregation measure for district "j" in the 2004/05 school year;

X_{1j} is total enrollment in school district "j;"

X_{2j} is the percentage of white students in school district "j;"

D_{3j} is a variable coded "1" when district "j" has "unitary status" and "0" otherwise; and

D_{4j} is a variable coded "1" when district "j" is a nonlitigant and "0" otherwise.

The effect of districts under court order is depicted by the constant, α_j. This basic model appears in panel C throughout this appendix's tables as model 10, or, for the entropy index, model 11.

The section B of chapter 5 the regression model is the same, substituting the change in value of the district's 1992/93 and 2004/05 indices for the dependent variable. In other words, $[\tilde{Y}_{I04j} - \tilde{Y}_{I93j}]$ replaces $[\tilde{Y}_{I04j}]$

where $[\tilde{Y}_{I04j} - \tilde{Y}_{I93j}]$ is the difference in the indices of dissimilarity for district "j" between school years 1992/93 and 2003/04.

This is model 12 in the tables of this appendix.

Indeed, the analyses of variance presented in this report are statistically depicted through regression models representing legal status as described in the formula above to explain the desegregation measure. Similarly, the formulae above are the regression representation for the analysis of covariance used herein, which, by definition, contains categorical explanatory factors (such as legal status) and scaled variables (such as district's enrollment).

Regression analysis may also reveal the statistically optimal explanation of two or more factors that are frequently associated together. To do so, one computes a series of regressions to determine the increase in the explained variance by adding one or more factors compared with a simpler model that excludes those factors. This method is used below in table A.7.

The regression results are subject to technical limitations that are common to all social science research. For accurate results, the researcher must avoid errors in the values of all variables, employ a regression model that truly depicts the relationships among factors, and remain sensitive to predictors that commonly occur together. The method of subtracting the explained variance of two regression models is one method to compensate for associations among predictors.

[23] *See* Blalock, *Social Statistics*, p. 392.

[24] *See SPSS Base 10.0 Applications Guide* (Chicago, IL: SPSS, Inc., 1999), pp. 198, 208.

explain variation in desegregation than the other. In these instances, table A.7 presents the R-square change and its associated statistical test of the difference (called the F-change), degrees of freedom (i.e., functions of the numbers of explanatory variables and school districts in these analyses), and significance (the probability that the increased explained variance could occur by chance, or the p-level).

Table A.7
Regression results: Explaining districts' desegregation with legal status and other factors

Model	The desegregation measure and explanatory factors in the analysis	Regression Model Summary		Selected Model Comparisons	Increase in explained variance from adding factors into the model			
		R square	Adjusted R square		R square change	F- change	Degrees of freedom	Statistical Significance
Panel A: Only legal status as an explanatory factor								
1	Dissimilarity index in 2004/05 school year	0.047	0.041					
2	Entropy index in 2004/05 school year	0.065	0.060					
3	Change in dissimilarity index from 1992/93 (or 1993/94) to 2004/05	0.021	0.014					
4	Change in entropy index from 1992/93 (or 1993/94) to 2004/05	0.001	-0.006					
Panel B: Legal status and state				**Testing the addition of state to legal status**				
5	Dissimilarity index in 2004/05 school year	0.107	0.091	Model 5 - 1	0.060	5.432	6, 486	.000*
6	Entropy index in 2004/05 school year	0.170	0.155	Model 6 - 2	0.105	10.234	6, 486	.000*
7	Change in dissimilarity index from 1992/93 (or 1993/94) to 2004/05	0.048	0.029	Model 7 - 3	0.027	2.101	6, 439	.052*
8	Change in entropy index from 1992/93 (or 1993/94) to 2004/05	0.026	0.006	Model 8 - 4	0.025	1.886	6, 439	.082
Panel C: Legal status, state, the log (base 10) of the district's enrollment, and district's percent of white students								
9	Dissimilarity index in 2004/05 school year	0.242	0.225					
10	Entropy index in 2004/05 school year	0.336	0.321					
11	Change in dissimilarity index from 1992/93 (or 1993/94) to 2004/05	0.083	0.060					
12	Change in entropy index from 1992/93 (or 1993/94) to 2004/05	0.030	0.006					

Continued

Table A.7 (continued)
Regression results: Explaining districts' desegregation with legal status and other factors

Model	The desegregation measure and explanatory factors in the analysis	Regression Model Summary		Selected Model Comparisons	Increase in explained variance from adding factors into the model			
		R square	Adjusted R square		R square change	F-change	Degrees of freedom	Statistical Significance
Panel D: Legal status and decade of unitary status				**Testing decade of unitary status in addition to legal status**				
13	Dissimilarity index in 2004/05 school year	0.086	0.073	Model 13 - 1	0.039	5.176	4, 488	.000*
14	Entropy index in 2004/05 school year	0.112	0.099	Model 14 - 2	0.046	6.357	4, 488	.000*
15	Change in dissimilarity index from 1992/93 (or 1993/94) to 2004/05	0.062	0.047	Model 15 - 3	0.041	4.789	4, 441	.001*
16	Change in entropy index from 1992/93 (or 1993/94) to 2004/05	0.048	0.033	Model 16 - 4	0.048	5.504	4, 441	.000*
Panel F: Legal status, whether the district obtained unitary status before or after 2000, state, the log (base 10) of the district's enrollment, and district's percent of white students				**Testing the effect of distinguishing districts that obtained unitary status before and after 2000 in the full model**				
21	Dissimilarity index in 2004/05 school year	0.261	0.243	Model 21 – 9	0.019	12.517	1, 483	.000*
22	Entropy index in 2004/05 school year	0.361	0.345	Model 22 - 10	0.025	18.942	1, 483	.000*
23	Change in dissimilarity index from 1992/93 (or 1993/94) to 2004/05	0.113	0.089	Model 23 - 11	0.030	14.620	1, 436	.000*
24	Change in entropy index from 1992/93 (or 1993/94) to 2004/05	0.071	0.046	Model 24 - 12	0.041	19.302	1, 436	.000*
Panel E: Legal status, decade of unitary status, state, the log (base 10) of the district's enrollment, and district's percent of white students				**Testing the effect of distinguishing districts that obtained unitary status in each of four decades in the full model**				
17	Dissimilarity index in 2004/05 school year	0.263	0.240	Model 17 - 21	0.002	0.459	3, 480	.711
18	Entropy index in 2004/05 school year	0.362	0.342	Model 18 - 22	0.002	0.405	3, 480	.749
19	Change in dissimilarity index from 1992/93 (or 1993/94) to 2004/05	0.118	0.087	Model 19 - 23	0.005	0.815	3, 433	.486
20	Change in entropy index from 1992/93 (or 1993/94) to 2004/05	0.081	0.049	Model 20 - 24	0.010	1.502	3, 433	.213

Continued

Table A.7 (continued)
Regression results: Explaining districts' desegregation with legal status and other factors

Model	The desegregation measure and explanatory factors in the analysis	Regression Model Summary		Selected Model Comparisons	Increase in explained variance from adding factors into the model			
		R square	Adjusted R square		R square change	F-change	Degrees of freedom	Statistical Significance
Panel G: The log (base 10) of the district's enrollment and district's percent of white students								
25	Dissimilarity index in 2004/05 school year	0.144	0.141					
26	Entropy index in 2004/05 school year	0.189	0.185					
27	Change in dissimilarity index from 1992/93 (or 1993/94) to 2004/05	0.042	0.037					
28	Change in entropy index from 1992/93 (or 1993/94) to 2004/05	0.003	-0.001					
Panel H: The log (base 10) of the district's enrollment, district's percent of white students, and state				**Testing the effect of state after the district's size and percent white enrollment**				
29	Dissimilarity index in 2004/05 school year	0.241	0.229	Model 29 - 25	0.097	10.383	6, 487	.000*
30	Entropy index in 2004/05 school year	0.335	0.324	Model 30 - 26	0.147	17.908	6, 487	.000*
31	Change in dissimilarity index from 1992/93 (or 1993/94) to 2004/05	0.081	0.065	Model 31 - 27	0.040	3.174	6, 440	.005*
32	Change in entropy index from 1992/93 (or 1993/94) to 2004/05	0.029	0.011	Model 32 - 28	0.026	1.941	6, 440	.073
Panel I: The log (base 10) of the district's enrollment, and district's percent of white students, state, and legal status				**Testing the effect of legal status after the district's size, percent white enrollment, and state**				
33	Dissimilarity index in 2004/05 school year	0.242	0.225	Model 33 - 29	0.001	0.199	3, 484	.897
34	Entropy index in 2004/05 school year	0.336	0.321	Model 34 - 30	0.000	0.107	3, 484	.956
35	Change in dissimilarity index from 1992/93 (or 1993/94) to 2004/05	0.083	0.060	Model 35 - 31	0.002	0.293	3, 437	.831
36	Change in entropy index from 1992/93 (or 1993/94) to 2004/05	0.030	0.006	Model 36 - 32	0.001	0.175	3, 437	.914

* Indicates significance at the 0.05 level.

Caption: In addition to legal status, distinguishing the state in which a district is located significantly increases the explained variation in most desegregation measures, but not in the change in the entropy index over time. The explained variation in all desegregation measures increases significantly in models that, in addition to using legal status, distinguish the decade in which districts obtained unitary status. Legal status does not produce a statistically significant explanation of variance once district size, percent white enrollment, and state location are included. The additional variance that the decade effect explains in racial imbalance measures arises from differences between districts receiving districts before and after 2000; distinctions among districts becoming unitary in the 1970s, 1980s, and 1990s do not contribute.

Source: Compiled by U.S. Commission on Civil Rights.

Panels A, B, and C show results for regression analysis with each of the desegregation measures explained by legal status only (panel A), legal status and state (panel B), and the initial full model using legal status, state, district size (the base 10 log of student enrollment), and the district's percent of white enrollment (panel C). For example, an R square of 0.047 indicates that legal status explains 4.7 percent of the variance in the 2004/05 dissimilarity index (panel A, model 1). Together legal status and the state in which the district is located explain 10.7 percent of the variance in the same measure (panel B, model 5). Legal status, state, district size, and the district's percent of white students explain 24.2 percent of the variation among districts' 2004/05 dissimilarity indices (panel C, model 9).

The right side of the table compares the results for different regression models. For example, compared to explaining the 2004/05 dissimilarity index with only the legal status (model 1), legal status and state (model 5) increase the R square from 4.7 percent to 10.7 percent, an R-square change of 6.0 percent. The right panel shows that this change is highly significant (F = 5.432, with 6 and 486 degrees of freedom; p < .001). Thus, as Chapter 5 reports, districts' dissimilarity indices vary according to the state in which they are located.

Panels D through F present regression models including a measure of when unitary districts received recognition of that status. Panel D shows the explained variance of regression models with legal status and the decade of unitary status (i.e., the 1970s, 1980s, 1990s, or 2000s). The right side of panel D shows that including legal status and decade of unitary status to explain the desegregation measures significantly increases the R squares compared to panel A models using only unitary status. For example, with the 2004/05 dissimilarity index, legal status and the decade effect explain 8.6 percent of the variance (panel D, model 13), an increase of 3.9 percent compared with the 4.7 percent of just legal status (in panel A, model 1). Indeed the increases in R square attributed to the addition of the decade effect are statistically significant with all four desegregation measures, e.g., the entropy index and the changes over time in the dissimilarity and entropy indices.

Panel F shows, for each desegregation measure, the full regression model—that is, with legal status, state, district size, the district's white enrollment (as a percent)—*and* a decade effect that represents the date unitary districts received their recognition simply *as before or after the year 2000*. The before and after dichotomy significantly increases the variance explained in all desegregation measures relative to the full model without any decade effect (panel C). For example, the explained variance in the 2004/05 dissimilarity index of the full model with the dichotomy (model 21, panel F) is 26.1 percent compared with the full model without the dichotomy (model 9, panel C)—24.2 percent—a statistically significant 1.9 percent increase (F=12.517, with 1 and 483 degrees of freedom, p=.001). In contrast, in Panel E, analyses represent the decade of unitary status recognition as during the 1970s, 1980s, 1990s, and 2000s. Although the R squares in panel E are larger than those in panel F, the R-square changes are not statistically significant. Thus, the decade effect explains variance in the desegregation measures because districts that obtained unitary status in the year 2000 and thereafter differ from those that received recognition in the earlier decades. In essence, the model comparisons in panel E indicate that distinctions among districts that became unitary in the 1970s, the 1980s, and the 1990s do not add to the explanation of the level of racial concentration.

The Commission's analyses show that district size, proportion of white students, and state bear strong relationships with districts' measures of racial concentration. The final panels of table A.7 explore whether legal status adds explanatory power to these potent variables or merely appears related to the level of racial concentration because unitary and court-supervised districts differ in size or the proportion of white enrollment. Panel G presents the R-squares for regression models with two explanatory factors—district size (the base 10 log of total enrollment) and district's percent of white students. Panel H adds state to these two factors. The district's state explains significantly more variance in three of the desegregation measures than the two factors alone (models 29, 30, and 31). However, the district's state-location does not explain additional variation in the over time change in the entropy index (model 32, panel H). Panel I (which contains the same models as panel C) shows the full model with size, white enrollment, state, and legal status. Legal status does not add statistically significant explained variance over the first three factors for any of the desegregation measures.

In summary, there is a general lack of significant effects of the legal status types in the analysis of variance results. Furthermore, legal status fails to increase the explained variance of the regression models beyond that of the few selected factors in these equations. Together, these results raise questions about whether court supervision of districts influences the racial/ethnic concentration of students in schools or whether recognition of unitary status has any adverse effects on the educational systems' racial balance thereafter. The analyses do reveal, however, other factors that are related to districts' measures of desegregation. Some further details of the parameters of these effects appear below.

Levels of racial concentration by state on desegregation measures

Analyses in table A.7 indicated that the state in which districts are located is related to districts' levels of desegregation for some of the measures. The regression results in panel B of the table showed that the amount of explained variance increased when the model included state along with legal status. Panel H of the table indicated further that state explained a unique proportion of variance in three of the desegregation measures. Compared with models that associate variation in the desegregation measures with district size and its percent of white students, the increase in explained variance attributable to the district's state is statistically significant for the 2004/05 dissimilarity and entropy indices and for the change over time in the dissimilarity index.

Changes in the entropy index over time are not explained by the state in which the district is located. The state location did not increase the explained variance in the change in time in entropy (e.g., in contrasting the regression model 32 of panel H with model 28 of panel G). Indeed, the ANOVA results in table A.5, panel B, revealed no statistically significant group differences among districts' over time entropy indices when they were classified by legal status and state (model 8, F= 1.304, p=.232, nonsignificant).

In chapter 5, tables 5.3 and 5.8 present results of the dissimilarity index by state for the 2004/05 school year and the change between 1992/93 (or 1993/94 for Georgia) and 2004/05. However, the particulars of state differences in the racial concentrations of their school districts are not the focus of the Commission's study. Hence, detailed effect parameters contrasting each state with every other one are not presented here.

Levels of racial concentration by district size and white enrollment

Many of the analyses suggest that district size and the percent of white enrollment explain substantial variation in the desegregation measures. Table A.8 shows the coefficients, both unstandardized and standardized, of these factors in the regression analysis along with a statistical test of their significance. The unstandardized coefficient represents the model's estimated increment in the measure of desegregation for each unit increase in the explanatory variable, i.e., the district size or percent white. The standardized coefficients express the relationship between desegregation and the explanatory variables in uniform units to facilitate comparisons with other factors that are scaled with different metrics. The models in table A.8 are keyed by number to those in earlier tables, specifically tables A.5 and A.7.

Table A.8
ANCOVA results: Explaining districts' desegregation with two covariates—district's size and white enrollment

Model key	The effect of district size (the base 10 log of district enrollment)				The effect of the district's percent of white enrollment			
	Unstandarized coefficient	Standardized coefficient	t-test	Significance (p-level)	Unstandarized coefficient	Standardized coefficient	t-test	Significance (p-level)
Panel C: Legal status, state, the log (base 10) of the district's enrollment, and district's percent of white students								
9	12.944	0.313	7.074	.000*	-0.181	-0.254	-5.875	.000*
10	7.153	0.301	7.273	.000*	-0.134	-0.327	-8.082	.000*
11	1.363	0.042	0.798	.425	-0.114	-0.199	-3.998	.000*
12	0.257	0.015	0.270	.787	-0.021	-0.067	-1.314	.190
Panel F: Legal status, whether the district obtained unitary status before or after 2000, state, the log (base 10) of the district's enrollment, and district's percent of white students								
21	12.172	0.294	6.683	.000*	-0.166	-0.234	-5.418	.000*
22	6.646	0.280	6.831	.000*	-0.124	-0.304	-7.574	.000*
23	0.692	0.021	0.409	.683	-0.103	-0.180	-3.646	.000*
24	-0.171	-0.010	-0.182	.856	-0.014	-0.044	-0.883	.378
Panel E: Legal status, decade of unitary status, state, the log (base 10) of the district's enrollment, and district's percent of white students								
17	12.008	0.290	6.547	.000*	-0.164	-0.231	-5.337	.000*
18	6.576	0.277	6.712	.000*	-0.123	-0.302	-7.501	.000*
19	0.439	0.013	0.258	.796	-0.099	-0.173	-3.489	.001*
20	-0.350	-0.020	-0.371	.710	-0.011	-0.036	-0.711	.478
Panel G: The log (base 10) of the district's enrollment and district's percent of white students								
25	10.817	0.262	6.276	.000*	-0.191	-0.269	-6.444	.000*
26	5.726	0.241	5.942	.000*	-0.145	-0.355	-8.746	.000*
27	1.797	0.055	1.188	.236	-0.112	-0.196	-4.223	.000*
28	0.423	0.024	0.506	.613	-0.016	-0.051	-1.076	.282
Panel H: The log (base 10) of the district's enrollment, district's percent of white students, and state								
29	12.822	0.310	7.222	.000*	-0.177	-0.249	-6.124	.000*
30	7.085	0.298	7.426	.000*	-0.132	-0.324	-8.524	.000*
31	1.432	0.044	0.864	.388	-0.117	-0.204	-4.363	.000*
32	0.183	0.010	0.198	.843	-0.017	-0.056	-1.167	.244

* Indicates significance at the 0.05 level.

Caption: Regardless of what other factors are in the model, each step-up in district size results in a statistically significant increase in the average 2004/05 dissimilarity index, an approximate 12 percent, and, similarly, in the average 2004/05 entropy index, an estimated 6 to 7 percent increase. District size does not have statistically significant effects on the change over time in either index. The district's percent of white students has a statistically significant negative effect on three of the desegregation measures, regardless of the other factors in the regression equation. A district's white enrollment does not significantly affect the change in entropy over time in any of the models.

Source: Compiled by U.S. Commission on Civil Rights.

The effect parameters for the district's size estimated in various models appears in the left side of table A.8. The results indicate for the dissimilarity index, nearly all models estimate a 12 percent or more increase in the average dissimilarity index of districts for each step-up in size. (See models 9, 21, 17, and 29.) Thus, districts with 10,000 to 99,999 students would need to reassign, on average, approximately 12 percent more pupils to achieve a perfect racial balance than schools with 1,000 to 9,999 students. Similarly, districts with enrollments greater than 100,000 would need to reassign, on average, about 12 percent more of their students than those with 10,000 to 99,999 pupils.

Using entropy, the results are about half as great. (See models 10, 22, 18, 26, and 30.) Districts with 10,000 to 99,999 students would need to reassign about 6 to 7 percent more of their students to achieve perfect racial balance than the next smaller category of districts.

These effects of district size are statistically significant for both the 2004/05 dissimilarity and entropy indices and whether or not the models include state, legal status, or a decade effect. However, district size does not have statistically significant effects on the change over time in dissimilarity and entropy indices, regardless of what other factors are in the model. (See models 11, 12, 23, 24, 19, 20, 27, 28, 31, and 32).

The analysis of the district's percent of white students, shown in the right side of table A.8, has a statistically significant effect on three of the four desegregation measures. The effect appears in each of the models for these three measures, regardless of the other factors in the regression equation. The statistically significant effect is *negative*. Thus, for example, for each 1 percent increase in a district's percent of white students, a district's dissimilarity index is about 0.2 percent lower (e.g., -0.181 in model 9, panel C). In chapter 5, table 5.4, for example, compared districts with white enrollments of less than 25 percent, 25 to less than 50 percent, and so forth. The effect shown in table A.8 associates a 4.5 percent decease in the dissimilarity index, for example, in model 9, with each 25 percent increase in white enrollment. The effects remain statistically significant but are smaller for the entropy index, and smaller still for the over time change in the dissimilarity index. The percent of the district's white enrollment is not a useful explanatory factor for the change in the entropy index over time. It is insignificant for that measure in all the models.

Levels of racial concentration by the decade of obtaining unitary status

Panel F of table A.7 showed that whether a district received its unitary status before or after the year 2000 explained a significant additional amount of variance relative to other variables in the model. This result occurred for all of the desegregation measures used in this study. Table A.9 shows the effects. The analysis estimates that, on average, a district that received unitary status in 2000 or after has a dissimilarity index that is 10.2 percent lower (note the unstandardized coefficient) than one that obtained release from court supervision earlier. Similarly, it has an entropy measure that is 6.7 percent lower; a decrease in dissimilarity index across more than a decade of 9.9 percent; and a reduction in the entropy index over time of 6.3 percent. All of these effects are statistically significant. Indeed, the starkly large effects for the change measures over time contrasts with insignificant results in most other analysis in tables A.5 to A.8.

Table A.9

Regression results: Explaining districts' desegregation with a distinction in unitary systems that received recognition for their status in the year 2000 or later

Model Key	The desegregation measure and explanatory factors in the analysis	The effect of receiving unitary status in 2000 or thereafter			
		Unstandarized coefficient	Standardized coefficient	t-test	Significance (p-level)
Panel F: Legal status, whether the district obtained unitary status before or after 2000, state, the log (base 10) of the district's enrollment, and district's percent of white students					
21	Dissimilarity index in 2004/05 school year	-10.179	-0.195	-3.538	.000*
22	Entropy index in 2004/05 school year	-6.688	-0.224	-4.352	.000*
23	Change in dissimilarity index from 1992/93 (or 1993/94) to 2004/05	-9.944	-0.234	-3.824	.000*
24	Change in entropy index from 1992/93 (or 1993/94) to 2004/05	-6.342	-0.275	-4.393	.000*

* Indicates significance at the 0.05 level.

Caption: For each of the desegregation measures, districts that received unitary status after the year 2000 had significantly less racial imbalance than districts recognized as unitary earlier. The imbalance is 10.2 percent less on the dissimilarity index, 6.7 percent lower on the entropy index, 9.9 percent less on the dissimilarity index over time, and a 6.3 percent reduction on the entropy index over time.

Source: Compiled by U.S. Commission on Civil Rights.

Conclusion

Technical details of the statistical analyses contained in this appendix bear out the conclusions found in chapter 5 of the report. A district's size, its proportion of white enrollment, and the state in which it is located have important effects on the racial/ethnic balance of students among its schools. Specifically, larger districts and those with small proportions of white students have greater racial/ethnic concentrations of students in schools.

Also important to a district's level of racial/ethnic concentration is whether or not the district received recognition of its unitary status since 2000. Districts that obtained unitary recognition in the 2000s have racial and ethnic groups spread more evenly throughout their schools than systems that became unitary in the 1970s, 1980s, and 1990s. The district's legal status is a determinant of the level of its racial imbalance because of differences arising from when districts gained recognition of their unitary status.

APPENDIX B: ALABAMA PUBLIC SCHOOLS' DESEGREGATION STATUS

Table B.1
Alabama Districts With Unitary Status

District Name	Case Name	Year Case Initiated	Intent regarding unitary status	Year Unitary Status attained
ALEXANDER CITY	Lee & U.S.& NEA v. Alexander City Bd. of Educ.	1963	N/A	2004
ANDALUSIA CITY	Lee & NEA & U.S. v. Andalusia City Bd. of Educ.	1963	N/A	2002
ATTALLA CITY	Lee & U.S. v. Macon County Bd. of Educ.	1966	N/A	2006
AUBURN CITY	Lee & U.S. & NEA v. Auburn City Bd. of Educ.	1966	N/A	2002
AUTAUGA COUNTY	Lee & U.S. & NEA v. Autauga County Bd. of Educ.	1963	N/A	2005
BALDWIN COUNTY	Lee & U.S. & NEA v. Baldwin County Bd. of Educ.	1966	N/A	1977
BESSEMER CITY	Brown & U.S. v. Bd. of Educ. of City of Bessemer	1965	N/A	2006
BIBB COUNTY	Lee, U.S. & Nat'l Educ. Ass'n, Inc. v. Macon County Bd. of Educ. (Bibb County Sch. Dist.)	1966	N/A	2006
BIRMINGHAM CITY	Armstrong & U.S. v. Bd. of Educ. of City of Birmingham	1960	N/A	1983
BLOUNT COUNTY	Lee & U.S. v. Macon County Bd. of Educ., et al.	1963	N/A	2005
BREWTON CITY	Lee & U.S. & NEA v. Brewton City Sch. Sys.	1966	N/A	1977
BULLOCK COUNTY	Harris & NEA & U.S. v. Bullock County Bd. of Educ.	1964	N/A	1999
BUTLER COUNTY	Lee & U.S. & NEA v. Butler County Bd. of Educ.	1966	N/A	2002
CHEROKEE COUNTY	Lee & U.S. v. Macon County Bd. of Educ., et al.	1963	N/A	2005
CHILTON COUNTY	Lee & U.S. & NEA v. Chilton County Bd. of Educ.	1963	N/A	2002
CLARKE COUNTY	Lee & U.S. & NEA v. Clarke County Bd. of Educ.	1966	N/A	1977
COFFEE COUNTY	Lee & NEA & U.S. v. Coffee County Bd. of Educ.	1963	N/A	2004
CONECUH COUNTY	Lee & U.S. v. Macon County Bd. of Educ.	1966	N/A	1979
COOSA COUNTY	Lee & National Education Association, Inc. v. Coosa County Bd. of Educ.	1963	N/A	2006
COVINGTON COUNTY	Lee & U.S. & NEA v. Covington County Bd. of Educ.	1963	N/A	2006
CRENSHAW COUNTY	Harris & U.S. & NEA v. Crenshaw County Bd. of Educ.	1966	N/A	2006
CULLMAN CITY	Lee & U.S. & NEA v. Macon County Bd. of Educ.	1966	N/A	2004
DALE COUNTY	Lee & NEA & U.S. v. Dale County Bd. of Educ.	1963	N/A	2005
DALEVILLE CITY	Lee & NEA & U.S. v. Daleville City Bd. of Educ.	1963	N/A	2002
DALLAS COUNTY	Lee & U.S. v. Dallas County Bd. of Educ.	1966	N/A	1977
DEKALB COUNTY	Lee & U.S. v. Macon County Bd. of Educ. (Dekalb County)	1966	N/A	2006

Continued

Table B.1 (continued)
Alabama Districts With Unitary Status

District Name	Case Name	Year Case Initiated	Intent regarding unitary status	Year Unitary Status attained
DEMOPOLIS CITY	Lee & U.S. v. Demoplis City School Sys.	1966	N/A	1979
ELBA CITY	Lee & NEA & U.S. v. Elba City Bd. of Educ.	1963	N/A	2004
ELMORE COUNTY	Lee & NEA & U.S. v. Elmore County Bd. of Educ.	1963	N/A	2004
ENTERPRISE CITY	Lee & NEA & U.S. v. Enterprise City Bd. of Educ.	1963	N/A	2003
ESCAMBIA COUNTY	Lee & U.S. & NEA v. Escambia County Bd. of Educ.	1966	N/A	1977
EUFAULA CITY	Lee & NEA & U.S. v. Eufaula City Bd. of Educ.	1963	N/A	2003
GADSDEN CITY	Miller & U.S. & NEA v. Bd. of Educ. of Gadsden	1963	N/A	2005
GENEVA COUNTY	Lee & U.S. & NEA v. Geneva County Bd. of Educ.	1963	N/A	2002
GREENE COUNTY	Lee & U.S. & NEA v. Macon County Bd. of Educ.	1966	N/A	2003
HALE COUNTY	U.S. v. Hale County Bd. of Educ.	1966	N/A	1982
HENRY COUNTY	Lee & NEA & U.S. v. Henry County Bd. of Educ.	1966	N/A	2006
JASPER CITY	Lee & U.S. & NEA v. Walker Co. & Jasper City Sch. Sys.	1966	N/A	1977
LEE COUNTY	Lee & U.S. & NEA v. Lee County BOE	1963	N/A	2005
LINDEN CITY	Lee & U.S. & NEA v. Linden City Sch. Sys.	1966	N/A	1977
LOWNDES COUNTY	U.S. v. Lowndes County Bd. of Educ.	1966	N/A	1991
MACON COUNTY	Lee & U.S. & NEA v. Macon County Bd. of Educ.	1963	N/A	2006
MARENGO COUNTY	Lee & U.S. v. Macon Co. Bd. of Educ.	1966	N/A	1983
MIDFIELD CITY	Stout & U.S. v. Bd. of Educ. of City of Midfield	1965	N/A	2006
MOBILE COUNTY	Davis & Gant & U.S. v. Bd. of Sch. Comm'nrs of Mobile Co.	1963	N/A	1997
MONROE COUNTY	Lee & U.S. & NEA v. Monroe County Bd. of Educ.	1966	N/A	1982
MONTGOMERY COUNTY	Carr & U.S. v. Montgomery County Bd. of Educ.	1964	N/A	1993
MT BROOK CITY[1]	Lee, U.S. & Nat'l Educ. Ass'n v. Macon County Bd. of Educ. (Mountain Brook Sch. Dist.)	1963	N/A	2005
ONEONTA CITY	Lee & U.S. v. Macon Co. Bd. of Educ.	1963	N/A	2005
OPELIKA CITY	Lee & U.S. & NEA v. Opelika City Bd. of Educ.	1963	N/A	2002
OPP CITY	Lee & U.S. & NEA v. Opp City Bd. of Educ.	1963	N/A	2002
OZARK CITY	Lee & U.S. & NEA v. Ozark City Bd. of Educ.	1963	N/A	2002
PERRY COUNTY	U.S. v. Perry County Bd. of Educ.	1966	N/A	1982
PHENIX CITY	Lee & U.S. & NEA v. Phoenix City Bd. of Educ.	1966	N/A	2005

Continued

Table B.1 (continued)
Alabama Districts With Unitary Status

District Name	Case Name	Year Case Initiated	Intent regarding unitary status	Year Unitary Status attained
PIKE COUNTY	Lee, U.S. & Nat'l Educ. Ass'n, Inc. v. Pike County Bd. of Educ.	1963	N/A	2007
ROANOKE CITY	Lee & U.S. v. Roanoke City Bd. of Educ.	1963	N/A	2007
RUSSELL COUNTY	Lee & U.S. & NEA v. Russell County Bd. of Educ.	1963	N/A	2002
SELMA CITY	Lee & U.S. & NEA v. Selma City Sch. Sys.	1966	N/A	1977
ST CLAIR COUNTY[2]	Lee & U.S. & NEA v. Macon County Bd. of Educ.	1963	N/A	2000
SYLACAUGA CITY	Lee & U.S. & NEA v. Sylacauga City Bd. of Educ.	1963	N/A	1995
TALLADEGA CITY	Lee & U.S. & NEA v. Talladega City Bd. of Educ.	1966	N/A	1993
TALLADEGA COUNTY	Lee & U.S. & NEA v. Talladega County Sch. Sys.	1966	N/A	1985
TALLAPOOSA COUNTY	Lee & U.S. & NEA v. Tallapoosa County Bd. of Educ.	1966	N/A	2004
TALLASSEE CITY	Lee & U.S. & NEA v. Tallassee City Bd. of Educ.	1963	N/A	2003
THOMASVILLE CITY	Lee & U.S. & NEA v. Thomasville City Bd. of Educ.	1966	N/A	1977
TROY CITY	Lee & U.S. & NEA v. Troy City Bd. of Educ.	1963	N/A	2005
TUSCALOOSA CITY	Lee & U.S. & NEA v. Macon County Bd. of Educ.	1963	N/A	2000
WALKER COUNTY	Lee & U.S. & NEA v. Walker Co. & Jasper City Sch. Sys.	1966	N/A	1977
WASHINGTON COUNTY	Lee & U.S. & NEA v. Washington County Bd. of Educ.	1966	N/A	1977
WILCOX COUNTY	U.S. v. Wilcox County Bd. of Educ.	1965	N/A	1979
WINSTON COUNTY	Lee & U.S. v. Winston County Bd. of Educ.	1963	N/A	2004

[1] Legal counsel for this school district maintains that "Mountain Brook has not been under the jurisdiction of the federal court in Alabama with regard to desegregation." Donald B. Sweeney, Jr., attorney, Mountain Brook City Board of Education, letter to David P. Blackwood, General Counsel, U.S. Commission on Civil Rights, July 6, 2007. The Commission could not independently confirm the district's claims, which are not reflected in U.S. Department of Justice (DOJ) records. *See* U.S. Department of Justice, Civil Rights Division (DOJ/CRD), Response to U.S. Commission on Civil Rights' (USCCR) Interrogatories and Document Requests, Exhibit 2, May 17, 2007.

[2] Commission records differ from U.S. Department of Justice, Civil Rights Division's Educational Opportunities Section (EOS) records for this district. EOS indicates that this case is still on their open case list, but the Commission's review of applicable court records indicates that this district was granted unitary status in 2000. Asheesh Agarwal, Deputy Assistant Attorney General, U.S. Department of Justice, letter to David Blackwood, General Counsel, U.S. Commission on Civil Rights, July 19, 2007, p. 1 (hereafter cited as "DOJ correspondence, July 19, 2007").

Source: Compiled by U.S. Commission on Civil Rights.

Table B.2
Alabama Districts Remaining Under Court Order

District Name	Case Name	Year Case Initiated	Intent regarding unitary status	Year Unitary Status attained
ANNISTON CITY	Lee & U.S. v. Macon County Bd. of Educ. (Anniston City Bd. of Educ.)	1963	District is working with DOJ towards a grant of unitary status	N/A
ATHENS CITY	Lee & U.S. v. Athens City Sch. Dist. (Limestone County)	1965	District is working with DOJ towards a grant of unitary status	N/A
BARBOUR COUNTY	Franklin & U.S. v. Barbour County Bd. of Educ.	1969	District is seeking unitary status	N/A
CALHOUN COUNTY	U.S. & Lee v. Macon County Bd. of Educ. (Calhoun County)	1966	District does not plan to seek unitary status	N/A
CHAMBERS COUNTY	U.S. & Lee v. Macon County Bd. of Educ. (Chambers County)	1966	District does not plan to seek unitary status	N/A
CHOCTAW COUNTY	U.S. v. Choctaw County Bd. of Educ.	1966	District does not plan to seek unitary status	N/A
CLAY COUNTY	U.S. & Lee v. Macon County Bd. of Educ. (Clay County)	1966	District is seeking unitary status	N/A
CLEBURNE COUNTY	U.S. & Lee v. Macon County Bd. of Educ. (Cleburne County)	1966	District has not made a decision about its intent	N/A
COLBERT COUNTY	U.S. & Lee v. Macon County Bd. of Educ. (Colbert County)	1966	District is working with DOJ towards a grant of unitary status	N/A
CULLMAN COUNTY	U.S. & Lee v. Macon County Bd. of Educ. (Cullman County)	1966	District did not reply to the Commission's inquiries	N/A

Continued

Table B.2 (continued)
Alabama Districts Remaining Under Court Order

District Name	Case Name	Year Case Initiated	Intent regarding unitary status	Year Unitary Status attained
DECATUR CITY	U.S. & Lee v. Macon County BOE (Decatur City)	1966	District is seeking unitary status	N/A
DOTHAN CITY	Lee & U.S. v. Dothan City Board of Education	1963	District is seeking unitary status	N/A
ETOWAH COUNTY[1]	U.S. & Lee v. Macon County Bd. of Educ. (Etowah County)	1966	District has not made a decision about its intent	N/A
FAIRFIELD CITY	U.S. & Boykins v. Bd. of Educ. of the City of Fairfield	1965	District does not plan to seek unitary status	N/A
FAYETTE COUNTY	U.S. & Lee v. Macon County Bd. of Educ. (Fayette County)	1966	District has not made a decision about its intent	N/A
FLORENCE CITY[2]	U.S. & Lee v. Macon County Bd. of Educ. (Florence City)	1966	District does not plan to seek unitary status	N/A
FORT PAYNE CITY	U.S. & Lee v. Macon County Bd. of Educ. (Fort Payne City)	1966	District is working with DOJ towards a grant of unitary status	N/A
FRANKLIN COUNTY	U.S. & Lee v. Macon Bd. of Educ. (Franklin County)	1966	District is working with DOJ towards a grant of unitary status	N/A
GUNTERSVILLE CITY	U.S. & Lee v. Macon Bd. of Educ. (Guntersville City)	1966	District is working with DOJ towards a grant of unitary status	N/A
HOMEWOOD CITY[3]	U.S. & Stout v. Homewood City Sch. Sys.	1966	District does not plan to seek unitary status	N/A
HOOVER CITY[4]	U.S. & Stout v. Hoover City Sch. Sys.	1966	District does not plan to seek unitary status	N/A
HOUSTON COUNTY	Lee & U.S. v. Houston County Bd. of Educ.	1963	District is seeking unitary status	N/A

Continued

Table B.2 (continued)
Alabama Districts Remaining Under Court Order

District Name	Case Name	Year Case Initiated	Intent regarding unitary status	Year Unitary Status attained
HUNTSVILLE CITY	U.S. & Hereford v. Huntsville City Sch. Dist.	1965	District plans to seek unitary status	N/A
JACKSON COUNTY	U.S. & Lee v. Macon County Bd. of Educ. (Jackson County)	1966	District is seeking unitary status	N/A
JACKSONVILLE CITY	U.S. & Lee v. Macon County Bd. of Educ. (Jacksonville City)	1966	District has not made a decision about its intent	N/A
JEFFERSON COUNTY	Stout & U.S. v. Jefferson County Bd. of Educ.	1965	District plans to seek unitary status	N/A
LAMAR COUNTY	U.S. & Lee v. Macon County Bd. of Educ. (Lamar County)	1966	District does not plan to seek unitary status	N/A
LANETT CITY	Lee & U.S. v. Lanett City Bd. of Educ.	1963	District does not plan to seek unitary status	N/A
LAUDERDALE COUNTY	U.S. & Lee v. Macon County Bd. of Educ. (Lauderdale County)	1966	District does not plan to seek unitary status	N/A
LAWRENCE COUNTY	U.S. & Horton v. Lawrence County Bd. of Educ.	1977	District is working with DOJ towards a grant of unitary status	N/A
LEEDS CITY[5]	U.S. & Stout v. City of Leeds Bd. of Educ.	1966	District does not plan to seek unitary status	N/A
LIMESTONE COUNTY	U.S. & Lee v. Macon County Bd. of Educ. (Limestone County)	1966	District is working with DOJ towards a grant of unitary status	N/A
MADISON COUNTY	Bennett & U.S. v. Madison County Bd. of Educ.	1965	District is seeking unitary status, case on appeal	N/A
MARION COUNTY	U.S. & Lee v. Macon County Bd. of Educ. (Marion County)	1966	District does not plan to seek unitary status	N/A

Continued

Table B.2 (continued)
Alabama Districts Remaining Under Court Order

District Name	Case Name	Year Case Initiated	Intent regarding unitary status	Year Unitary Status attained
MARSHALL COUNTY	U.S. & Lee v. Macon County Bd. of Educ. (Marshall County)	1966	District disputes status	N/A
MORGAN COUNTY	Lee & U.S. v. Macon County Bd. of Educ. (Morgan County School District)	1963	District is seeking unitary status	N/A
MUSCLE SHOALS CITY	Lee & U.S. v. Macon County Bd. of Educ. (Muscle Shoals School District)	1963	District disputes status	N/A
OXFORD CITY	Lee & U.S. v. Macon County Bd. of Educ. (Oxford City Board of Education)	1963	District plans to seek unitary status	N/A
PELL CITY	Lee & U.S. v. Macon County Bd. of Educ. (Pell City Board of Education)	1965	District is seeking unitary status	N/A
PICKENS COUNTY	Lee & U.S. v. Macon County Bd. of Educ. (Pickens County School System)	1963	District is working with DOJ towards a grant of unitary status	N/A
PIEDMONT CITY	Lee & U.S. v. Macon County Bd. of Educ. (Piedmont City School District)	1963	District has not made a decision about its intent	N/A
RANDOLPH COUNTY	Lee & U.S. v. Randolph County Bd. of Educ.	1963	District has not made a decision about its intent	N/A
RUSSELLVILLE CITY	U.S. & Lee v. Russellville Bd. of Educ.	1963	District is working with DOJ towards a grant of unitary status	N/A
SCOTTSBORO CITY	Lee & U.S. v. Macon County Bd. of Educ. (Scottsboro City School District)	1963	District does not plan to seek unitary status	N/A
SHEFFIELD CITY[6]	Lee & U.S. v. Colbert County Sch. Sys. (Sheffield City Bd. of Educ.)	1963	District is waiting for DOJ initiative	N/A
SHELBY COUNTY	U.S. & Lee v. Macon County Bd. of Educ. (Shelby County Sch. Dist.)	1963	District disputes status	N/A
SUMTER COUNTY	Lee & U.S. v. Macon County Bd. of Educ. (Sumter County Sch. Sys.)	1963	District did not reply to the Commission's inquiries	N/A

Continued

Table B.2 (continued)
Alabama Districts Remaining Under Court Order

District Name	Case Name	Year Case Initiated	Intent regarding unitary status	Year Unitary Status attained
TARRANT CITY	Lee & U.S. v. Macon County Bd. of Educ. (Tarrant City Bd. of Educ.)	1963	District has not made a decision about its intent	N/A
TRUSSVILLE CITY	Stout & United States v. Trussville City (Jefferson County Bd. of Educ.)	1965	Uncertain	N/A
TUSCALOOSA COUNTY	U.S. & Lee v. Macon County Bd. of Educ. (Tuscaloosa County)	1966	District disputes status	N/A
TUSCUMBIA CITY	Lee & U.S. v. Macon County Bd. of Educ. (City of Tuscumbia)	1963	District disputes status	N/A
VESTAVIA HILLS BOARD OF EDUCATION[7]	U.S. & Stout v. Vestavia Hills Bd. of Educ.	1965	District is seeking unitary status	N/A
WINFIELD CITY	Lee &. U.S. v. Macon County Bd. of Educ. (Winfield City School District)	1963	District does not plan to seek unitary status	N/A

[1] The Etowah County School District received unitary status on July 16, 2007. *See Lee & U.S. v. Etowah County Board of Education*, C.A. No. 70-251-S (N.D. Ga. July 16, 2007) (order granting unitary status). The Commission received this information after the final analyses were run, and thus the district's revised status is not reflected in the analyses.

[2] Legal counsel for this school district maintains that "The school district has been declared unitary and has been released from the court mandated desegregation order." J.R. Brooks, attorney, Florence City Board of Education, letter to David P. Blackwood, General Counsel, U.S. Commission on Civil Rights, July 10, 2007. The Commission could not independently confirm the district's claims, which are not reflected in DOJ records. *See* DOJ/CRD, Response to USCCR Interrogatories, Exhibit 1.

[3] Commission records differ from EOS records for this district. This district is one of several that were partitioned from the Jefferson County School District. EOS indicates that the initial court action date for such districts "is the date that the court approved the formation of the separate school districts." DOJ correspondence, July 19, 2007. The Commission traces the initial court action date to the original order affecting Jefferson County School District.

[4] Ibid.

[5] Ibid.

[6] Legal counsel for this school district maintains that "Sheffield School District was determined to be a unitary school system in 1979." Vincent McAlister, attorney, Sheffield City School District, letter to David P. Blackwood, General Counsel, U.S. Commission on Civil Rights, July 16, 2007. The Commission could not independently confirm the district's claims, which are not reflected in DOJ records. *See* U.S. DOJ/CRD, Response to USCCR Interrogatories, Exhibit 1.

[7] Commission records differ from EOS records for this district. This district is one of several that were partitioned from the Jefferson County School District. EOS indicates that the initial court action date for such districts "is the date that the court approved the formation of the separate school districts." DOJ correspondence, July 19, 2007. The Commission traces the initial court action date to the original order affecting Jefferson County School District.

Source: Compiled by U.S. Commission on Civil Rights.

Table B.3
Alabama Districts Not Subject to School Desegregation Litigation

District Name	Case Name	Year Case Initiated	Intent regarding unitary status	Year Unitary Status attained
ALBERTVILLE CITY	N/A	N/A	N/A	N/A
ARAB CITY	N/A	N/A	N/A	N/A
BOAZ CITY	N/A	N/A	N/A	N/A
GENEVA CITY	N/A	N/A	N/A	N/A
HALEYVILLE CITY	N/A	N/A	N/A	N/A
HARTSELLE CITY	N/A	N/A	N/A	N/A
MADISON CITY	N/A	N/A	N/A	N/A

Source: Compiled by U.S. Commission on Civil Rights.

APPENDIX C: FLORIDA PUBLIC SCHOOLS' DESEGREGATION STATUS

Table C.1
Florida Districts With Unitary Status

District Name	Case Name	Year Case Initiated	Intent regarding unitary status	Year Unitary Status attained
ALACHUA COUNTY SCHOOL DISTRICT	Wright v. Bd. of Pub. Instr. of Alachua County	{1964}	N/A	{1971}
BREVARD COUNTY SCHOOL DISTRICT	Weaver v. Pub. Instr. of Brevard County	1966	N/A	1976
SCHOOL BOARD OF BROWARD COUNTY	Washington v. Sch. Bd. of Broward County	1970	N/A	1996
COLUMBIA COUNTY SCHOOL DISTRICT	Zinnerman & U.S. v. Columbia Bd. of Pub. Instr.	{1970}	N/A	{1987}
DADE COUNTY SCHOOL DISTRICT	Gibson v. Dade County Schools Pate v. Dade County Sch. Bd.	1956 1969	N/A	2002
DUVAL COUNTY SCHOOL DISTRICT	Braxton v. Bd. of Pub. Instr. of Duval County	1960	N/A	1999
ESCAMBIA COUNTY SCHOOL DISTRICT	Augustus v. Sch.. of Escambia	1960	N/A	1999
GADSDEN COUNTY SCHOOL DISTRICT	U.S. v. Gadsden County Sch. Dist.	1970	N/A	1983
HILLSBOROUGH COUNTY SCHOOL DISTRICT	Manning v. Bd. of Pub. Instr. of Hillsborough County	1958	N/A	2001
LEE COUNTY SCHOOL DISTRICT	Blalock & U.S. v. Bd. of Pub. Instr. of Lee County	1964	N/A	1999
LEON COUNTY SCHOOL DISTRICT	Steele et al. v. Bd. of Pub. Instr. of Leon County	1962	N/A	1974
MARION COUNTY SCHOOL DISTRICT	U.S. v. Marion County Sch. Dist.	1978	N/A	2007
PALM BEACH COUNTY SCHOOL DISTRICT	Holland v. Bd. of Pub Instr. of Palm Beach County	1956	N/A	1979
PINELLAS COUNTY SCHOOL DISTRICT	Bradley v. Pinellas County Sch. Bd.	1964	N/A	2000
POLK COUNTY SCHOOL DISTRICT	Mills & U.S. v. Sch. Bd. of Polk County	1963	N/A	2000
SARASOTA COUNTY SCHOOL DISTRICT	Mays v. Sarasota County Bd. of Pub. Instruction	{1963}	N/A	1971
SEMINOLE COUNTY SCHOOL DISTRICT	U.S. v. Seminole County Sch. Dist.	1970	N/A	2006
ST. LUCIE COUNTY SCHOOL DISTRICT	U.S. v. Bd. of Pub Instr. of St. Lucie County	1970	N/A	1997
VOLUSIA COUNTY SCHOOL DISTRICT	Tillman v. Bd. of Pub. Instr. of Volusia County	1960	N/A	1970

{ } Brackets around years indicate Commission staff were unable to verify these years through the process described in the methodology section of chapter 4.
Source: Compiled by U.S. Commission on Civil Rights.

Table C.2
Florida Districts Remaining Under Court Order

District Name	Case Name	Year Case Initiated	Intent regarding unitary status	Year Unitary Status attained
BAKER COUNTY SCHOOL DISTRICT	U.S. v. Baker County, et. al.	1970	District does not plan to seek unitary status	N/A
BAY COUNTY SCHOOL DISTRICT	Youngblood v. Board of Pub. Instr. of Bay County	1966	Uncertain	N/A
BRADFORD COUNTY SCHOOL DISTRICT	U.S. v. Bradford County Sch. Dist.	1969	District is seeking unitary status	N/A
FLAGLER COUNTY SCHOOL DISTRICT	U.S. v. Baker County, et. al.	1970	District intends to seek unitary status	N/A
GULF COUNTY SCHOOL DISTRICT	U.S. v. Gadsden County, et. al.	1970	District does not plan to seek unitary status	N/A
HENDRY COUNTY SCHOOL DISTRICT[1]	U.S. v. Hendry County, et. al.	1970	Uncertain	N/A
INDIAN RIVER COUNTY SCHOOL DISTRICT	Sharpton v. Bd. of Pub. Instr. of Indian River County	1965	District does not plan to seek unitary status	N/A
JACKSON COUNTY SCHOOL DISTRICT	U.S. v. Gadsden County, et. al.	1970	Uncertain	N/A
JEFFERSON COUNTY SCHOOL DISTRICT	U.S. v. Gadsden County, et. al.	1970	District is working with DOJ towards a grant of unitary status	N/A
LAFAYETTE COUNTY SCHOOL DISTRICT	U.S. v. Gadsden County, et. al.	1970	District does not plan to seek unitary status	N/A
MANATEE COUNTY SCHOOL DISTRICT	Harvest v. Bd. of Pub. Instr. of Manatee County	1965	District does not plan to seek unitary status	N/A
ORANGE COUNTY SCHOOL DISTRICT	Ellis v. Bd. of Pub. Instr. of Orange County	1970	District is seeking unitary status	N/A
PASCO COUNTY SCHOOL DISTRICT[2]	U.S. v. Baker County, et. al.	1970	District does not plan to seek unitary status	N/A

Continued

Table C.2 (continued)
Florida Districts Remaining Under Court Order

District Name	Case Name	Year Case Initiated	Intent regarding unitary status	Year Unitary Status attained
ST. JOHNS COUNTY SCHOOL DISTRICT	U.S. v. Baker County, et. al.	1970	District does not plan to seek unitary status	N/A
WAKULLA COUNTY SCHOOL DISTRICT	U.S. v. Gadsden County, et. al.	1970	District does not plan to seek unitary status	N/A

[1]The superintendent of this district maintains that "the Hendry County School District obtained unitary status in 1975." Thomas W. Conner, superintendent, Hendry County School Board, letter to David P. Blackwood, General Counsel, U.S. Commission on Civil Rights, July 9, 2007. The Commission could not independently confirm the district's claims, which are not reflected in U.S. Department of Justice records. *See* U.S. Department of Justice, Civil Rights Division (DOJ/CRD), Response to U.S. Commission on Civil Rights' (USCCR) Interrogatories and Document Requests, Exhibit 1, May 17, 2007.

[2] An assistant superintendent for the school district maintains that "it is my belief that Pasco County schools were never subject to court ordered desegregation, and that any outstanding issues that existed between the District School Board of Pasco County and Department of Justice were resolved through the 1973 consent decree in which the courts granted the District School Board of Pasco County unitary status." Renalia DuBose, Assistant Superintendent for Administration, District School Board of Pasco County, letter to David P. Blackwood, General Counsel, U.S. Commission on Civil Rights, July 13, 2007. The Commission could not independently confirm the district's claims, which are not reflected in DOJ records. *See* DOJ/CRD, Response to USCCR Interrogatories, Exhibit 1.

Source: Compiled by U.S. Commission on Civil Rights.

Table C.3
Florida Districts Not Subject to School Desegregation Litigation

District Name	Case Name	Year Case Initiated	Intent regarding unitary status	Year unitary status attained
CALHOUN COUNTY SCHOOL DISTRICT	N/A	N/A	N/A	N/A
CHARLOTTE COUNTY SCHOOL DISTRICT	N/A	N/A	N/A	N/A
CITRUS COUNTY SCHOOL DISTRICT	N/A	N/A	N/A	N/A
CLAY COUNTY SCHOOL DISTRICT	N/A	N/A	N/A	N/A
COLLIER COUNTY SCHOOL DISTRICT	N/A	N/A	N/A	N/A
DESOTO COUNTY SCHOOL DISTRICT	N/A	N/A	N/A	N/A
DIXIE COUNTY SCHOOL DISTRICT	N/A	N/A	N/A	N/A
FRANKLIN COUNTY SCHOOL DISTRICT	N/A	N/A	N/A	N/A
GILCHRIST COUNTY SCHOOL DISTRICT	N/A	N/A	N/A	N/A
GLADES COUNTY SCHOOL DISTRICT	N/A	N/A	N/A	N/A
HAMILTON COUNTY SCHOOL DISTRICT	N/A	N/A	N/A	N/A
HARDEE COUNTY SCHOOL DISTRICT	N/A	N/A	N/A	N/A
HERNANDO COUNTY SCHOOL DISTRICT	N/A	N/A	N/A	N/A
HIGHLANDS COUNTY SCHOOL DISTRICT	N/A	N/A	N/A	N/A
HOLMES COUNTY SCHOOL DISTRICT	N/A	N/A	N/A	N/A
LAKE COUNTY SCHOOL DISTRICT	N/A	N/A	N/A	N/A
LEVY COUNTY SCHOOL DISTRICT	N/A	N/A	N/A	N/A
LIBERTY COUNTY SCHOOL DISTRICT	N/A	N/A	N/A	N/A

Continued

Table C.3 (continued)
Florida Districts Not Subject to School Desegregation Litigation

District Name	Case Name	Year Case Initiated	Intent regarding unitary status	Year unitary status attained
MADISON COUNTY SCHOOL DISTRICT	N/A	N/A	N/A	N/A
MARTIN COUNTY SCHOOL DISTRICT	N/A	N/A	N/A	N/A
MONROE COUNTY SCHOOL DISTRICT	N/A	N/A	N/A	N/A
NASSAU COUNTY SCHOOL DISTRICT	N/A	N/A	N/A	N/A
OKALOOSA COUNTY SCHOOL DISTRICT	N/A	N/A	N/A	N/A
OKEECHOBEE COUNTY SCHOOL DISTRICT	N/A	N/A	N/A	N/A
OSCEOLA COUNTY SCHOOL DISTRICT	N/A	N/A	N/A	N/A
PUTNAM COUNTY SCHOOL DISTRICT	N/A	N/A	N/A	N/A
SANTA ROSA COUNTY SCHOOL DISTRICT	N/A	N/A	N/A	N/A
SUMTER COUNTY SCHOOL DISTRICT	N/A	N/A	N/A	N/A
SUWANNEE COUNTY SCHOOL DISTRICT	N/A	N/A	N/A	N/A
TAYLOR COUNTY SCHOOL DISTRICT	N/A	N/A	N/A	N/A
UNION COUNTY SCHOOL DISTRICT	N/A	N/A	N/A	N/A
WALTON COUNTY SCHOOL DISTRICT	N/A	N/A	N/A	N/A
WASHINGTON COUNTY SCHOOL DISTRICT	N/A	N/A	N/A	N/A

Source: Compiled by U.S. Commission on Civil Rights.

APPENDIX D: GEORGIA PUBLIC SCHOOLS' DESEGREGATION STATUS

Table D.1
Georgia Districts With Unitary Status

District Name	Case Name	Year Case Initiated	Intent regarding unitary status	Year Unitary Status attained
ATLANTA CITY	Vivian Calhoun v. Ed. S. Cook	1958	N/A	1979
BAKER COUNTY	U.S. & Ridley v. State of Georgia (Baker County Sch. Dist.)	1969	N/A	2007
BLECKLEY COUNTY	U.S. & Ridley v. State of Georgia (Bleckley County School. Dist.)	1969	N/A	2006
BROOKS COUNTY	U.S. & Ridley v. State of Georgia (Brooks)	1969	N/A	2005
BULLOCH COUNTY	U.S. v. The Bd. of Ed. of Bulloch County, Georgia, et al.	Uncertain	N/A	2001
BUTTS COUNTY	U.S. & Ridley v. State of Georgia (Butts)	1969	N/A	2005
CHATHAM COUNTY	Stell v. Savannah-Chatham	1962	N/A	1994
CHATTAHOOCHEE COUNTY	U.S. & Ridley v. State of Georgia (Chattahoochee)	1969	N/A	2006
CLAY COUNTY	U.S. & Ridley v. State of Georgia (Clay)	1969	N/A	2006
CLAYTON COUNTY[1]	U.S. v. Bd. of Ed. Of Clayton County	Uncertain	N/A	1977
COFFEE COUNTY	U.S. v. Coffee County	1969	N/A	1995
DEKALB COUNTY	Mills v. Freeman	1968	N/A	1996
ECHOLS COUNTY	U.S. & Ridley v. State of Georgia (Echols)	1969	N/A	2005
FULTON COUNTY	Hightower v. West	1970	N/A	2003
HANCOCK COUNTY	U.S. & Ridley v. State of Georgia (Hancock County Sch. Dist.)	1969	N/A	2007
JACKSON COUNTY	U.S. v. Jackson County	1969	N/A	1985
JASPER COUNTY	U.S. & Ridley v. State of Georgia (Jasper)	1969	N/A	2006
JEFFERSON CITY	U.S. v. Jackson County	1969	N/A	1985
LONG COUNTY	U.S. v. Bd. of Educ. Long County	1969	N/A	2003
LOWNDES COUNTY	U.S. v. Bd. of Educ. of Lowndes County	1968	N/A	2006
MCINTOSH COUNTY	U.S. & Ridley v. State of Georgia (McIntosh County Sch. Dist.)	1969	N/A	2006

Continued

Table D.1 (continued)
Georgia Districts With Unitary Status

District Name	Case Name	Year Case Initiated	Intent regarding unitary status	Year Unitary Status attained
MORGAN COUNTY	U.S. & Ridley v. State of Georgia (Morgan County Sch. Dist.)	1969	N/A	2006
MUSCOGEE COUNTY	Lockett v. Bd. of Educ. of Muscogee County	1971	N/A	1997
PELHAM CITY	U.S. & Ridley v. State of Georgia (Pelham City)	1969	N/A	2006
PUTNAM COUNTY	U.S. & Ridley v. State of Georgia (Putnam County Sch. Dist.)	1969	N/A	2007
QUITMAN COUNTY	U.S. & Ridley v. State of Georgia (Quitman County Sch. Dist.)	1969	N/A	2006
SCHLEY COUNTY	U.S. & Ridley v. State of Georgia (Schley County Sch. Dist.)	1969	N/A	2005
SEMINOLE COUNTY	United States v. State of Georgia (Seminole County Sch. Dist.)	1969	N/A	2006
THOMAS COUNTY	U.S. & Ridley v. State of Georgia (Thomas County Sch. Dist.)	1969	N/A	2006
TREUTLEN COUNTY	U.S. & Ridley v. State of Georgia (Treutlen County Sch. Dist.)	1969	N/A	2007
TROUP COUNTY	U.S. & Ridley v. State of Georgia (Troup)	1969	N/A	2003
WEBSTER COUNTY	U.S. & Bd. of Educ. of Webster County	1967	N/A	2006
WILKES COUNTY	U.S. & Ridley v. State of Georgia (Wilkes)	1969	N/A	2005

[1] The superintendent of this school district maintains that there is no federal school desegregation case with regard to Clayton County Public Schools. Barbara Pulliam, superintendent, Clayton County Public Schools, facsimile to David P. Blackwood, General Counsel, U.S. Commission on Civil Rights, July 11, 2007. The Commission disagrees. *See U.S. v. The Board of Education of Clayton County, Georgia,* C.A. No. 14709 (D. Ga. Mar. 11, 1977) (order dismissing action).

Source: Compiled by U.S. Commission on Civil Rights.

Table D.2
Georgia Districts Remaining Under Court Order

District Name	Case Name	Year Case Initiated	Intent regarding unitary status	Year Unitary Status attained
APPLING COUNTY	U.S. v. State of Georgia, et al.	1969	District does not plan to seek unitary status	N/A
ATKINSON COUNTY	U.S. v. State of Georgia, et al.	1969	District does not plan to seek unitary status	N/A
BALDWIN COUNTY	U.S. v. Baldwin County	1968	District is working with DOJ towards a grant of unitary status	N/A
BARROW COUNTY	U.S. v. State of Georgia, et al.	1969	District does not plan to seek unitary status	N/A
BEN HILL COUNTY	U.S. v. Ben Hill County Sch. Dist.	1967	District does not plan to seek unitary status	N/A
BIBB COUNTY[1]	Bivins v. Bibb County Bd. of Educ.	1965	District is seeking unitary status	N/A
BRYAN COUNTY	U.S. v. State of Georgia, et al.	1969	District does not plan to seek unitary status	N/A
CALHOUN COUNTY	U.S. v. State of Georgia, et al.	1969	Uncertain	N/A
CAMDEN COUNTY	U.S. v. State of Georgia, et al.	1969	District does not plan to seek unitary status	N/A
CANDLER COUNTY	U.S. v. State of Georgia, et al.	1969	District is working with DOJ towards a grant of unitary status	N/A
CHARLTON COUNTY	U.S. v. State of Georgia, et al.	1969	District did not reply to the Commission's inquiries	N/A
CLINCH COUNTY	U.S. v. Bd. of Educ. of Clinch County	1969	District did not reply to the Commission's inquiries	N/A

Continued

Table D.2 (continued)
Georgia Districts Remaining Under Court Order

District Name	Case Name	Year Case Initiated	Intent regarding unitary status	Year Unitary Status attained
COLQUITT COUNTY	Harrington v. Colquitt County Bd. of Educ.	1971	District intends to seek unitary status	N/A
COLUMBIA COUNTY	U.S. v. State of Georgia, et al.	1969	Uncertain	N/A
COOK COUNTY	U.S. v. State of Georgia, et al.	1969	District did not reply to the Commission's inquiries	N/A
COWETA COUNTY	U.S. v. State of Georgia, et al.	1969	District is working with DOJ towards a grant of unitary status	N/A
CRAWFORD COUNTY	U.S. v. State of Georgia, et al.	1969	Uncertain	N/A
CRISP COUNTY	U.S. v. Bd. of Educ. of Crisp County Schools	1968	District is working with DOJ towards a grant of unitary status	N/A
DECATUR CITY	U.S. v. State of Georgia, et al.	1969	District is working with DOJ towards a grant of unitary status	N/A
DECATUR COUNTY	U.S. v. Bd. of Educ. of Decatur County	1967	District does not plan to seek unitary status	N/A
DODGE COUNTY	U.S. v. Bd. of Educ. of Dodge County	1969	District does not plan to seek unitary status	N/A
DOOLY COUNTY	U.S. v. State of Georgia, et al.	1969	District does not plan to seek unitary status	N/A
DOUGHERTY COUNTY	Shirley Gaines, et al. v. Dougherty County Bd. of Educ., et al.	1963	District is seeking unitary status	N/A
DUBLIN CITY	U.S. v. State of Georgia, et al.	1969	District is seeking unitary status	N/A

Continued

Table D.2 (continued)
Georgia Districts Remaining Under Court Order

District Name	Case Name	Year Case Initiated	Intent regarding unitary status	Year Unitary Status attained
EARLY COUNTY	U.S. v. State of Georgia, et al.	1969	District does not plan to seek unitary status	N/A
ELBERT COUNTY	U.S. v. State of Georgia, et al.	1969	District did not reply to the Commission's inquiries	N/A
EMANUEL COUNTY	U.S. v. Bd. of Educ. of Emanuel County	1969	District does not plan to seek unitary status	N/A
GLASCOCK COUNTY	U.S. v. Bd. of Educ. of Glascock County	1969	District does not plan to seek unitary status	N/A
GLYNN COUNTY	Harris v. Glynn County	1963	District does not plan to seek unitary status	N/A
GRADY COUNTY	U.S. v. State of Georgia, et al.	1969	Uncertain	N/A
HARRIS COUNTY	U.S. v. State of Georgia, et al.	1969	District does not plan to seek unitary status	N/A
HART COUNTY	U.S. v. State of Georgia, et al.	1969	District does not plan to seek unitary status	N/A
IRWIN COUNTY	U.S. v. State of Georgia, et al.	1969	District does not plan to seek unitary status	N/A
JEFF DAVIS COUNTY	U.S. v. State of Georgia, et al.	1969	Uncertain	N/A
JEFFERSON COUNTY	U.S. v. State of Georgia, et al.	1969	District did not reply to the Commission's inquiries	N/A
JENKINS COUNTY	U.S. v. State of Georgia, et al.	1969	District does not plan to seek unitary status	N/A
JOHNSON COUNTY	U.S. v. Bd. of Educ. of Johnson County	1967	District does not plan to seek unitary status	N/A

Continued

Table D.2 (continued)
Georgia Districts Remaining Under Court Order

District Name	Case Name	Year Case Initiated	Intent regarding unitary status	Year Unitary Status attained
JONES COUNTY	U.S. v. State of Georgia, et al.	1969	District is working with DOJ towards a grant of unitary status	N/A
LAMAR COUNTY[2]	U.S. v. State of Georgia, et al.	1969	District does not plan to seek unitary status	N/A
LAURENS COUNTY[3]	U.S. v. State of Georgia, et al.	1969	District does not plan to seek unitary status	N/A
LEE COUNTY	U.S. v. State of Georgia, et al.	1969	District does not plan to seek unitary status	N/A
LINCOLN COUNTY	U.S. v. Lincoln County	1968	District does not plan to seek unitary status	N/A
MACON COUNTY	U.S. v. State of Georgia, et al.	1969	District did not reply to the Commission's inquiries	N/A
MARION COUNTY	U.S. v. State of Georgia, et al.	1969	District does not plan to seek unitary status	N/A
MCDUFFIE COUNTY	U.S. v. State of Georgia, et al.	1969	District did not reply to the Commission's inquiries	N/A
MERIWETHER COUNTY	U.S. & Ridley v. State of Georgia (Meriwether County Sch. Dist.)	1965	District is seeking unitary status	N/A
MILLER COUNTY	U.S. v. State of Georgia, et al.	1969	District does not plan to seek unitary status	N/A
MITCHELL COUNTY	U.S. v. State of Georgia, et al.	1969	District did not reply to the Commission's inquiries	N/A

Continued

Table D.2 (continued)
Georgia Districts Remaining Under Court Order

District Name	Case Name	Year Case Initiated	Intent regarding unitary status	Year Unitary Status attained
MONROE COUNTY	U.S. v. State of Georgia, et al.	1969	District does not plan to seek unitary status	N/A
MONTGOMERY COUNTY	U.S. v. State of Georgia, et al.	1969	District does not plan to seek unitary status	N/A
NEWTON COUNTY	U.S. v. State of Georgia, et al.	1969	District is undecided	N/A
PEACH COUNTY	U.S. v. State of Georgia, et al.	1969	District does not plan to seek unitary status	N/A
PULASKI COUNTY	U.S. v. State of Georgia, et al.	1969	District does not plan to seek unitary status	N/A
RANDOLPH COUNTY	U.S. v. State of Georgia, et al.	1969	District does not plan to seek unitary status	N/A
RICHMOND COUNTY	Acree v. Bd. of Educ. of Richmond County	1972	District did not reply to the Commission's inquiries	N/A
ROME CITY	U.S. v. State of Georgia, et al.	1969	District does not plan to seek unitary status	N/A
SCREVEN COUNTY	U.S. v. Bd. of Educ. Screven County	1969	District is working with DOJ towards a grant of unitary status	N/A
SUMTER COUNTY	U.S. v. State of Georgia, et al.	1969	District does not plan to seek unitary status	N/A
TATTNALL COUNTY[4]	U.S. v. State of Georgia, et al.	1969	District did not reply to the Commission's inquiries	N/A

Continued

Table D.2 (continued)
Georgia Districts Remaining Under Court Order

District Name	Case Name	Year Case Initiated	Intent regarding unitary status	Year Unitary Status attained
TAYLOR COUNTY	U.S. v. State of Georgia, et al.	1969	Uncertain	N/A
TELFAIR COUNTY	U.S. v. Bd. of Educ. of Telfair County	1969	District is working with DOJ towards a grant of unitary status	N/A
TERRELL COUNTY	U.S. v. State of Georgia, et al.	1969	District did not reply to the Commission's inquiries	N/A
TOOMBS COUNTY	U.S. v. State of Georgia, et al.	1969	District does not plan to seek unitary status	N/A
TURNER COUNTY	U.S. v. State of Georgia, et al.	1968	District is working with DOJ towards a grant of unitary status	N/A
TWIGGS COUNTY	U.S. v. State of Georgia, et al.	1969	District did not reply to the Commission's inquiries	N/A
VALDOSTA CITY	U.S. v. Bd. of Educ. of Valdosta City	1970	District intends to seek unitary status	N/A
VIDALIA CITY	U.S. v. State of Georgia, et al.	1969	District does not plan to seek unitary status	N/A
WALKER COUNTY	U.S. v. State of Georgia, et al.	1969	District is working with DOJ towards a grant of unitary status	N/A
WALTON COUNTY	Graves v. Walton County Bd. of Educ.	1963	District is seeking unitary status	N/A
WARREN COUNTY	U.S. v. State of Georgia, et al.	1969	District did not reply to the Commission's inquiries	N/A

Continued

Table D.2 (continued)
Georgia Districts Remaining Under Court Order

District Name	Case Name	Year Case Initiated	Intent regarding unitary status	Year Unitary Status attained
WASHINGTON COUNTY	Hilson v. Ouzts & Washington County Bd. of Educ.	1970	District did not reply to the Commission's inquiries	N/A
WAYNE COUNTY	U.S. v. State of Georgia, et al.	1969	District did not reply to the Commission's inquiries	N/A
WHEELER COUNTY	U.S. v. Wheeler County	1969	Uncertain	N/A
WILCOX COUNTY	U.S. v. State of Georgia, et al.	1969	District has not made a decision about its intent	N/A
WILKINSON COUNTY	U.S. v. State of Georgia, et al.	1969	District is seeking unitary status	N/A
WORTH COUNTY	U.S. v. State of Georgia, et al.	1969	District did not reply to the Commission's inquiries	N/A

[1] The Bibb County School District received unitary status on March 20, 2007. *See Garrett v. The Board of Public Education of Bibb County, Georgia*, No. 5:63-CV-1926 (D. Ga. Mar. 20, 2007) (order granting unitary status). The Commission received this information after the final analyses were run, and thus the district's revised status is not reflected in the analyses.

[2] The Lamar County School District received unitary status on June 18, 2007. *See U.S. v. State of Georgia, et al.*, C.A. No. 2771 (D. Ga. June 18, 2007) (order granting unitary status). The Commission received this information after the final analyses were run, and thus the district's revised status is not reflected in the analyses.

[3] Legal counsel for this school district maintains that the "Laurens County School District is not the subject of any Desegregation Order." Donald W. Gillis, attorney, Laurens County School District, letter to David P. Blackwood, General Counsel, U.S. Commission on Civil Rights, July 18, 2007. The Commission could not independently confirm the district's claims, which are not reflected in U.S. Department of Justice records. *See* U.S. Department of Justice, Civil Rights Division, Response to U.S. Commission on Civil Rights' Interrogatories and Document Requests, Exhibit 1, May 17, 2007.

[4] Legal counsel for the Tattnall County School District takes the position that the only order in effect is one issued by the United States District Court for the Southern District of Georgia in 1974 imposing a permanent injunction on the school district and not the initial desegregation order. B. Daniel Dubberly, Jr., attorney Tattnall County School District letter to the Office of General Counsel, U.S. Commission on Civil Rights, Aug. 16, 2007.

Source: Compiled by U.S. Commission on Civil Rights.

Table D.3
Georgia Districts Not Subject to School Desegregation Litigation

District Name	Case Name	Year Case Initiated	Intent regarding unitary status	Year Unitary Status attained
BACON COUNTY	N/A	N/A	N/A	N/A
BANKS COUNTY	N/A	N/A	N/A	N/A
BARTOW COUNTY	N/A	N/A	N/A	N/A
BERRIEN COUNTY	N/A	N/A	N/A	N/A
BRANTLEY COUNTY	N/A	N/A	N/A	N/A
BREMEN CITY	N/A	N/A	N/A	N/A
BUFORD CITY	N/A	N/A	N/A	N/A
BURKE COUNTY	N/A	N/A	N/A	N/A
CALHOUN CITY	N/A	N/A	N/A	N/A
CARROLL COUNTY	N/A	N/A	N/A	N/A
CARROLLTON CITY	N/A	N/A	N/A	N/A
CARTERSVILLE CITY	N/A	N/A	N/A	N/A
CATOOSA COUNTY	N/A	N/A	N/A	N/A
CHATTOOGA COUNTY	N/A	N/A	N/A	N/A
CHEROKEE COUNTY	N/A	N/A	N/A	N/A
CHICKAMAUGA CITY	N/A	N/A	N/A	N/A
CLARKE COUNTY	N/A	N/A	N/A	N/A
COBB COUNTY	N/A	N/A	N/A	N/A
COMMERCE CITY	N/A	N/A	N/A	N/A
DADE COUNTY	N/A	N/A	N/A	N/A
DALTON CITY	N/A	N/A	N/A	N/A
DAWSON COUNTY	N/A	N/A	N/A	N/A
DOUGLAS COUNTY	N/A	N/A	N/A	N/A
EFFINGHAM COUNTY	N/A	N/A	N/A	N/A
EVANS COUNTY	N/A	N/A	N/A	N/A
FANNIN COUNTY	N/A	N/A	N/A	N/A
FAYETTE COUNTY	N/A	N/A	N/A	N/A
FLOYD COUNTY	N/A	N/A	N/A	N/A
FORSYTH COUNTY	N/A	N/A	N/A	N/A
FRANKLIN COUNTY	N/A	N/A	N/A	N/A
GAINESVILLE CITY	N/A	N/A	N/A	N/A
GILMER COUNTY	N/A	N/A	N/A	N/A
GORDON COUNTY	N/A	N/A	N/A	N/A
GREENE COUNTY	N/A	N/A	N/A	N/A

Continued

Table D.3 (continued)
Georgia Districts Not Subject to School Desegregation Litigation

District Name	Case Name	Year Case Initiated	Intent regarding unitary status	Year Unitary Status attained
GWINNETT COUNTY	N/A	N/A	N/A	N/A
HABERSHAM COUNTY	N/A	N/A	N/A	N/A
HALL COUNTY	N/A	N/A	N/A	N/A
HARALSON COUNTY	N/A	N/A	N/A	N/A
HEARD COUNTY	N/A	N/A	N/A	N/A
HENRY COUNTY	N/A	N/A	N/A	N/A
HOUSTON COUNTY	N/A	N/A	N/A	N/A
LANIER COUNTY	N/A	N/A	N/A	N/A
LIBERTY COUNTY	N/A	N/A	N/A	N/A
LUMPKIN COUNTY	N/A	N/A	N/A	N/A
MADISON COUNTY	N/A	N/A	N/A	N/A
MARIETTA CITY	N/A	N/A	N/A	N/A
MURRAY COUNTY	N/A	N/A	N/A	N/A
OCONEE COUNTY	N/A	N/A	N/A	N/A
OGLETHORPE COUNTY	N/A	N/A	N/A	N/A
PAULDING COUNTY	N/A	N/A	N/A	N/A
PICKENS COUNTY	N/A	N/A	N/A	N/A
PIERCE COUNTY	N/A	N/A	N/A	N/A
PIKE COUNTY	N/A	N/A	N/A	N/A
POLK COUNTY	N/A	N/A	N/A	N/A
RABUN COUNTY	N/A	N/A	N/A	N/A
ROCKDALE COUNTY	N/A	N/A	N/A	N/A
SOCIAL CIRCLE CITY	N/A	N/A	N/A	N/A
SPALDING COUNTY	N/A	N/A	N/A	N/A
STEPHENS COUNTY	N/A	N/A	N/A	N/A
STEWART COUNTY	N/A	N/A	N/A	N/A
TALBOT COUNTY	N/A	N/A	N/A	N/A
TALIAFERRO COUNTY	N/A	N/A	N/A	N/A
THOMASTON-UPSON COUNTY	N/A	N/A	N/A	N/A
THOMASVILLE CITY	N/A	N/A	N/A	N/A
TIFT COUNTY	N/A	N/A	N/A	N/A
TOWNS COUNTY	N/A	N/A	N/A	N/A
TRION CITY	N/A	N/A	N/A	N/A
UNION COUNTY	N/A	N/A	N/A	N/A
WARE COUNTY	N/A	N/A	N/A	N/A
WHITE COUNTY	N/A	N/A	N/A	N/A
WHITFIELD COUNTY	N/A	N/A	N/A	N/A

Source: Compiled by U.S. Commission on Civil Rights.

APPENDIX E: LOUISIANA PUBLIC SCHOOLS' DESEGREGATION STATUS

Table E.1
Louisiana Districts With Unitary Status

District Name	Case Name	Year Case Initiated	Intent regarding unitary status	Year Unitary Status attained
ACADIA PARISH SCHOOL BOARD	Battiste v. Acadia Parish Sch. Bd.	1965	N/A	1981
ASCENSION PARISH SCHOOL BOARD	U.S. & Charles v. Ascension Parish Sch. Bd.	1965	N/A	2004
EAST BATON ROUGE PARISH SCHOOL BOARD	U.S. & Davis v. E. Baton Rouge Parish Sch. Bd.	1956	N/A	2003
GRANT PARISH SCHOOL BOARD	U.S. v. Grant Parish Sch. Bd.	1966	N/A	2007
IBERIA PARISH SCHOOL BOARD	Henderson v. Iberia Parish Sch. Bd.	1965	N/A	1970
IBERVILLE PARISH SCHOOL BOARD	U.S. & Williams v. Iberville Parish Sch. Bd.	1964	N/A	2002
LAFAYETTE PARISH SCHOOL BOARD	Alfreda Trahan, et al. v. Sch. Bd. of Lafayette, et al.	1965	N/A	2006
LIVINGSTON PARISH SCHOOL BOARD	U.S. & Dunn v. Livingston Parish Sch. Bd.	1965	N/A	2001
RAPIDES PARISH SCHOOL BOARD	U.S. & Valley v. Rapides Parish Sch. Bd.	1969	N/A	2006
RED RIVER PARISH SCHOOL BOARD	U.S. v. Red River Parish Sch. Bd.	1969	N/A	2005

Continued

Table E.1 (continued)
Louisiana Districts With Unitary Status

District Name	Case Name	Year Case Initiated	Intent regarding unitary status	Year Unitary Status attained
SAINT BERNARD PARISH SCHOOL BOARD	U.S. v. St. Bernard Parish Sch. Bd.	1966	N/A	2006
SAINT MARTIN PARISH SCHOOL BOARD[1]	U.S. v. St. Martin Sch. Bd.	1965	N/A	1974
SAINT MARY PARISH SCHOOL BOARD[2]	Gwen Boudreaux v. St. Mary Parish Sch. Bd.	1965	N/A	Uncertain
TENSAS PARISH SCHOOL BOARD	U.S. v. Tensas Parish Sch. Bd.	1966	N/A	2005
VERMILION PARISH SCHOOL BOARD[3]	Vira Celestain v. Vermilion Parish Sch. Bd.	1966	N/A	1974
WEST FELICIANA PARISH SCHOOL BOARD	Carter & U.S. v. Sch. Bd. of West Feliciana	1983	N/A	2007

[1] Commission records differ from U.S. Department of Justice, Civil Rights Division's Educational Opportunities Section (EOS) records for this district. EOS indicates that this case is still on their open case list, but the Commission's review of applicable court records indicates that this district was granted unitary status in 1974. Asheesh Agarwal, Deputy Assistant Attorney General, U.S. Department of Justice, letter to David Blackwood, General Counsel, U.S. Commission on Civil Rights , July 19, 2007, p. 1 (hereafter cited as "DOJ correspondence, July 19, 2007").

[2] The superintendent contends that the St. Mary Parish School Board "was declared a unitary system" on April 9, 1975. Donald W. Aguillard, superintendent, St. Mary Parish School Board, letter to David P. Blackwood, General Counsel, U.S. Commission on Civil Rights, July 10, 2007. Since the district continued to submit bi-annual reports to the court until 1983, the Commission remains uncertain about the year in which the district gained unitary status. *Boudreaux v. St. Mary Parish School Board, et al.*, C.A. No. 11351, U.S. District Court for the Western District of Louisiana, Civil Docket Sheet.

[3] Commission records differ from EOS records for this district. EOS indicates that this case is still on their open case list, but the Commission's review of applicable court records indicates that this district was granted unitary status in 1974. DOJ correspondence, July 19, 2007.

Source: Compiled by U.S. Commission on Civil Rights.

Table E.2
Louisiana Districts Remaining Under Court Order

District Name	Case Name	Year Case Initiated	Intent regarding unitary status	Year Unitary Status attained
AVOYELLES PARISH SCHOOL BOARD	U.S. v. Avoyelles Parish Sch. Bd.	1966	District did not reply to the Commission's inquiries	N/A
BIENVILLE PARISH SCHOOL BOARD	U.S. v. Bienville	1966	District has not made a decision about its intent	N/A
BOSSIER PARISH SCHOOL BOARD	Lemon & U.S. v. Bossier Parish Sch. Bd.	1964	District is seeking unitary status	N/A
CADDO PARISH SCHOOL BOARD	Jones & U.S. v. Caddo Parish Sch. Bd.	1965	District has not made a decision about its intent	N/A
CALCASIEU PARISH SCHOOL BOARD	Conley v. Lake Charles Sch. Bd.	1968	District intends to seek unitary status	N/A
CALDWELL PARISH SCHOOL BOARD	U.S. v. Caldwell	1971	District does not plan to seek unitary status	N/A
CATAHOULA PARISH SCHOOL BOARD	U.S. v. Catahoula	1966	District intends to seek unitary status	N/A
CITY OF BOGALUSA SCHOOL BOARD	Jenkins & U.S. v. Sch. Bd. of Bogalusa City	1965	District has not made a decision about its intent	N/A
CITY OF MONROE SCHOOL BOARD	Andrews & U.S. v. Monroe City Sch. Bd.	1978	District does not plan to seek unitary status	N/A
CLAIBORNE PARISH SCHOOL BOARD	Banks & U.S. v. Claiborne Parish Sch. Bd.	1965	District does not plan to seek unitary status	N/A
CONCORDIA PARISH SCHOOL BOARD	Smith & U.S. v. Concordia Parish Sch. Bd.	1966	District does not plan to seek unitary status	N/A
DESOTO PARISH SCHOOL BOARD	U.S. v. DeSoto Parish Sch. Bd.	1967	District does not plan to seek unitary status	N/A

Continued

Table E.2 (continued)
Louisiana Districts Remaining Under Court Order

District Name	Case Name	Year Case Initiated	Intent regarding unitary status	Year Unitary Status attained
EAST CARROLL PARISH SCHOOL BOARD	U.S. v. E. Carroll	1967	District did not reply to the Commission's inquiries	N/A
EAST FELICIANA PARISH SCHOOL BOARD	Hall v. St. Helena Sch. Bd.	1965	District is seeking unitary status	N/A
EVANGELINE PARISH SCHOOL BOARD	U.S. & Graham v. Evangeline	1971	District is seeking unitary status	N/A
FRANKLIN PARISH SCHOOL BOARD	U.S. v. Franklin	1970	District intends to seek unitary status	N/A
JACKSON PARISH SCHOOL BOARD	U.S. & Johnson v. Jackson	1966	District did not reply to the Commission's inquiries	N/A
JEFFERSON DAVIS PARISH SCHOOL BOARD	Gordon v. Jeff. Davis Parish Sch. Bd.	1970	District is seeking unitary status	N/A
JEFFERSON PARISH SCHOOL BOARD	Dandridge v. Jefferson Parish Sch. Bd.	1969	District has not made a decision about its intent	N/A
LAFOURCHE PARISH SCHOOL BOARD	Hill v. Lafourche Parish Sch. Bd.	1967	District did not reply to the Commission's inquiries	N/A
LASALLE PARISH SCHOOL BOARD	U.S. v. LaSalle	1966	District has no position on seeking unitary status	N/A
LINCOLN PARISH SCHOOL BOARD	U.S. v. Lincoln	1966	District does not plan to seek unitary status	N/A

Continued

Table E.2 (continued)
Louisiana Districts Remaining Under Court Order

District Name	Case Name	Year Case Initiated	Intent regarding unitary status	Year Unitary Status attained
MADISON PARISH SCHOOL BOARD	Williams v. Kimbrough	1969	District has no position on seeking unitary status	N/A
MOREHOUSE PARISH SCHOOL BOARD	U.S. v. Morehouse	1969	District does not plan to seek unitary status	N/A
NATCHITOCHES PARISH SCHOOL BOARD	Robertson v. Nat. Parish Sch. Bd.	1970	District has no position on seeking unitary status	N/A
ORLEANS PARISH SCHOOL BOARD	Bush v. Orleans Parish Sch. Bd.	1956	District did not reply to the Commission's inquiries	N/A
OUACHITA PARISH SCHOOL BOARD	Taylor v. Ouachita Parish Sch. Bd.	1970	District plans to seek unitary status	N/A
PLAQUEMINES PARISH SCHOOL BOARD	U.S. v. Plaquemines Parish Bd. of Educ.	1966	Uncertain	N/A
POINTE COUPEE PARISH SCHOOL BOARD	U.S. & Boyd v. Ponte Coupee	1966	District does not plan to seek unitary status	N/A
RICHLAND PARISH SCHOOL BOARD	U.S. v. Richland	1966	District has not made a decision about its intent	N/A
SABINE PARISH SCHOOL BOARD	U.S. v. Sabine	1977	District does not plan to seek unitary status	N/A
SAINT HELENA PARISH SCHOOL BOARD	U.S. & Hall v. St. Helena	1965	District plans to seek unitary status	N/A
SAINT JAMES PARISH SCHOOL BOARD	U.S. & Banks v. St. James	1966	District did not reply to the Commission's inquiries	N/A

Continued

Table E.2 (continued)
Louisiana Districts Remaining Under Court Order

District Name	Case Name	Year Case Initiated	Intent regarding unitary status	Year Unitary Status attained
SAINT JOHN THE BAPTIST PARISH SCHOOL BOARD	Duhon & U.S. v. St. John The Baptist Sch. Bd.	1966	District has not made a decision about its intent	N/A
SAINT LANDRY PARISH SCHOOL BOARD	U.S. v. St. Landry	1969	District is seeking unitary status	N/A
SAINT TAMMANY PARISH SCHOOL BOARD	U.S. & Smith v. St. Tamany	1966	District disputes status	N/A
TANGIPAHOA PARISH SCHOOL BOARD	Moore v. Tang. Parish Sch. Bd.	1968	District is seeking unitary status	N/A
TERREBONNE PARISH SCHOOL BOARD	Redman v. Terrebonne Parish Sch. Bd.	1967	District does not plan to seek unitary status	N/A
UNION PARISH SCHOOL BOARD	Cleveland v. Union Parish Sch. Bd.	1969	District plans to seek unitary status	N/A
WASHINGTON PARISH SCHOOL BOARD	Moses v. Washington Parish Sch. Bd.	1967	District did not reply to the Commission's inquiries	N/A
WEBSTER PARISH SCHOOL BOARD	Gilbert v. Webster Parish Sch. Bd.	1974	District did not reply to the Commission's inquiries	N/A
WEST BATON ROUGE PARISH SCHOOL BOARD	U.S. & Davis v. W. Baton Rouge	1969	District does not plan to seek unitary status	N/A
WEST CARROLL PARISH SCHOOL BOARD	U.S. v. W. Carroll	1969	District is seeking unitary status	N/A

Source: Compiled by U.S. Commission on Civil Rights.

Table E.3
Louisiana Districts Not Subject to School Desegregation Litigation

District Name	Case Name	Year Case Initiated	Intent regarding unitary status	Year Unitary Status attained
ALLEN PARISH SCHOOL BOARD	N/A	N/A	N/A	N/A
ASSUMPTION PARISH SCHOOL BOARD	N/A	N/A	N/A	N/A
BEAUREGARD PARISH SCHOOL BOARD	N/A	N/A	N/A	N/A
CAMERON PARISH SCHOOL BOARD	N/A	N/A	N/A	N/A
CITY OF BAKER SCHOOL DISTRICT	N/A	N/A	N/A	N/A
SAINT CHARLES PARISH SCHOOL BOARD	N/A	N/A	N/A	N/A
VERNON PARISH SCHOOL BOARD	N/A	N/A	N/A	N/A
WINN PARISH SCHOOL BOARD	N/A	N/A	N/A	N/A
ZACHARY COMMUNITY SCHOOL DISTRICT	N/A	N/A	N/A	N/A

Source: Compiled by U.S. Commission on Civil Rights.

APPENDIX F: MISSISSIPPI PUBLIC SCHOOLS' DESEGREGATION STATUS

Table F.1
Mississippi Districts With Unitary Status

District Name	Case Name	Year Case Initiated	Intent regarding unitary status	Year Unitary Status attained
BILOXI PUBLIC SCHOOL DISTRICT	Gilbert R. Maso, Jr., et al. v. Biloxi Municipal Separate Sch. Dist.	1963	N/A	2002
CALHOUN COUNTY SCHOOL DISTRICT	US. v. Calhoun	1966	N/A	2007
COFFEEVILLE SCHOOL DISTRICT	US. v. Coffeeville Sch. Dist.	1969	N/A	2007
CORINTH SCHOOL DISTRICT	U.S. v. Corinth MSSD	1966	N/A	1976
EAST TALLAHATCHIE CONSOLIDATED SCHOOL DISTRICT	U.S. v. East Tallahatchie	1970	N/A	2003
GREENVILLE PUBLIC SCHOOLS	Edwards v. Greenville	1970	N/A	1994
GRENADA SCHOOL DISTRICT	Cunningham v. Grenada	1966	N/A	1985
HARRISON COUNTY SCHOOL DISTRICT	U.S. v. State of Mississippi & Harrison County	1970	N/A	2003
HATTIESBURG PUBLIC SCHOOL DISTRICT	U.S. v. State of Mississippi & Hattiesburg	1970	N/A	1997
HAZLEHURST CITY SCHOOL DISTRICT	U.S. v. State of Mississippi & Hazlehurst	1970	N/A	2005
HINDS COUNTY SCHOOL DISTRICT	U.S. v. Hinds Co. Bd. of Educ.	1967	N/A	1984
HUMPHREYS COUNTY SCHOOL DISTRICT	U.S. v. Humphreys County	1966	N/A	2003
LEFLORE COUNTY SCHOOL DISTRICT	Young v. LeFlore	1966	N/A	2005
MADISON COUNTY SCHOOL DISTRICT	Anderson & U.S. v. Madison County	1965	N/A	2006
MARSHALL COUNTY SCHOOL DISTRICT	Clarence M. Anthony, et al. v. Marshall County	1968	N/A	2005
NATCHEZ-ADAMS SCHOOL DISTRICT	U.S. v. Natchez Special MSSD	1965	N/A	2003
NEWTON COUNTY SCHOOL DISTRICT	U.S. v. State of Mississippi & Newton County	1970	N/A	2003
NOXUBEE COUNTY SCHOOL DISTRICT	U.S. v. Noxubee	1966	N/A	2004

Continued

Table F.1 (continued)
Mississippi Districts With Unitary Status

District Name	Case Name	Year Case Initiated	Intent regarding unitary status	Year Unitary Status attained
OXFORD SCHOOL DISTRICT	Robert Earl Quarles, et al. v. Oxford MSSD	1969	N/A	1988
SOUTH DELTA SCHOOL DISTRICT	Jeremiah Blackwell & U.S. v. South Delta Sch. Dist.	1966	N/A	2004
SUNFLOWER COUNTY SCHOOL DISTRICT	U.S. v. Sunflower County	1966	N/A	2003
TISHOMINGO COUNTY SP MUN SCHOOL DISTRICT	U.S. Tishomingo County	1966	N/A	2005
WEST TALLAHATCHIE SCHOOL DISTRICT	U.S. v. West Tallahatchie	1970	N/A	2006
WILKINSON COUNTY SCHOOL DISTRICT	U.S. v. Wilkinson County Sch. Bd.	1966	N/A	2004

Source: Compiled by U.S. Commission on Civil Rights.

Table F.2
Mississippi Districts Remaining Under Court Order

District Name	Case Name	Year Case Initiated	Intent regarding unitary status	Year Unitary Status attained
ABERDEEN SCHOOL DISTRICT	U.S. v. Aberdeen	1965	District is working with DOJ towards a grant of unitary status	N/A
AMITE COUNTY SCHOOL DISTRICT	U.S. v. Amite County	1966	District could not confirm status	N/A
ATTALA COUNTY SCHOOL DISTRICT	U.S. v. Attla	1970	District has not made a decision about its intent	N/A
BENTON COUNTY SCHOOL DISTRICT	U.S. & Baird v. Benton County	1966	District does not plan to seek unitary status	N/A
BROOKHAVEN SCHOOL DISTRICT	U.S. v. Brookhaven	1965	District did not reply to the Commission's inquiries	N/A
CANTON PUBLIC SCHOOL DISTRICT	Anderson & U.S. v. Canton	1965	District did not reply to the Commission's inquiries	N/A

Continued

Table F.2 (continued)
Mississippi Districts Remaining Under Court Order

District Name	Case Name	Year Case Initiated	Intent regarding unitary status	Year Unitary Status attained
CARROLL COUNTY SCHOOL DISTRICT	U.S. v. Carroll County	1965	District does not plan to seek unitary status	N/A
CHOCTAW COUNTY SCHOOL DISTRICT	U.S. v. Choctaw County	1970	District does not plan to seek unitary status	N/A
CLARKSDALE MUNICIPAL SCHOOL DISTRICT	Henry v. Clarksdale Municipal	1970	District does not plan to seek unitary status	N/A
CLEVELAND SCHOOL DISTRICT	Cowan & U.S. v. Cleveland City	1983	District has no position on seeking unitary status	N/A
CLINTON PUBLIC SCHOOL DISTRICT	U.S. v. Clinton MSSD	1967	District does not plan to seek unitary status	N/A
COAHOMA COUNTY SCHOOL DISTRICT	Taylor v. Coahoma County	Uncertain	District does not plan to seek unitary status	N/A
COLUMBIA SCHOOL DISTRICT	U.S. v. Columbia MSSD	1967	District could not confirm status	N/A
COLUMBUS MUNICIPAL SCHOOL DISTRICT	U.S. v. Columbus	1970	District is seeking unitary status	N/A
COPIAH COUNTY SCHOOL DISTRICT	U.S. v. Copiah	1970	Uncertain	N/A
COVINGTON COUNTY SCHOOLS	U.S. v. Covington County	1968	District does not plan to seek unitary status	N/A
DURANT PUBLIC SCHOOL DISTRICT	U.S. & Alexander v. Holmes County	1965	District does not plan to seek unitary status	N/A
ENTERPRISE SCHOOL DISTRICT	Killingsworth v. Enterprise Consol. Sch. Dist. & Quitman Consol. Sch. Dist.	1970	District is seeking unitary status	N/A
FORREST COUNTY SCHOOL DISTRICT	U.S. & Lee v. Forrest County	1965	District could not confirm status	N/A

Continued

Table F.2 (continued)
Mississippi Districts Remaining Under Court Order

District Name	Case Name	Year Case Initiated	Intent regarding unitary status	Year Unitary Status attained
FRANKLIN COUNTY SCHOOL DISTRICT	U.S. v. Franklin County	1968	District does not plan to seek unitary status	N/A
GREENWOOD PUBLIC SCHOOL DISTRICT	U.S. v. Greenwood	1966	District does not plan to seek unitary status	N/A
HOLLANDALE SCHOOL DISTRICT	Williams v. Hollandale Consol.	1971	District does not plan to seek unitary status	N/A
HOLLY SPRINGS SCHOOL DISTRICT	Anthony v. Marshall County	1969	District could not confirm status	N/A
HOLMES COUNTY SCHOOL DISTRICT	U.S. & Alexander v. Holmes County	1965	District could not confirm status	N/A
INDIANOLA SCHOOL DISTRICT	U.S. v. Indianola	1966	District is working with DOJ towards a grant of unitary status	N/A
JACKSON PUBLIC SCHOOL DISTRICT	Singleton v. Jackson Municipal Sch. Dist.	1969	District does not plan to seek unitary status	N/A
JONES COUNTY SCHOOL DISTRICT	U.S. v. State of Mississippi & Jones County	1991	District does not plan to seek unitary status	N/A
KEMPER COUNTY SCHOOL DISTRICT	U.S. v. Kemper County	1966	District does not plan to seek unitary status	N/A
KOSCIUSKO SCHOOL DISTRICT	U.S. v. Kosciusko	1970	District does not plan to seek unitary status	N/A
LAFAYETTE COUNTY SCHOOL DISTRICT	U.S. v. Hinds County	1969	District does not plan to seek unitary status	N/A
LAUDERDALE COUNTY SCHOOL DISTRICT	U.S. v. Hinds County Sch. Bd. (Lauderdale County Sch. Dist.)	1966	District does not plan to seek unitary status	N/A

Continued

Table F.2 (continued)
Mississippi Districts Remaining Under Court Order

District Name	Case Name	Year Case Initiated	Intent regarding unitary status	Year Unitary Status attained
LAUREL SCHOOL DISTRICT	U.S. v. State of Mississippi & Laurel	1970	District is seeking unitary status	N/A
LAWRENCE COUNTY SCHOOL DISTRICT	U.S. v. Lawrence County	1967	District is seeking unitary status	N/A
LEAKE COUNTY SCHOOL DISTRICT	U.S. & Hudson v. Leake County	1965	District does not plan to seek unitary status	N/A
LINCOLN COUNTY SCHOOL DISTRICT	U.S. v. Lincoln County	1966	District does not plan to seek unitary status	N/A
LOUISVILLE MUNICIPAL SCHOOL DISTRICT	U.S. v. Louisville County	1969	District is undecided	N/A
LOWNDES COUNTY SCHOOL DISTRICT	U.S. v. Lowndes County	1965	District is seeking unitary status	N/A
MARION COUNTY SCHOOL DISTRICT	U.S. v. Marion County Sch. Dist.	1967	District does not plan to seek unitary status	N/A
MCCOMB SCHOOL DISTRICT	U.S. v. State of Mississippi & McComb Municipal Separate Sch. Dist.	1970	District is seeking unitary status	N/A
MERIDIAN PUBLIC SCHOOL DISTRICT	U.S. & Barnhardt v. Meridian Mun. Separate Sch. Dist.	1965	District is working with DOJ towards a grant of unitary status	N/A
MONTGOMERY COUNTY SCHOOL DISTRICT	U.S. v. Montgomery County	1967	District does not plan to seek unitary status	N/A
NESHOBA COUNTY SCHOOL DISTRICT	U.S. v. Neshoba County	1967	District does not plan to seek unitary status	N/A
NETTLETON SCHOOL DISTRICT	U.S. v. Nettleton Line Consol.	1969	District is seeking unitary status	N/A

Continued

Table F.2 (continued)
Mississippi Districts Remaining Under Court Order

District Name	Case Name	Year Case Initiated	Intent regarding unitary status	Year Unitary Status attained
NORTH BOLIVAR SCHOOL DISTRICT	U.S. v. Bolivar Co. No. 4	1965	Uncertain	N/A
NORTH PIKE SCHOOL DISTRICT	U.S. v. North Pike County	1965	District does not plan to seek unitary status	N/A
NORTH TIPPAH SCHOOL DISTRICT	U.S. v. North Tippah	1968	District does not plan to seek unitary status	N/A
OKTIBBEHA COUNTY SCHOOL DISTRICT	Cowan & U.S. v. Oktibbeha County	1965	District does not plan to seek unitary status	N/A
PHILADELPHIA PUBLIC SCHOOL DISTRICT	U.S. v. Philadelphia County	1966	District is working with DOJ towards a grant of unitary status	N/A
PONTOTOC COUNTY SCHOOL DISTRICT[1]	U.S. v. Pontotoc	1967	District does not plan to seek unitary status	N/A
POPLARVILLE SEPARATE SCHOOL DISTRICT	U.S. v. Poplarville	1970	District is working with DOJ towards a grant of unitary status	N/A
QUITMAN COUNTY SCHOOL DISTRICT	Franklin v. Quitman County	Uncertain	District has not made a decision about its intent	N/A
QUITMAN SCHOOL DISTRICT	Killingsworth v. Enterprise Consol. Sch. Dist. & Quitman Consol. Sch. Dist.	1970	District does not plan to seek unitary status	N/A
RANKIN COUNTY SCHOOL DISTRICT	U.S. & Adams v. Rankin County	1971	District does not plan to seek unitary status	N/A
SCOTT COUNTY SCHOOL DISTRICT	U.S. v. Scott County	1970	District did not reply to the Commission's inquiries	N/A

Continued

Table F.2 (continued)
Mississippi Districts Remaining Under Court Order

District Name	Case Name	Year Case Initiated	Intent regarding unitary status	Year Unitary Status attained
SENATOBIA MUNICIPAL SCHOOL DISTRICT	Alexander v. Senatobia	1970	District does not plan to seek unitary status	N/A
SIMPSON COUNTY SCHOOL DISTRICT	U.S. v. Simpson County	1970	District is seeking unitary status	N/A
SMITH COUNTY SCHOOL DISTRICT	U.S. v. State of Mississippi & Smith County	1970	Uncertain	N/A
SOUTH PIKE SCHOOL DISTRICT	U.S. v. South Pike	1966	District does not plan to seek unitary status	N/A
SOUTH TIPPAH SCHOOL DISTRICT	U.S. v. South Tippah	1968	District does not plan to seek unitary status	N/A
STARKVILLE SCHOOL DISTRICT	Montgomery v. Starkville	1969	District does not plan to seek unitary status	N/A
TATE COUNTY SCHOOL DISTRICT	McNeal v. Tate County	Uncertain	District does not plan to seek unitary status	N/A
TUNICA COUNTY SCHOOL DISTRICT	U.S. v. Tunica County	1966	District has not made a decision about its intent	N/A
UNION COUNTY SCHOOL DISTRICT	U.S. v. Union County	1970	District has not made a decision about its intent	N/A
UNION PUBLIC SCHOOL DISTRICT	U.S. v. State of Mississippi	1970	District did not reply to the Commission's inquiries	N/A
VICKSBURG WARREN SCHOOL DISTRICT	U.S. v. Vicksburg-Warren County	1970	District does not plan to seek unitary status	N/A
WALTHALL COUNTY SCHOOL DISTRICT	U.S. v. Walthall County	1970	District has not made a decision about its intent	N/A
WAYNE COUNTY SCHOOL DISTRICT	U.S. v. Wayne County	1970	District is seeking unitary status	N/A

Continued

Table F.2 (continued)
Mississippi Districts Remaining Under Court Order

District Name	Case Name	Year Case Initiated	Intent regarding unitary status	Year Unitary Status attained
WEBSTER COUNTY SCHOOL DISTRICT	U.S. v. State of Mississippi	1970	District did not reply to the Commission's inquiries	N/A
WESTERN LINE SCHOOL DISTRICT	Ayers v. Western Line Consol.	Uncertain	District does not plan to seek unitary status	N/A
YAZOO CITY MUNICIPAL SCHOOL DISTRICT	Harris & U.S. v. Yazoo City	1970	District does not plan to seek unitary status	N/A
YAZOO COUNTY SCHOOL DISTRICT	Harris & U.S. v. Yazoo County	1970	District does not plan to seek unitary status	N/A

[1] Legal counsel for the school district states that "the local federal district court granted the school district unitary status and released the school district from the prior order." Philip L. Tutor, attorney, Pontotoc County School District, letter to David P. Blackwood, General Counsel, U.S. Commission on Civil Rights, July 11, 2007. The Commission received this information after the final analyses were run, and thus the district's revised status is not reflected in the analyses. *See U.S. v. Pontotoc County School District*, C.A. No. WC6735-K (D. Miss. May 14, 2007) (order granting unitary status).

Source: Compiled by U.S. Commission on Civil Rights.

Table F.3
Mississippi Districts Not Subject to School Desegregation Litigation

District Name	Case Name	Year Case Initiated	Intent regarding unitary status	Year Unitary Status attained
ALCORN SCHOOL DISTRICT	N/A	N/A	N/A	N/A
AMORY SCHOOL DISTRICT	N/A	N/A	N/A	N/A
BALDWYN SCHOOL DISTRICT	N/A	N/A	N/A	N/A
BAY ST LOUIS WAVELAND SCHOOL DISTRICT	N/A	N/A	N/A	N/A
BENOIT SCHOOL DISTRICT	N/A	N/A	N/A	N/A
BOONEVILLE SCHOOL DISTRICT	N/A	N/A	N/A	N/A
CHICKASAW COUNTY SCHOOL DISTRICT	N/A	N/A	N/A	N/A
CLAIBORNE COUNTY SCHOOL DISTRICT	N/A	N/A	N/A	N/A

Continued

Table F.3 (continued)
Mississippi Districts Not Subject to School Desegregation Litigation

District Name	Case Name	Year Case Initiated	Intent regarding unitary status	Year Unitary Status attained
CLAY COUNTY SCHOOL DISTRICT	N/A	N/A	N/A	N/A
DESOTO COUNTY SCHOOL DISTRICT	N/A	N/A	N/A	N/A
DREW SCHOOL DISTRICT	N/A	N/A	N/A	N/A
EAST JASPER CONSOLIDATED SCHOOL DISTRICT	N/A	N/A	N/A	N/A
FOREST MUNICIPAL SCHOOL DISTRICT	N/A	N/A	N/A	N/A
GEORGE COUNTY SCHOOL DISTRICT	N/A	N/A	N/A	N/A
GREENE COUNTY SCHOOL DISTRICT	N/A	N/A	N/A	N/A
GULFPORT SCHOOL DISTRICT	N/A	N/A	N/A	N/A
HANCOCK COUNTY SCHOOL DISTRICT	N/A	N/A	N/A	N/A
HOUSTON SCHOOL DISTRICT	N/A	N/A	N/A	N/A
ITAWAMBA COUNTY SCHOOL DISTRICT	N/A	N/A	N/A	N/A
JACKSON COUNTY SCHOOL DISTRICT	N/A	N/A	N/A	N/A
JEFFERSON COUNTY SCHOOL DISTRICT	N/A	N/A	N/A	N/A
JEFFERSON DAVIS COUNTY SCHOOL DISTRICT	N/A	N/A	N/A	N/A
LAMAR COUNTY SCHOOL DISTRICT	N/A	N/A	N/A	N/A
LEE COUNTY SCHOOL DISTRICT	N/A	N/A	N/A	N/A
LONG BEACH SCHOOL DISTRICT	N/A	N/A	N/A	N/A
LUMBERTON PUBLIC SCHOOL DISTRICT	N/A	N/A	N/A	N/A
MONROE COUNTY SCHOOL DISTRICT	N/A	N/A	N/A	N/A
MOSS POINT SEPARATE SCHOOL DISTRICT	N/A	N/A	N/A	N/A

Continued

Table F.3 (continued)
Mississippi Districts Not Subject to School Desegregation Litigation

District Name	Case Name	Year Case Initiated	Intent regarding unitary status	Year Unitary Status attained
MOUND BAYOU PUBLIC SCHOOL	N/A	N/A	N/A	N/A
NEW ALBANY PUBLIC SCHOOLS	N/A	N/A	N/A	N/A
NEWTON MUNICIPAL SCHOOL DISTRICT	N/A	N/A	N/A	N/A
NORTH PANOLA SCHOOLS	N/A	N/A	N/A	N/A
OCEAN SPRINGS SCHOOL DISTRICT	N/A	N/A	N/A	N/A
OKOLONA SEPARATE SCHOOL DISTRICT	N/A	N/A	N/A	N/A
PASCAGOULA SCHOOL DISTRICT	N/A	N/A	N/A	N/A
PASS CHRISTIAN PUBLIC SCHOOL DISTRICT	N/A	N/A	N/A	N/A
PEARL PUBLIC SCHOOL DISTRICT	N/A	N/A	N/A	N/A
PEARL RIVER COUNTY SCHOOL DISTRICT	N/A	N/A	N/A	N/A
PERRY COUNTY SCHOOL DISTRICT	N/A	N/A	N/A	N/A
PETAL SCHOOL DISTRICT[1]	N/A	N/A	N/A	N/A
PICAYUNE SCHOOL DISTRICT	N/A	N/A	N/A	N/A
PONTOTOC CITY SCHOOLS	N/A	N/A	N/A	N/A
PRENTISS COUNTY SCHOOL DISTRICT	N/A	N/A	N/A	N/A
RICHTON SCHOOL DISTRICT	N/A	N/A	N/A	N/A
SHAW SCHOOL DISTRICT	N/A	N/A	N/A	N/A
SOUTH PANOLA SCHOOL DISTRICT	N/A	N/A	N/A	N/A
STONE COUNTY SCHOOL DISTRICT	N/A	N/A	N/A	N/A
TUPELO PUBLIC SCHOOL DISTRICT	N/A	N/A	N/A	N/A

Continued

Table F.3 (continued)
Mississippi Districts Not Subject to School Desegregation Litigation

District Name	Case Name	Year Case Initiated	Intent regarding unitary status	Year Unitary Status attained
WATER VALLEY SCHOOL DISTRICT	N/A	N/A	N/A	N/A
WEST BOLIVAR SCHOOL DISTRICT	N/A	N/A	N/A	N/A
WEST JASPER CONSOLIDATED SCHOOLS	N/A	N/A	N/A	N/A
WEST POINT SCHOOL DISTRICT[2]	N/A	N/A	N/A	N/A
WINONA SEPARATE SCHOOL DISTRICT	N/A	N/A	N/A	N/A

[1] Legal counsel for this school district maintains that "the Petal School District continues to operate under a desegregation order" originating in the late 1960s. William H. Jones, attorney, Petal School District, letter to David P. Blackwood, General Counsel, U.S. Commission on Civil Rights, July 9, 2007. The district's legal counsel provided some evidence that the district has a history of litigation: *Buford A. Lee v. United States*, No. 28030 & 28042 (D. Miss. filed Dec. 17, 1969). The Commission received this information after the final analyses were run, and thus the district's revised status is not reflected in the analyses.

[2] The superintendent of this school district maintains that the West Point School District currently operates under a federal school desegregation order: *Hugh Larry Bell v. West Point Municipal Separate School District* (1971). Steve Montgomery, superintendent, West Point School District, letter to David P. Blackwood, General Counsel, U.S. Commission on Civil Rights, July 6, 2007. The Commission received this information after the final analyses were run, and thus the district's revised status is not reflected in the analyses.

Source: Compiled by U.S. Commission on Civil Rights.

Table F.4
Mississippi Districts With Uncertain Legal Status

District Name	Case Name	Year Case Initiated	Intent regarding unitary status	Year Unitary Status attained
LELAND SCHOOL DISTRICT	Young v. Leland Consolidated School District	Uncertain	Uncertain	Uncertain

Source: Compiled by U.S. Commission on Civil Rights.

APPENDIX G: NORTH CAROLINA PUBLIC SCHOOLS' DESEGREGATION STATUS

Table G.1
North Carolina Districts With Unitary Status

District Name	Case Name	Year Case Initiated	Intent regarding unitary status	Year Unitary Status attained
ANSON COUNTY SCHOOLS	U.S. & Freddie M. Singleton v. Anson County Bd. of Educ.	1967	N/A	1973
BLADEN COUNTY SCHOOLS	Smith & U.S v. North Carolina State Bd. of Educ. (Bladen)	1970	N/A	1997
CHARLOTTE-MECKLENBURG SCHOOLS	Swann v. Charlotte-Mecklenburg	1965	N/A	1999
CUMBERLAND COUNTY SCHOOLS	Ford v. the Cumberland County Bd. of Educ.	1964	N/A	1978
EDGECOMBE COUNTY SCHOOLS	Smith & U.S v. North Carolina State Bd. of Educ. (Edgecombe)	1970	N/A	1979
GUILFORD COUNTY SCHOOLS[1]	Smith & U.S v. North Carolina State Bd. of Educ. (Guilford)	1970	N/A	1972
JONES COUNTY SCHOOLS	U.S. v. Jones County Bd. of Educ.	1967	N/A	1997
NASH-ROCKY MOUNT SCHOOLS	Smith & U.S v. North Carolina State Bd. of Educ. (Rocky Mount City)	1970	N/A	1998
NEW HANOVER COUNTY SCHOOLS	Carolyn Eaton v. New Hanover County	1971	N/A	1983
NORTHAMPTON COUNTY SCHOOLS	U.S. v. Northampton County Bd. of Educ.	1967	N/A	1976
UNION COUNTY PUBLIC SCHOOLS	Smith & U.S v. North Carolina State Bd. of Educ. (Union)	1970	N/A	1972
WILSON COUNTY SCHOOLS	Cynthia Whitley & Will Whitley, Judith Lewis & U.S. v. Wilson County Bd. of Educ.	1970	N/A	1997

[1] Legal counsel for this school district maintains that Guilford County School District, as it exists today, was formed when "three school systems merged in 1993 into a unitary school system. The district further states that the "school system has never been under Court order or otherwise challenged with regard to its student assignment issues on the basis of race." Jill R. Wilson, attorney, Guilford County Board of Education, letter to David P. Blackwood, General Counsel, U.S. Commission on Civil Rights, July 12, 2007. Based on applicable court records, the Commission retains its assessment of the school district's status.

Source: Compiled by U.S. Commission on Civil Rights.

Table G.2
North Carolina Districts Remaining Under Court Order

District Name	Case Name	Year Case Initiated	Intent regarding unitary status	Year Unitary Status attained
ALAMANCE-BURLINGTON SCHOOL SYSTEM	U.S. v. Burlington City Bd. of Educ. & Brank Proffitt	1971	District is seeking unitary status	N/A
ASHEVILLE CITY SCHOOLS	Allen v. Asheville City Schools	1968	District is undecided	N/A
BEAUFORT COUNTY SCHOOLS	Barrow v. Washington City	1964	District disputes status	N/A
BERTIE COUNTY SCHOOLS	U.S. v. Bertie County Bd. of Educ.	1976	District is seeking unitary status	N/A
BUNCOMBE COUNTY SCHOOLS	Bowditch v. Buncombe County	1965	District does not plan to seek unitary status	N/A
CASWELL COUNTY SCHOOLS	Jeffers, et al. v. Whitley	1968	District does not plan to seek unitary status	N/A
DURHAM PUBLIC SCHOOLS	McKissick v. Durham City	1968	District disputes status	N/A
EDENTON/CHOWAN SCHOOLS	Felton v. Edenton-Chowan Sch. Dist.	1968	District does not plan to seek unitary status	N/A
FRANKLIN COUNTY SCHOOLS	Coppedge v. Franklin County	1966	District does not plan to seek unitary status	N/A
HALIFAX COUNTY SCHOOLS[1]	U.S. v. Halifax County	1966	District did not reply to the Commission's inquiries	N/A
HARNETT COUNTY SCHOOLS	Felder v. Harnett County	1965	District does not plan to seek unitary status	N/A

Continued

Table G.2 (continued)
North Carolina Districts Remaining Under Court Order

District Name	Case Name	Year Case Initiated	Intent regarding unitary status	Year Unitary Status attained
PERSON COUNTY SCHOOLS	Clayton v. Person County Bd. of Educ.	1964	District does not plan to seek unitary status	N/A
PITT COUNTY SCHOOLS	Teel v. Pitt County	1964	District does not plan to seek unitary status	N/A
WARREN COUNTY SCHOOLS	Turner v. Warren County	1970	District does not plan to seek unitary status	N/A
WILKES COUNTY SCHOOLS[2]	Burns v. Wilkes County Bd. of Educ.	1964	District did not reply to the Commission's inquiries	N/A

[1] The superintendent of this school district maintains that the district is not currently under a school desegregation court order. Geraldine Middleton, superintendent, Halifax County School District, letter to David P. Blackwood, General Counsel, U.S. Commission on Civil Rights, July 10, 2007. The Commission could not independently confirm the district's claims, which are not reflected in U.S. Department of Justice records. *See* U.S. Department of Justice, Civil Rights Division, Response to U.S. Commission on Civil Rights' Interrogatories and Document Requests, Exhibit 1, May 17, 2007.

[2] Legal counsel for this school district maintains that their "research does not indicate that the Wilkes County (North Carolina) Board of Education has been involved in any school desegregation litigation." Frederick G. Johnson, attorney, Wilkes County School District, letter to David P. Blackwood, General Counsel, U.S. Commission on Civil Rights, July 5, 2007. The Commission was unable to confirm this contention, and has retained its assessment of the school district's status.

Source: Compiled by U.S. Commission on Civil Rights.

Table G.3
North Carolina Districts Not Subject to School Desegregation Litigation

District Name	Case Name	Year Case Initiated	Intent regarding unitary status	Year Unitary Status attained
ALEXANDER COUNTY SCHOOLS	N/A	N/A	N/A	N/A
ALLEGHANY COUNTY SCHOOLS	N/A	N/A	N/A	N/A
ASHE COUNTY SCHOOLS	N/A	N/A	N/A	N/A
ASHEBORO CITY SCHOOLS	N/A	N/A	N/A	N/A
AVERY COUNTY SCHOOLS	N/A	N/A	N/A	N/A
BRUNSWICK COUNTY SCHOOLS	N/A	N/A	N/A	N/A

Continued

Table G.3 (continued)
North Carolina Districts Not Subject to School Desegregation Litigation

District Name	Case Name	Year Case Initiated	Intent regarding unitary status	Year Unitary Status attained
BURKE COUNTY SCHOOLS	N/A	N/A	N/A	N/A
CABARRUS COUNTY SCHOOLS	N/A	N/A	N/A	N/A
CALDWELL COUNTY SCHOOLS	N/A	N/A	N/A	N/A
CAMDEN COUNTY SCHOOLS	N/A	N/A	N/A	N/A
CARTERET COUNTY PUBLIC SCHOOLS	N/A	N/A	N/A	N/A
CATAWBA COUNTY SCHOOLS	N/A	N/A	N/A	N/A
CHAPEL HILL-CARRBORO SCHOOLS	N/A	N/A	N/A	N/A
CHATHAM COUNTY SCHOOLS	N/A	N/A	N/A	N/A
CHEROKEE COUNTY SCHOOLS	N/A	N/A	N/A	N/A
CLAY COUNTY SCHOOLS	N/A	N/A	N/A	N/A
CLEVELAND COUNTY SCHOOLS	N/A	N/A	N/A	N/A
CLINTON CITY SCHOOLS	N/A	N/A	N/A	N/A
COLUMBUS COUNTY SCHOOLS	N/A	N/A	N/A	N/A
CURRITUCK COUNTY SCHOOLS	N/A	N/A	N/A	N/A
DARE COUNTY SCHOOLS	N/A	N/A	N/A	N/A
DAVIDSON COUNTY SCHOOLS	N/A	N/A	N/A	N/A
DAVIE COUNTY SCHOOLS	N/A	N/A	N/A	N/A
DUPLIN COUNTY SCHOOLS	N/A	N/A	N/A	N/A
ELKIN CITY SCHOOLS	N/A	N/A	N/A	N/A
GASTON COUNTY SCHOOLS	N/A	N/A	N/A	N/A
GATES COUNTY SCHOOLS	N/A	N/A	N/A	N/A

Continued

Table G.3 (continued)
North Carolina Districts Not Subject to School Desegregation Litigation

District Name	Case Name	Year Case Initiated	Intent regarding unitary status	Year Unitary Status attained
GRAHAM COUNTY SCHOOLS	N/A	N/A	N/A	N/A
GRANVILLE COUNTY SCHOOLS	N/A	N/A	N/A	N/A
GREENE COUNTY SCHOOLS	N/A	N/A	N/A	N/A
HAYWOOD COUNTY SCHOOLS	N/A	N/A	N/A	N/A
HENDERSON COUNTY SCHOOLS	N/A	N/A	N/A	N/A
HERTFORD COUNTY SCHOOLS	N/A	N/A	N/A	N/A
HOKE COUNTY SCHOOLS	N/A	N/A	N/A	N/A
HYDE COUNTY SCHOOLS	N/A	N/A	N/A	N/A
JACKSON COUNTY SCHOOLS	N/A	N/A	N/A	N/A
KANNAPOLIS CITY SCHOOLS	N/A	N/A	N/A	N/A
LEE COUNTY SCHOOLS	N/A	N/A	N/A	N/A
LEXINGTON CITY SCHOOLS	N/A	N/A	N/A	N/A
LINCOLN COUNTY SCHOOLS	N/A	N/A	N/A	N/A
MACON COUNTY SCHOOLS	N/A	N/A	N/A	N/A
MADISON COUNTY SCHOOLS	N/A	N/A	N/A	N/A
MARTIN COUNTY SCHOOLS	N/A	N/A	N/A	N/A
MCDOWELL COUNTY SCHOOLS	N/A	N/A	N/A	N/A
MITCHELL COUNTY SCHOOLS	N/A	N/A	N/A	N/A
MONTGOMERY COUNTY SCHOOLS	N/A	N/A	N/A	N/A
MOORE COUNTY SCHOOLS	N/A	N/A	N/A	N/A

Continued

Table G.3 (continued)
North Carolina Districts Not Subject to School Desegregation Litigation

District Name	Case Name	Year Case Initiated	Intent regarding unitary status	Year Unitary Status attained
MOORESVILLE CITY SCHOOLS	N/A	N/A	N/A	N/A
MOUNT AIRY CITY SCHOOLS	N/A	N/A	N/A	N/A
NEWTON CONOVER CITY SCHOOLS	N/A	N/A	N/A	N/A
ONSLOW COUNTY SCHOOLS	N/A	N/A	N/A	N/A
ORANGE COUNTY SCHOOLS	N/A	N/A	N/A	N/A
ELIZABETH CITY-PASQUOTANK SCHOOLS	N/A	N/A	N/A	N/A
PENDER COUNTY SCHOOLS	N/A	N/A	N/A	N/A
PERQUIMANS COUNTY SCHOOLS	N/A	N/A	N/A	N/A
RANDOLPH COUNTY SCHOOLS	N/A	N/A	N/A	N/A
RICHMOND COUNTY SCHOOLS	N/A	N/A	N/A	N/A
ROANOKE RAPIDS CITY SCHOOLS	N/A	N/A	N/A	N/A
ROWAN-SALISBURY SCHOOLS	N/A	N/A	N/A	N/A
RUTHERFORD COUNTY SCHOOLS	N/A	N/A	N/A	N/A
SCOTLAND COUNTY SCHOOLS	N/A	N/A	N/A	N/A
STANLY COUNTY SCHOOLS	N/A	N/A	N/A	N/A
STOKES COUNTY SCHOOLS	N/A	N/A	N/A	N/A
SURRY COUNTY SCHOOLS	N/A	N/A	N/A	N/A
SWAIN COUNTY SCHOOLS	N/A	N/A	N/A	N/A
THOMASVILLE CITY SCHOOLS	N/A	N/A	N/A	N/A

Continued

Table G.3 (continued)
North Carolina Districts Not Subject to School Desegregation Litigation

District Name	Case Name	Year Case Initiated	Intent regarding unitary status	Year Unitary Status attained
TRANSYLVANIA COUNTY SCHOOLS	N/A	N/A	N/A	N/A
TYRRELL COUNTY SCHOOLS	N/A	N/A	N/A	N/A
VANCE COUNTY SCHOOLS	N/A	N/A	N/A	N/A
WASHINGTON COUNTY SCHOOLS	N/A	N/A	N/A	N/A
WATAUGA COUNTY SCHOOLS	N/A	N/A	N/A	N/A
WAYNE COUNTY PUBLIC SCHOOLS	N/A	N/A	N/A	N/A
WELDON CITY SCHOOLS	N/A	N/A	N/A	N/A
WHITEVILLE CITY SCHOOLS	N/A	N/A	N/A	N/A
YADKIN COUNTY SCHOOLS	N/A	N/A	N/A	N/A
YANCEY COUNTY SCHOOLS	N/A	N/A	N/A	N/A

Source: Compiled by U.S. Commission on Civil Rights.

Table G.4
North Carolina Districts With Uncertain Legal Status

District Name	Case Name	Year Case Initiated	Intent regarding unitary status	Year Unitary Status attained
CRAVEN COUNTY SCHOOLS	Hickman v. Craven County Bd. of Educ.	Uncertain	Uncertain	Uncertain
FORSYTH COUNTY SCHOOLS[1]	Winston Salem-Forsyth County v. Scott	Uncertain	Uncertain	Uncertain
HICKORY CITY SCHOOLS	Uncertain	Uncertain	Uncertain	Uncertain
IREDELL-STATESVILLE SCHOOLS	Uncertain	Uncertain	Uncertain	Uncertain
JOHNSTON COUNTY SCHOOLS[2]	Godwin v. Johnston County	Uncertain	Uncertain	Uncertain
LENOIR COUNTY PUBLIC SCHOOLS	Uncertain	Uncertain	Uncertain	Uncertain
PAMLICO COUNTY SCHOOLS[3]	Uncertain	Uncertain	Uncertain	Uncertain
POLK COUNTY SCHOOLS	Uncertain	Uncertain	District did not reply to the Commission's inquiries	Uncertain
ROBESON COUNTY SCHOOLS	Uncertain	Uncertain	District did not reply to the Commission's inquiries	Uncertain
ROCKINGHAM COUNTY SCHOOLS[4]	Uncertain	Uncertain	District did not reply to the Commission's inquiries	Uncertain
SAMPSON COUNTY SCHOOLS[5]	Uncertain	Uncertain	Uncertain	Uncertain
WAKE COUNTY SCHOOLS	Holt v. Raleigh City Board of Education	Uncertain	Uncertain	Uncertain

[1] The General Counsel for the Board of Education maintains that multiple desegregation orders were issued from 1970 through 1971; that the district was granted unitary status in 1971; and that the district was released from the desegregation order in 1981. The case cited is *Catherin Scott v. Winston-Salem/Forsyth County Board of Education*. Drew H. Davis, General Counsel, Winston-Salem/Forsyth County Board of Education, facsimile to David P. Blackwood, General Counsel, U.S. Commission on Civil Rights, July 3, 2007. The Commission could not confirm this contention and has retained its assessment of the school district's status.

[2] The superintendent of this school district maintains that the district was placed under a court order in 1968 and granted unitary status in 1995. Anthony L. Parker, superintendent, Johnston County Schools, letter to David P. Blackwood, General Counsel, U.S. Commission on Civil Rights, July 3, 2007. The Commission could not confirm this contention and has retained its assessment of the school district's status.

[3] The superintendent of this school district maintains that the district was subject to a court issued desegregation order in *Jones, et al. v. Pamlico County Board of Education* (1967). Rick Sherrill, superintendent, Pamlico County Schools, letter to David P. Blackwood, General Counsel, U.S. Commission on Civil Rights, July 6, 2007. The Commission could not confirm this contention and has retained its assessment of the school district's status.

[4] Legal counsel states that, "In 1993, the four school systems that previously existed in Rockingham County (the Eden City Board of Education, the Rockingham County Board of Education, the Western Rockingham County Board of Education, and the Reidsville City Board of Education) merged to form one school system. At the time of merger, none of the four school systems were under order to desegregate." Jill R. Wilson, attorney, Rockingham County Board of Education, letter to David P. Blackwood, General Counsel, U.S. Commission on Civil Rights, July 12, 2007. The Commission was unable to confirm this contention, and remains uncertain of the school district's status.

[5] The superintendent submitted a number of documents to clarify the school district's history with respect to desegregation. Stewart Hobbs, superintendent, Sampson County Schools, letter to David P. Blackwood, General Counsel, U.S. Commission on Civil Rights, July 10, 2007. These documents indicate that the district may have been placed under a court order in the late 1960s and granted unitary status in 1981. *Peggie Bowden v. The Sampson County Board of Education*, C.A. No. 798 (D. NC. Aug. 17, 1981) (order approving the consent judgment). The Commission received this information after the final analyses were run, and thus the district's revised status is not reflected in the analyses.

Source: Compiled by U.S. Commission on Civil Rights.

APPENDIX H: SOUTH CAROLINA PUBLIC SCHOOLS' DESEGREGATION STATUS

Table H.1
South Carolina Districts With Unitary Status

District Name	Case Name	Year Case Initiated	Intent regarding unitary status	Year Unitary Status attained
ABBEVILLE COUNTY SCHOOL DISTRICT	U.S. v. Abbeville County Sch. Dist. No. 60	1969	N/A	1984
ANDERSON COUNTY SCHOOL DISTRICT 03	U.S. v. Anderson County Sch. Dist. No. 3	1968	N/A	2005
BAMBERG COUNTY SCHOOL DISTRICT 02	Albert & U.S. v. Denmark-Olar Dist. No. 2 (Bamberg Dist. No. 2)	1969	N/A	2004
BARNWELL COUNTY SCHOOL DISTRICT 45	U.S. v. Barnwell School Dist. No. 45 of Barnwell County, SC	1969	N/A	2002
BERKELEY COUNTY SCHOOL DISTRICT	U.S. v. Berkeley County Sch. Dist.	1970	N/A	2004
CLARENDON COUNTY SCHOOL DISTRICT 02	Miller & U.S. v. Sch. Dist. No. 2, Clarendon County, SC	1965	N/A	2004
COLLETON COUNTY SCHOOL DISTRICT	U.S. v. Colleton County Sch. Dist.	1970	N/A	2004
DARLINGTON COUNTY SCHOOL DISTRICT	Stanley & U.S. v. Darlington County Sch. Dist.	1962	N/A	2000
FAIRFIELD COUNTY SCHOOL DISTRICT	U.S. v. Fairfield County Sch. Dist.	1970	N/A	2006
FLORENCE COUNTY SCHOOL DISTRICT 04	U.S. v. Florence County Sch. Dist. No. 4	1970	N/A	2005
GREENVILLE COUNTY SCHOOL DISTRICT	Whittenberg v. Sch. Dist. of Greenville County	1969	N/A	1985
HAMPTON COUNTY SCHOOL DISTRICT NO. 1	U.S. v. Hampton County Sch. Dist. No. 1	1969	N/A	2004
HAMPTON COUNTY SCHOOL DISTRICT NO. 2	U.S. v. Hampton County Sch. Dist. No. 2	1970	N/A	2005
LEE COUNTY SCHOOL DISTRICT	Scott v. Lee County School Dist. No. 1	1969	N/A	2001
LEXINGTON COUNTY SCHOOL DISTRICT 01	U.S. v. Lexington Dist. No. 1	1966	N/A	2005
MCCORMICK COUNTY SCHOOL DISTRICT	U.S. v. McCormik County Sch. Dist.	1970	N/A	2003
ORANGEBURG COUNTY SCHOOL DISTRICT 03	U.S. v. Orangeburg Co. Consol. Sch. Dist. No. 3	1970	N/A	2006
SALUDA COUNTY SCHOOL DISTRICT	U.S. v. Saluda County Sch. Dist. No. 1 of Saluda County, SC	1969	N/A	2002

Source: Compiled by U.S. Commission on Civil Rights.

Table H.2
South Carolina Districts Remaining Under Court Order

District Name	Case Name	Year Case Initiated	Intent regarding unitary status	Year Unitary Status attained
ALLENDALE COUNTY SCHOOL DISTRICT	U.S. v. Allendale County Sch. Dist.	1968	District does not plan to seek unitary status	N/A
BARNWELL COUNTY SCHOOL DISTRICT 19	U.S. v. Barnwell County Sch. Dist. No. 19, et al.	1970	District does not plan to seek unitary status	N/A
CALHOUN COUNTY SCHOOL DISTRICT	U.S. v. Calhoun County Sch. Dist. One, Two & Three	1970	District does not plan to seek unitary status	N/A
CHESTERFIELD COUNTY SCHOOL DISTRICT	U.S. v. Chesterfield County Sch. Dist.	1969	District is seeking unitary status	N/A
CLARENDON COUNTY SCHOOL DISTRICT 01	Brunson v. Board of Clarendon County Sch. Dist. No. 1	1962	District does not plan to seek unitary status	N/A
CLARENDON COUNTY SCHOOL DISTRICT 03	Wheeler v. Board of Clarendon County Sch. Dist. No. 3	1969	District does not plan to seek unitary status	N/A
DORCHESTER COUNTY SCHOOL DISTRICT 02	U.S. v. Dorchester County Sch. Dist. No. 2	1968	District does not plan to seek unitary status	N/A
DORCHESTER COUNTY SCHOOL DISTRICT 04	U.S. v. Sch. Dist. No. 1-4, Dorchester County	1968	District does not plan to seek unitary status	N/A
FLORENCE COUNTY SCHOOL DISTRICT 01	U.S. v. Florence County Sch. Dist. No. 1	1970	District does not plan to seek unitary status	N/A
GEORGETOWN COUNTY SCHOOL DISTRICT	U.S. v. Georgetown County Sch. Dist.	1969	District is seeking unitary status	N/A
LEXINGTON COUNTY SCHOOL DISTRICT 04	McDaniel v. Lexington County Sch. Dist. No. 4	1969	District does not plan to seek unitary status	N/A
NEWBERRY COUNTY SCHOOL DISTRICT	Carter v. Newberry County Sch. Dist.	1969	District does not plan to seek unitary status	N/A
ORANGEBURG COUNTY SCHOOL DISTRICT 05	Adams v. Orangeburg County Sch. Dist. No. 5	1964	District does not plan to seek unitary status	N/A
SUMTER COUNTY SCHOOL DISTRICT 02	Hood v. Board of Sumter County Sch. Dist. No. 2	1956	District did not reply to the Commission's inquiries	N/A

Source: Compiled by U.S. Commission on Civil Rights.

Table H.3
South Carolina Districts Not Subject to School Desegregation Litigation

District Name	Case Name	Year Case Initiated	Intent regarding unitary status	Year Unitary Status attained
AIKEN COUNTY SCHOOL DISTRICT	N/A	N/A	N/A	N/A
ANDERSON COUNTY SCHOOL DISTRICT 01	N/A	N/A	N/A	N/A
ANDERSON COUNTY SCHOOL DISTRICT 02	N/A	N/A	N/A	N/A
ANDERSON COUNTY SCHOOL DISTRICT 04	N/A	N/A	N/A	N/A
ANDERSON COUNTY SCHOOL DISTRICT 05	N/A	N/A	N/A	N/A
BAMBERG COUNTY SCHOOL DISTRICT 01	N/A	N/A	N/A	N/A
BARNWELL COUNTY SCHOOL DISTRICT 29	N/A	N/A	N/A	N/A
BEAUFORT COUNTY SCHOOL DISTRICT	N/A	N/A	N/A	N/A
CHARLESTON COUNTY SCHOOL DISTRICT[1]	N/A	N/A	N/A	N/A
CHEROKEE COUNTY SCHOOL DISTRICT	N/A	N/A	N/A	N/A
CHESTER COUNTY SCHOOL DISTRICT	N/A	N/A	N/A	N/A
DILLON COUNTY SCHOOL DISTRICT 01	N/A	N/A	N/A	N/A
DILLON COUNTY SCHOOL DISTRICT 02	N/A	N/A	N/A	N/A
DILLON COUNTY SCHOOL DISTRICT 03	N/A	N/A	N/A	N/A
EDGEFIELD COUNTY SCHOOL DISTRICT	N/A	N/A	N/A	N/A
FLORENCE COUNTY SCHOOL DISTRICT 02	N/A	N/A	N/A	N/A
FLORENCE COUNTY SCHOOL DISTRICT 03	N/A	N/A	N/A	N/A
FLORENCE COUNTY SCHOOL DISTRICT 05	N/A	N/A	N/A	N/A

Continued

Table H.3 (continued)
South Carolina Districts Not Subject to School Desegregation Litigation

District Name	Case Name	Year Case Initiated	Intent regarding unitary status	Year Unitary Status attained
GREENWOOD 50 COUNTY SCHOOL DISTRICT	N/A	N/A	N/A	N/A
GREENWOOD 51 COUNTY SCHOOL DISTRICT	N/A	N/A	N/A	N/A
GREENWOOD 52 COUNTY SCHOOL DISTRICT	N/A	N/A	N/A	N/A
HORRY COUNTY SCHOOL DISTRICT	N/A	N/A	N/A	N/A
JASPER COUNTY SCHOOL DISTRICT	N/A	N/A	N/A	N/A
KERSHAW COUNTY SCHOOL DISTRICT	N/A	N/A	N/A	N/A
LANCASTER COUNTY SCHOOL DISTRICT	N/A	N/A	N/A	N/A
LAURENS COUNTY SCHOOL DISTRICT 55	N/A	N/A	N/A	N/A
LAURENS COUNTY SCHOOL DISTRICT 56	N/A	N/A	N/A	N/A
LEXINGTON COUNTY SCHOOL DISTRICT 02	N/A	N/A	N/A	N/A
LEXINGTON COUNTY SCHOOL DISTRICT 03	N/A	N/A	N/A	N/A
LEXINGTON COUNTY SCHOOL DISTRICT 05	N/A	N/A	N/A	N/A
MARION COUNTY SCHOOL DISTRICT 01	N/A	N/A	N/A	N/A
MARION COUNTY SCHOOL DISTRICT 02	N/A	N/A	N/A	N/A
MARION COUNTY SCHOOL DISTRICT 07	N/A	N/A	N/A	N/A
MARLBORO COUNTY SCHOOL DISTRICT	N/A	N/A	N/A	N/A
OCONEE COUNTY SCHOOL DISTRICT	N/A	N/A	N/A	N/A

Continued

Table H.3 (continued)
South Carolina Districts Not Subject to School Desegregation Litigation

District Name	Case Name	Year Case Initiated	Intent regarding unitary status	Year Unitary Status attained
ORANGEBURG COUNTY SCHOOL DISTRICT 04	N/A	N/A	N/A	N/A
SCHOOL DISTRICT OF PICKENS COUNTY	N/A	N/A	N/A	N/A
RICHLAND COUNTY SCHOOL DISTRICT 01	N/A	N/A	N/A	N/A
RICHLAND COUNTY SCHOOL DISTRICT 02	N/A	N/A	N/A	N/A
SPARTANBURG COUNTY SCHOOL DISTRICT 01	N/A	N/A	N/A	N/A
SPARTANBURG COUNTY SCHOOL DISTRICT 02	N/A	N/A	N/A	N/A
SPARTANBURG COUNTY SCHOOL DISTRICT 03	N/A	N/A	N/A	N/A
SPARTANBURG COUNTY SCHOOL DISTRICT 04	N/A	N/A	N/A	N/A
SPARTANBURG COUNTY SCHOOL DISTRICT 05	N/A	N/A	N/A	N/A
SPARTANBURG COUNTY SCHOOL DISTRICT 06	N/A	N/A	N/A	N/A
SPARTANBURG COUNTY SCHOOL DISTRICT 07	N/A	N/A	N/A	N/A
SUMTER COUNTY SCHOOL DISTRICT 17	N/A	N/A	N/A	N/A
UNION COUNTY SCHOOL DISTRICT	N/A	N/A	N/A	N/A
WILLIAMSBURG COUNTY SCHOOL DISTRICT	N/A	N/A	N/A	N/A
YORK COUNTY SCHOOL DISTRICT 01	N/A	N/A	N/A	N/A
YORK COUNTY SCHOOL DISTRICT 02	N/A	N/A	N/A	N/A
YORK COUNTY SCHOOL DISTRICT 03	N/A	N/A	N/A	N/A
YORK COUNTY SCHOOL DISTRICT 04	N/A	N/A	N/A	N/A

[1] Legal counsel for the Charleston County School District (CCSD) maintains that "the eight school districts in Charleston County, South Carolina, were consolidated into the CCSD in 1967. Several, if not all of those former districts, did have desegregation orders." Furthermore, "in an Order, dated June 28, 1994, Judge Blatt affirmed his prior holding that the CCSD 'operates, in all respects, as a unitary school system.'" Alice F. Paylor, attorney, Charleston County School District, letter to David P. Blackwood, General Counsel, U.S. Commission on Civil Rights, July 5, 2007. *See Richard Ganaway, II v. Charleston County School District*, C.A. Nos. 2:81-0050-8, 2:82-2921-8 (D. SC June 28, 1994). The Commission received this information after the final analyses were run, and thus the district's revised status is not reflected in the analyses.

Source: Compiled by U.S. Commission on Civil Rights.

JOINT STATEMENT OF COMMISSIONERS MELENDEZ AND YAKI

We commend Commission staff for their efforts and largely support the findings and recommendations in this report *Becoming Less Separate? School Desegregation, Justice Department Enforcement, and the Pursuit of Unitary Justice.*

***

This September 2007 is the 50th anniversary of the U.S. Commission on Civil Rights and it is fitting that this year's statutory report should be an update on school desegregation efforts. The struggle to desegregate our nation's schools is a cornerstone of this nation's civil rights movement. We must not forget how brave men and women risked their loved ones and their own lives in the wave of integration that followed the *Brown v. Board of Education of Topeka* decision in 1954.

Today the struggle for integration continues in many communities. Even if those efforts no longer draw bloodshed and armed government intervention, the stakes are still extraordinary. The opportunity for our nation's children to grow up and be educated alongside faces of many colors, races, and ethnicities (and have access to equal facilities and teachers, an inextricably linked concern in segregated school districts) remains a goal all Americans should strive for. At a time when the worst effects of government-sanctioned segregation have been erased, we must not cease to give attention to those communities still plagued by the effects of discrimination or where changing economics have created new *de facto* segregation of schools.

This report gives a useful snapshot of the racial balance in seven Southern states, how many school districts remain under court order, and how the Department of Justice monitors and enforces desegregation orders and relevant statutes. The data shows that school districts in the South still experience significant segregation, even when looking at all races, not just the ratios of black and white students. Importantly, the study suggests that small school districts are less likely to obtain unitary status from courts despite having (on average) less racial clustering than districts of over 10,000 students. This finding should inform debate about the incentives and costs for school districts to seek lifting of desegregation orders, many of which have been in place since the 1960s.

However, there are several important limitations to this Commission report and issues we think bear caution:

- The report data arise from the agency's study of just seven states—Alabama, Georgia, Florida, Louisiana, Mississippi, North Carolina, and South Carolina. The trends seen in these states may or may not be representative of larger national patterns of racial segregation and re-segregation. In particular, reports of re-segregation in large, urban school districts throughout the country and racial isolation of Hispanic school children cannot be assessed from this data. Moreover, even within these states, the report body contains little information or assessment of localized problems of racial concentration within particular school districts. While a useful piece of the puzzle, further research is needed to understand desegregation efforts at the local and national levels.

- Commission staff ran regressions to determine the significance of several factors underlying racial concentration. Besides considering whether districts were subject to court desegregation orders, these regressions included: size of a district's student population, the percentage of white student enrollment, and the state in which the district is located. Unfortunately, the study design did not explore other possible factors and these limited analyses seem to hide as much as they reveal. While the report shows tremendous variation in school districts' racial concentration by state, such variation may be due to state differences in education policies, residential patterns, economics, or a host of other causes. It is simply beyond the scope of this study to name the current causes of racial isolation beyond noting the relative insignificance of court status (whether a school district is under a desegregation order) and the relative importance of school district size. We hope researchers will carry out more detailed analysis using the data compiled by the Commission.

- Report data comparing differences in integration from the early 1990s to 2004/05 indicate there is no general trend toward re-segregation among school districts that gained unitary status (see Finding 25). However, we have reservations about the strength of this finding. The vast majority of all studied school districts to have gained unitary status have done so since 2000 and the fact that significant backsliding isn't apparent by 2004/05 is not a reliable indicator that it will not occur. Ongoing, significant shifts in these states' overall demographics also indicate that further tracking of districts that have gained unitary status is necessary to get a firm sense of the effects of coming off court desegregation orders.

- The report recommends that states and school districts should seek to remove extrajudicial barriers to unitary status (see Recommendation 6). While we of course agree that all parties should work toward fulfillment of court orders and the full integration of schools, it must not be forgotten that a school district's decision to seek unitary status is a nuanced, local decision. There may be legitimate reasons why a particular school district wishes to remain under a court desegregation order. For example, unitary status can seriously affect overall funding, moneys for magnet schools, and many other matters that some might label "extrajudicial barriers" to unitary status. We think each school district must carefully weigh these matters and, if it wishes to pursue unitary status, should have the full support of state and federal officials in providing funding and other resources to remove barriers.

There were several procedural problems with the issuance of this report that have prevented us from analyzing the information as thoroughly as we would have liked. Not a single deadline was met in completion of this project and Commissioners were given little time for comment. In addition, we note the lack of any external review of this report[1] and the agency's continued lack of protocol for statistical analysis. Apart from these missteps, however, it appears that agency quality control procedures were followed. We trust the work of the Commission's civil servants and expect the outside research community will thoroughly review and correct the report's data and findings.

***

In our opinion, statutory reports like this one, that are data-driven, original, thorough, and carefully reviewed by qualified agency staff, should be the focus of all agency reporting. This project was a major endeavor, taking over a year for completion and involving multiple agency divisions as well as several State Advisory Committees. The original research at the root of the report provides an adequate basis to be issuing findings and recommendations to Congress and the President—the first time during our tenure as Commissioners. We are well aware that our current agency resources would not permit many such reports. However, we think that just one or two quality publications like this annually, based on original research and fact-finding, could genuinely advance civil rights and restore the agency's reputation. Our partisan differences are few when the Commission grounds its work in well-researched facts.

The experiment our fellow Commissioners have conducted over the last two years by issuing findings and recommendations to the Congress and President in so-called "briefing reports" rather than statutory or hearing reports must be ended. The quality of the agency's reports has declined because it has tried to do too much with too little. Hour-and-a-half long monthly (or sometimes bimonthly) briefings with a few guest speakers can at best do nothing more than recycle commonly known truths about civil rights problems. At worst, such briefings serve as thinly-veiled political cover for the Commission majority to issue ideological policy statements to influence pending legislation, administrative decisions or reviews, and judicial cases.[2] It is shameful to trade on the Commission's past reputation for quality work in this way. We need to return our focus to doing original social science research and fact-finding through hearings—vetting all documents with quality control checks.

---

[1] Current agency procedures require an "external reviewer" to verify that procedures were followed, but that review merely entails a few minutes inspection of a checklist. The external reviewer does not do a substantive review of the work as is done at other agencies and as the U.S. Government Accountability Office suggested in its May 2006 report on the Commission. Underscoring the rubber stamp nature of the current external review process, the reviewer on this project was an attorney (not a social scientist) who signed off as complete a form certifying procedures for the "final draft" dated July 7—yet the final draft with many staff alterations was not even completed until weeks later.

[2] *See, e.g.*, U.S. Commission on Civil Rights (USCCR) *Briefing Report on Native Hawaiian Government Reorganization Act of 2005* (May 2006); USCCR *Affirmative Action in Law Schools* (August 2007); USCCR *Briefing Report on Benefits of Racial and Ethnic Diversity in Elementary and Secondary Education* (November 2006).

***

This report provides new, useful data on the status of school desegregation for the civil rights community. There are significant limitations to this study, particularly its lack of causal explanations for variation in racial isolation by state. We hope that independent researchers will further review the data and analyses. We also regret the majority of Commissioners was unwilling to make the minor changes we requested in order that we might join in full approval of this report. However, we hope (and will work to ensure) that future agency work follows the model of this report and provides carefully researched, fact-based, and data-driven reports to the Congress, President, and civil rights community.

As the struggle to achieve fully integrated schoolrooms continues and evolves in 2007, so does the U.S. Commission on Civil Rights. We hope this agency will renew its commitment to report difficult facts about discrimination and raise the voices of those who are unheard. We hope this nation's children are given the opportunity to learn and grow in richly diverse classrooms.

U.S. COMMISSION ON CIVIL RIGHTS
WASHINGTON, DC 20425

VISIT US ON THE WEB: WWW.USCCR.GOV

www.ingramcontent.com/pod-product-compliance
Lightning Source LLC
Chambersburg PA
CBHW081118170526
45165CB00008B/2485